A COURSE IN PHONETICS AND SPOKEN ENGLISH

A COURSE IN PHONETICS AND SPOKEN ENGLISH

Sonu Marwah

ANMOL PUBLICATIONS PVT. LTD.
NEW DELHI-110 002 (INDIA)

ANMOL PUBLICATIONS PVT. LTD.
Regd. Office: 4360/4, Ansari Road, Daryaganj,
New Delhi-110002 (India)
Tel.: 23278000, 23261597, 23286875, 23255577
Fax: 91-11-23280289
Email: anmolpub@gmail.com
Visit us at: www.anmolpublications.com

Branch Office: No. 1015, Ist Main Road, BSK IIIrd Stage
IIIrd Phase, IIIrd Block, Bangalore-560 085 (India)
Tel.: 080-41723429 • Fax: 080-26723604
Email: anmolpublicationsbangalore@gmail.com

A Course in Phonetics and Spoken English

First Edition, 2010

ISBN 978-81-261-4611-6

PRINTED IN INDIA

Printed at Mehra Offset Press, Delhi.

Contents

Preface *vii*

1. The English Alphabet 1
2. Phonetic English 11
3. Consonants and Vowels 19
4. Mechanism of Speech 229
5. Rules for Learning Spoken English 236
6. Basic and Advanced Spoken Lessons 241
7. Studying Verb 250
8. Success in Spoken English 255
9. English Language 262

Index 295

Preface

Speech is an exceedingly complex human activity, and it took a great deal of scientific exploration, experimentation, development, as well as considerable computational power to deal successfully with speech. Moreover, the challenge hasn't been fully met yet. Change the way you pronounce your commands ever so subtly.

Or put even good computer speech and human speech side by side, and most listeners will still show a clear preference for human speech. As a result, the race is on to improve computer speech interfaces, a race that has recently been joined by some of the world's major computer firms. It can be expected that over the next ten years, major efforts will be launched to create competing products, and to improve on existing software.

Moreover, the world is a multilingual place, and at least the synthesis side of speech will have a distinctly international flavour. The recognition side may initially be handled in language-independent fashion, but in the long run, even in this area, "one size may not fit all". Increasingly, the aim will be to create and understand natural, error-free and truly pronounce speech.

Author

Chapter 1

The English Alphabet

The English alphabet has 26 letters. Each letter has a lower and upper case form. The letters A, E, I, O, U are vowels.

A	a	[ei]	N	n	[en]
B	b	[bi:]	O	o	[ou]
C	c	[si:]	P	p	[pi:]
D	d	[di:]	Q	q	[kju:]
E	e	[i:]	R	r	[a:]
F	f	[ef]	S	s	[es]
G	g	[d_3i:]	T	t	[ti:]
H	h	[ei^{t}ʃ]	U	u	[ju:]
I	i	[ai][el]	V	v	[vi:]
J	j	[$d_3$ei]	W	w	[d^blju:]
K	k	[kei]	X	x	[eks]
L	l	[el]	Y	y	[wai]
M	m	[em]	Z	z	[zed] or [AmE zi:]

PHONETICS AND PHONOLOGY

Phonetics (from the Greek word *phone* = *sound/voice*) is a fundamental branch of Linguistics and itself has three different aspects:

- *Articulatory Phonetics*: Describes how vowels and consonants are produced or "articulated" in various parts of the mouth and throat;
- *Acoustic Phonetics*: A study of how speech sounds are transmitted: when sound travels through the air from the speaker's mouth to the hearer's ear it does so in the form of vibrations in the air;

- *Auditory Phonetics*: A study of how speech sounds are perceived: looks at the way in which the hearer's brain decodes the sound waves back into the vowels and consonants originally intended by the speaker. The actual sound produced, such as a simple vowel or consonant sound is called phone.
- *Closely associated with*: Phonetics is another branch of Linguistics known as Phonology. Phonology deals with the way speech sounds behave in particular languages or in languages generally. This focuses on the way languages use differences between sounds in order to convey differences of meaning between words. All theories of phonology hold that spoken language can be broken down into a string of sound units (phonemes). A phoneme is the smallest 'distinctive unit sound' of a language. It distinguishes one word from another in a given language. This means changing a phoneme in a word, produces another word, that has a different meaning. In the pair of words (minimal pairs) 'cat' and 'bat', the distinguishing sounds/c/and/b/are both phonemes. The phoneme is an abstract term (a speech sound as it exists in the mind of the speaker) and it is specific to a particular language.

  A phoneme may have several allophones, related sounds that are distinct but do not change the meaning of a word when they are interchanged. The sounds corresponding to the letter "t" in the English words 'tea' and 'trip' are not in fact quite the same. The position of the tongue is slightly different, which causes a difference in sound detectable by an instrument such as a speech spectrograph. Thus the [t] in 'tea' and the [t] in 'trip' are allophones of the phoneme/t/.

  Phonology is the link between Phonetics and the rest of Linguistics. Only by studying both the phonetics and the phonology of English is it possible to acquire a full understanding of the use of sounds in English speech.

ENGLISH PRONUNCIATION

We use the term 'accents' to refer to differences in pronunciations. Pronunciation can vary with cultures, regions and speakers, but there are two major standard varieties in English pronunciation: British English and American English.

Within British English and American English there are also a variety of accents. Some of them have received more attention than others from phoneticians and phonologists. These are Received pronunciation (RP)* and General American (GA).

Received pronunciation is a form of pronunciation of the English language, sometimes defined as the *"educated spoken English of southeastern England"*. RP is close to BBC English (the kind spoken by British newscasters) and it is represented in the pronunciation schemes of most British dictionaries. RP is rather a social accent than regional, associated with the educated upper classes (and/or people who have attended public schools) in Britain. English pronunciation is also divided into two main accent groups, the rhotic and the non-rhotic, depending on when the phoneme /r/ is pronounced. Rhotic speakers pronounce written "r" in all positions.

They will pronounce the "r" in stork, whereas non-rhotic speakers won't, making no distinction between stork and stalk. Non-rhotic speakers pronounce "r" only if it is followed by a vowel right, rain, room, Robert, far awey, etc.

Non-rhotic accents are British Received Pronunciation and some other types of British English, Australian, New Zealand and South African English. American English is rhotic (the "r" is always pronounced), with the notable exception of the Boston area and New York City. Rhotic accents can be found also in most of Canada. SE Britain is apparently the source of non-rhotic. England is non-rhotic, apart from the south-western England and some ever-diminishing northern areas. Scotland and Ireland are rhotic.

SOUNDS OF ENGLISH AND THEIR REPRESENTATION

In English, there is no one-to-one relation between the system of writing and the system of pronunciation. The alphabet which we use to write English has 26 letters but in (Standard British) English there are approximately 44 speach sounds.

The number of speech sounds in English varies from dialect to dialect, and any actual tally depends greatly on the interpretation of the researcher doing the counting. To represent the basic sound of spoken languages linguists use a set of phonetic symbols called the International Phonetic Alphabet (IPA). The chart below contains all of the IPA symbols used to represent the sounds of the English language. This is the standard set of phonemic symbols for English (RP and similar accents).

i:	I	ʊ	u:	Iə	eI		
ε	ə		ɔ:	ʊə	ɔI	əʊ	
æ	^	a:	ɒ	eə	ai	aʊ	
p	b	t	d	tʃ	dʒ	k	g
f	v	θ	ð	s	z	ʃ	ʒ
m	n	ŋ	h	l	r	w	j

[I] - small capital letter I
[ε] -'epsilon' – a Greek letter
[ʊ] - sometimes called'upsilon'
[æ] -'ash'; digraph a-e -- usually just"digraph"
[a] - script A
[ɔ] - open O
[^] -'caret'
-'eng' (right-tail n)
[ð] -'eth'
[θ] -'theta'
[ə] -'schwa'

The colon/:/represents longer duration in pronunciation and is found in long vowels such as/i:/,/a:/,/u:/, etc.

VOWELS AND CONSONANTS

Sounds can be classified into two major categories: vowels and consomants.

Vowels:/ΓΛacHͷ/- Vowels are made by opening the mouth and letting air come out freely. Dictionaries say that there are 20 vowel sounds in English. Phonetically there are three distinct kind of vowels used in English: short vowels, long vowels and diphthongs. All vowels are voiced by definition.

Short Vowels /*KpaTKͷ ΓΛacHͷ*/

I	ship, city, sit	(*KpaTbK 3ByK MeЖ Ay 6bΛΓapcKO TO* И И)
e		
ε	pen, bed, head	(*KbCO e, 6ΛИ3KO AO 6bΛΓapcK OTO e*)
ʊ	book, foot, put	(*KbCO y, KaTO 6bΛΓapcKOTO y*)
ɒ	hot, rock, sock	(*MaΛKO πO-OTBOpeHa OT 6bΛΓapc KO TO O; И3ΓOBapя ce cbBceM* Ш И *pOKO B AmE*)

PHONETIC ALPHABET FOR ENGLISH

A proposed phonetic alphabet for English which provides a one to one correlation between pronunciation and spelling.

Using this alphabet, when you hear a word, you will know how to spell it, and when you see a word, you will know how to pronounce it (except for stress). This makes teaching and learning to read and write much easier than the present orthography. Only familiar letters are used, with either an Umlaut (two dots) or a Macron (a short line) over some vowels to make enough symbols for the twelve different vowel sounds of English.

Macron vowels (with a short bar over the letter), Ā ā, etc., are preferred to the Umlaut vowels (with two dots over the letter), Macron is preferred to the Umlaut as quicker to write and easier to read.

Note: The dotless lower case i is preferred for this alphabet, since it provides a better contrast with the Umlaut i. In some fonts, a Greek iota can be used for a dotless i.

Letter = traditional spelling (phonetic spelling)[name]

1. Δ δ = a in father (fδqur), o in mop (mδp) [δ]
2. A a = a in can (kan) [a]

3. B b = b in bib (b|b) [bπ]
4. D d = d in dead (ded) [dπ]
5. Q q = th in thus (qus) [qu]
6. Λ Λ = a in make (mΛk) [Λ]
7. E e = e in set (set) [e]
8. F f = f in fife (fδ|f), ph in Phòenix (Fπn|ks) [ef]
9. G g = g in gag (gag) [ag]
10. H h = h in ham (ham) [hΛ]
11. Π π = i in machine (musjπn), ee in meet (mπt) [π]
12. I | = i in sit (s|t) [|]
13. J j = y in yes (jes), i in union (jünjun), h in ship (sj|p) [je]
14. K k = k in kite (kδ|t), c in cut (kut), ch in ache (Λk) [kΛ]
15. L l = l in lull (lul) [el]
16. M m = m in maim (mΛm) [em]
17. N n = n in nine (nδ|n) [nπ]
18. Ö ö = o in lone (lön) [ö]
19. O o = o in log (log), au in Pause (poz), aw in laws (loz) [o]
20. P p = p in pipe (pδ|p) [pπ]
21. R r = r in roar (ruör) [ar]
22. S s = s in sister (s|stur) [es]
23. T t = t in tight (tδ|t) [tπ]
24. C c = th in think (cπnk), c in ciencia {Castilian} (cπ|ncπu) [cπ]
25. Ü ü = u in plume (plüm), oo in boot (büt) [ü]
26. U u = u in run (run), o in union (jünjun), a1 and a3 in banana (bunanu), e in nerve (nurv) [u]
27. V v = v in verve (vurv) [vπ]
28. W w = w in way (wΛ) [wΛ]
29. X x = ch in loch (lδx), x in Quixote (KπxötΛ), X {Greek Chi}in X?????? {Christos} (Xrπstös), X {Russian Khah} in XpyùθB {Khrushchov} (Xrüsjtsjov) [δx]
30. Ÿ ÿ = ow in cow (kÿ), a in Albert (Ÿlburt), ou in couch (kÿtsj) [ÿ]
31. Y y = oo in book (byk), use for u in une {French} (yn), y in Physik {German} (fyzπk) [y]

32. Z z = z in zebra (zπbru), s in is (I z) [zπ]
Combination sounds:
- δI = i in like (lδIk), y in my (mδI)
- jü = u in fume (fjüm)
- hw = wh in what (hwδt)
- kw = qu in queen (kwπn)
- sj = sh in shirt (sjurt), ch in chic (sjπk)
- tsj = ch in church (tsjurtsj)
- zj = z in azure (uzjyr), s in treasure (trezjyr)
- dzj = j in jail (dzjΛl), g in age (Λdzj)
- ng = ng in sing (sπng)
- ndzj = nge in singe (sIndzj)

Some examples of words written in the Phonetic Alphabet: (Sum ekzamplz δv wurds rItIn In qπ FönetIk Ÿlfubet) philosophy (fIlosöfπ), biology (bδIδlödzjπ), Johnson (Dzjδnsun) caught (kot), thought (cot), cot (kδt), cat (kat), kite (kδIt), then (qIn), thin (cIn)

Dialect and regional accents will present problems with any phonetic alphabet. The simple answer is to accept variant spellings and list them in the dictionary. This is done now with Aluminum and Aluminium, tire and tyre, jail and gaol, etc. Some examples of words with variable pronounciation: grass (gras, grδs), amino (umπnö, umδInö), vitamin (vδItImIn, vItImIn), pecan (pπkδn, pπkan), research (rπsurtsj, rIsurtsj), schedule (skedjül, sjedjül).

Choice of symbols Q q and C c for th sounds: The th in then could be represented by Icelandic Eth, Þ ð, or by Greek Delta, Δ δ. The th in thin could be represented by Icelandic Thorn, ⊖ θ, or by Greek Theta, Θ θ. I chose Q and C because they are already present on English keyboards. Lower case q can be looked at as an upside down d, to which its sound (th in then) is related, and c does have this sound (th in thin) in Castilian Spanish.

LETTER MATRIX TABLE

The following table is copied from "Letter Matrix: Orthographic Demons - Phoneme Grapheme Correspondences for different writing systems. Problematic sound signs." It is part of "New Follick, An Alfabet for English, by Steve Bett, 1997" at I have eliminated the columns for those orthographic schemes which use a mixture of upper and lower case letters for different sounds, as these strike me as totally impractical. I have added my Fönetlk Ÿlfubet as the first column. Follick and SR1 P-A (Spelling Reform Stage 1 Phonetic Alphabet) seem to fit the needs the best of the other systems except for not distinguishing δ (q, dh) from θ (c, th) and hw (wh) from w. The distinction between the short u sound of up and cut and the schwa sound of acute is not one I hear, so I have made no allowance for it.

The modification of the vowels by a following r is more meaningful in the "received pronunciation" of southern England than it is in American, perhaps because the r in the middle of a word is usually not pronounced. There is no difference between the er sound in air and fare versus error and care in American usage, though apparently there is in some British. The word party is a good example of this confusion, since the southern English pronunciation sounds like potty, not party, to an American.

HISTORY.

Being mildly dyslexic, it have always been acutely aware of the non-phonetic nature of standard English orthography. When it went to England as a graduate student in the early 1960's, it encountered the Initial Teaching Alphabet and heard of the Shavian Alphabet. I began tinkering with a phonetic spelling system for English at that time, so this alphabet is the result of about forty years of development, even though it only got around to putting it on the Internet in June of 2001. While it was inspired by the Shavian alphabet, it uses only conventional letters of the Roman alphabet as found on an English keyboard (with one diacritical mark), whereas the Shavian alphabet uses all new characters.

Dyslexia is a genetic syndrome which causes certain learning problems. Those of us with dyslexia can learn the letters in a word (or digits in a phone number) but not be at all sure of their order. Languages like English and French, with silent letters and multiple sounds for the same letter and multiple ways of representing the same sound, cause dyslexics much grief. Dyslexics are able to use phonics to learn to read and therefore can learn to read a phonetically spelt language much faster than English, since they can sound out the letters instead of having to memorize the words.

See the article on dyslexia at English Spelling Reform for a discussion of dyslexia as a function of non-phonetic spelling. Even children without dyslexia frequently have difficulty learning to spell English correctly because of its lack of sound to letter correspondence, as do speakers of other languages trying to learn English.

A language like Spanish, where every letter always has the same sound, is very much easier to learn to read. Having been exposed to several European languages like German, Dutch, Spanish, French, Russian and Greek, plus a few African ones (Shona, Swahili and Bemba), I have become convinced that the standard spelling of English is a major problem for those learning the language, and that it is much worse than the spelling of any of these other languages.

I was not aware of all the other attempts that have been made to develop a phonetic spelling for English until I put my webpage on the Internet and found that the Open Directory already had several other ones there. Some of them are obviously much more sophisticated than mine, being produced by people with formal linguistics training, and would represent the full range of sounds including the length that a vowel sound is held in speaking and the modifying effects of the letter r on a preceding vowel. I feel this over-complicates the system and makes it much harder to learn. My intention is to enable people to easily learn to spell English correctly, not represent every nuance of enunciation. I have tried to keep the number of different characters to a minimum and still have a character for every unique sound in the language.

My list of 32 letters, 12 vowels and 20 consonants, is pretty minimal, I believe. It agrees with the number the number of unmixed vowels and has two less unmixed consonants than

Steve Bett has in the table for Phoneme Inventory. The difference is j in jail and ch in church, which are mixed, actually, which he notes.

The ideas for the orthography which I have proposed come from other languages, not from other earlier alphabets. The use of sj for the sh sound comes from Dutch, the use of c for the th in thin comes from Castilian Spanish, the use of umlauts to produce six new vowels comes from German, though the actual sounds are not those of German. The use of umlauts rather than macrons, which would be preferred if they were more readily available, is a function of the letter sets available on the PC. An umlaut can be produced by typing control+: before typing the letter in MS Word and some other programmes, there is no such code for a macron. This is just a suggestion, it amenable to changes or to having parts lifted for other systems. After impressed by SR1 P-A and Follick now that it have seen them (since posting the first page on the Internet), I think they could be improved by adopting the q and c for the th in then and the th in thin from my alphabet. Note that they all use the well-defined consonants of traditional orthography, b, d, f, g, k, l, m, n, p, r, s, t, v, and z, so these letters are not shown on the table.

Chapter 2

Phonetic English

BEGINNING OF PHONETICS

If there had not been so much money to be so easily acquired in information technology, there's a good chance that I would have pursued a career in linguistics. I've always been fascinated by languages, by the different ways that information can be expressed and understood in symbolic forms. Indeed, I think that's a big part of the reason why computer science appealed to me.

This post is pretty off-topic for this blog, so it's hidden behind the jump. You're invited to continue if you'd like.

I need to preface all of this with a huge disclaimer, lest any true linguist geeks see this and lose all respect for me. I am a linguaphile, but not any kind of serious linguistic scholar. Like anyone who uses a tool day in and day out, I have a lot of opinions about languages, and I like to think that I perhaps think a bit more than the average joe about the language I speak, but I'm certainly not any kind of expert, per se. If you're looking for very well-written blog posts from lingual experts, check out The Language Log. I can't even pretend to compete with the wonderful authors of that site. I lose about 6 hours every time I check the bookmark.

In high school, I studied Latin for 4 years. In college, I studied Spanish for 2. Today I couldn't really hold a conversation in either, but what always seemed so interesting to me is that both those languages are almost obsessively phonetic, whereas English is so far from phonetic that native English speakers often don't even really understand what a "vowel" really is. They'll happily recite "a e i o u and sometimes y", but the *concept* is lost. In fact, y is not "sometimes" a vowel—it's *always* a vowel, but often part of a diphthong.

In a spoken language, sound is made by passing air over tightened vocal chords through a particularly shaped chamber. The chamber can be opened and closed in various different ways, and can be shaped in different ways. Consonants define the method by which the chamber is opened or closed (sound is started or stopped) while vowels define the shape of the chamber while sound is being created. Nasals are sound that is passed through the nose, where air does not escape the mouth.

When the chamber is changed during the sound from one shape into another, that is a diphthong, or combination of vowels. If you can pronounce the sound on its own without moving your tongue, and it doesn't have a clear start or end, then it's most likely a vowel. (It could also be a nasal like n, m, and ng, or a sibilant consonant, like s or z. Perhaps there are others, I'm not sure)

I've been thinking a lot the last few weeks about how English might be made phonetic. The first step is identifying the vowels and diphthongs that we use in our spoken language, and forget everything we now know about spelling. Where possible, I believe that it would make sense to use the Spanish vowels, since they are so widely known and seem to be fairly consistent in most languages:

a = "ah" as in "father"
e = "eh" as in "bed"
i = "ee" as in "feet"
o = "oh" as in "go"
u = "oo" as in "boot"

The first thing that struck me is that we have a lot of other vowel sounds that simply don't exist in Spanish.

For example:

"r" as in "they're grrrrrrreat!"
"a" as in "bat"
"i" as in "bit"

There's already a letter for "r", but the "short a" needs a new symbol. Since "y" is wholly unnecessary, being more properly expressed as "i," we can use y as the short i sound. C is always either a "k" or "s" sound, except when it's part of "ch," so let's make c into "ch". Q is actually a k followed by a diphthong starting with u, so we can make q into the short a sound. (It's kind of like an a with a tail, anyway) The short "oo" sound is tricky, as well. X is also just a "ks", so we can use that. The short "u" as in "but" is also missing. W is actually just a diphthong that starts with "u", so let's use that.

So:

y = "i" as in "bit"

q = "a" as in "bat"

x = "oo" as in "book"

w = "u" as in "but"

c = "ch" as in "chess"

A lot of the so-called vowels in English are actually diphthongs. Spanish mostly gets these right.

For example,

"i" as in "bite" is actually ai

"ai" as in "wait" is actually ei

So, uat du ui faind hir? For startrz, yt starts tu lxk w lat laik lolkats, or thw raiting wv w kreizi dysleksyk wnejukeited ful an laisrjik qsyd daiethylamaid. Houevr, yt dwz get izir tu rid uons u hqv sin mor wv yt. Thi er yz veri klir tudei, thi wethr meiks mi w hqpi boi. Ai qm yn iur yntrnets, kloging iur tubz. Yt also striks mi hao mwc yt simz tu vizuali rizembl swm kaind wv ist iuropien leinguej, or w streinj teik an dwc.

Thi bygest prablem wyth thys speling yzynt thqt yts hard tu wndrstqnd, bwt rqthr thqt ui form hqbyts uyc ar hard tu breik. Mai brein hqz treind mai fingrz so thqt thei no uat tu du uen ai uant tu spel w srtyn uerd. Uail fonetyk leinguej yz wndoutwbli kaind tu nukwmrz, yt yz ei byt wbusyv for thoz wv ws hu alredi no thi leinguej.

Also, srtyn uerdz bigyn tu sho wp thqt ar shr tu koaz prablemz. For eksqmpel, thi inglysh "we" qnd "you" lwk veri dyfrent. Houevr, yn fonetyk inglysh, thi seim uerdz ar speld "ui" qnd "iu", rispektyvli. Ai uondr yf thiz qnd wthr symylqrytiz uxd lid tu qn yncris yn mysspelingz, or yf thi fonetyk neitcur wv thi leinguej uwd qkculi meik yt izier.

Ok, enough of that craziness...

So, why not just use Kirshenbaum or some other IPA for day-to-day writing? After all, if you're going to be phonetic, why not *be* phonetic?

The problem with that is that, while these alphabets are extremely useful in the analysis of speech and dialects, they are *too* precise to serve as a written language, as different dialects would then have completely different spellings. For example, "tour" in America is pronouced "tŠy," but in the UK, it would be pronounced By simply saying that "r" is "r as in tour", it makes it much easier for different dialects to pronounce each vowel different from one another, and yet have a consistent spelling that all can use. The "r" vowel may be pronounced differently in America than England (and indeed, there is a lot of variation with respect to the letter "r" on this side of the pond,) individual Americans and Brits each pronounce "r" consistently, and thus, we can all use the same letter for it, even if we sound a little different.

However, the IPA alphabets do get one thing very right: "th" should really be either "θ" (th as in thing) or "ð" (th as in breathe) Or, perhaps they should be the same symbol, since some words like "the" can be pronounced either way, depending on dialect. Speaking of "the," assuming we go with θ as a symbol, would it properly be spelled "θi" or "θw"? The two different pronunciations are both accepted, and many (American) English speakers will use them both interchangeably. When speaking quickly, as in the middle of this sentence, we tend to say θw. However, when announcing a title or something of great import, as in "President of the United States of America," or when placed before another vowel as in "the alphabet," we tend to favour θi.

PHONETICS AND PHONOLOGY

SPEECH GENERATION

Speech is achieved by compression of the lung volume

causing air flow which may be made audible if set into vibration by the activity of the larynx. This sound can then be made into speech by various modifications of the supralaryngeal vocal tract.

- Lungs provide the energy source - Respiration
- Vocal folds convert the energy into audible sound - Phonation
- Articulators transform the sound into intelligible speech – Articulation

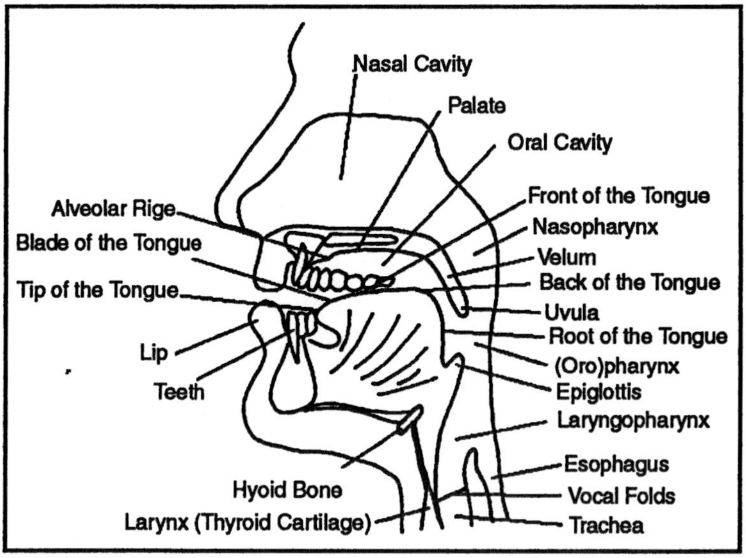

Fig. An Overview of the Vocal Tract

An overview of the vocal tract showing structures that are important in speech sound production and speech articulation

LUNG STRUCTURE AND FUNCTION

Expanding the thoracic cavity by expanding the rib cage (raising the ribs) and by lowering the diaphragm increases lung volume, decreases air pressure in the lungs and so air is drawn in from the from the outside to equalise pressure. Contracting the thoracic cavity by contracting the rib cage (lowering the ribs) and by raising the diaphragm decreases lung volume, increases air pressure in the lungs and so air is expelled from the lungs to equalise pressure with the outside air.a flow chart overview of the above processes.

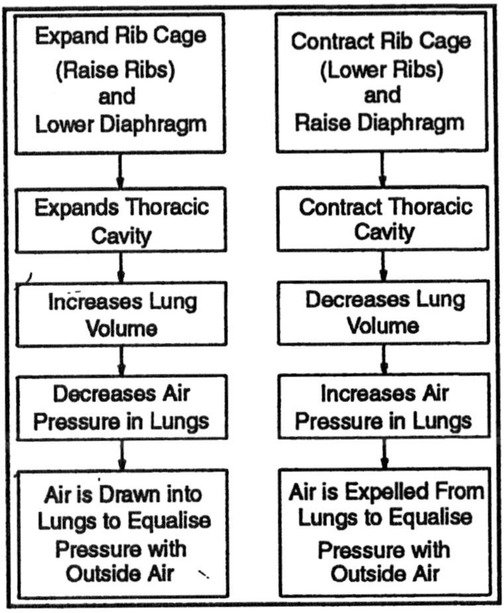

Fig. Flow Chart of Lung Function

See a simplified diagram of the lungs' function as the energy generator in speech production.A Simplified Diagram of the Vocal Tract.

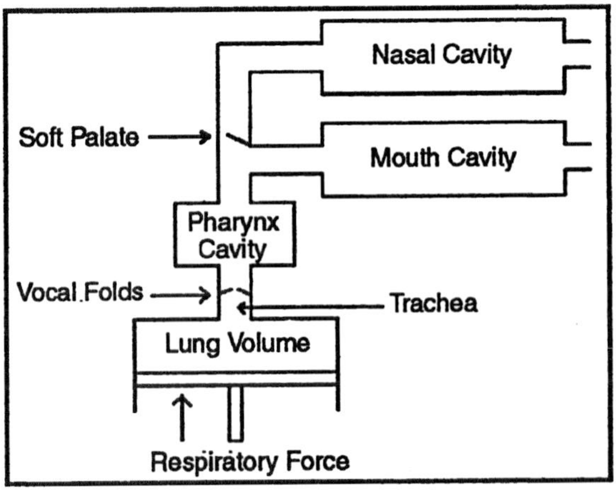

A simplified diagram of the vocal tract showing the energy generation function of the lungs.

Above the vocal folds are the various cavities that can be modified in size and shape to cause changes in the sound quality of the speech sounds.

LARYNX STRUCTURE AND FUNCTION

The larynx is a continuation of the trachea but the cartilage structures of the larynx are highly specialised. The main cartilages are the thyroid, cricoid and arytenoid cartilages. These cartilages variously rotate and tilt to affect changes in the vocal folds.

The vocal folds (also known as the vocal cords) stretch across the larynx and when closed they separate the pharynx from the trachea. When the vocal folds are open breathing is permitted. The opening between the vocal folds is known as the glottis.

When air pressure below closed vocal folds (sub-glottal pressure) is high enough the vocal folds are forced open, the vocal folds then spring back closed under both elastic and aerodynamic forces, pressure builds up again, the vocal folds open again... and so on for as along as the vocal folds remain closed and a sufficient sub-glottal pressure can be maintained. This continuous periodic process is known as phonation and produces a "voiced" sound source.

Different laryngeal adjustments affect the way that the vocal folds vibrate and can result in different voice qualities, some of which are important linguistically in some languages.

ARTICULATION

When sound is produced at the larynx, that sound can be modified by altering the shape of the vocal tract above the larynx (supralaryngeal or supraglottal).

The shape can be changed by opening or closing the velum (which opens or closes the nasal cavity connection into the oropharynx), by moving the tongue or by moving the lips or the jaw.

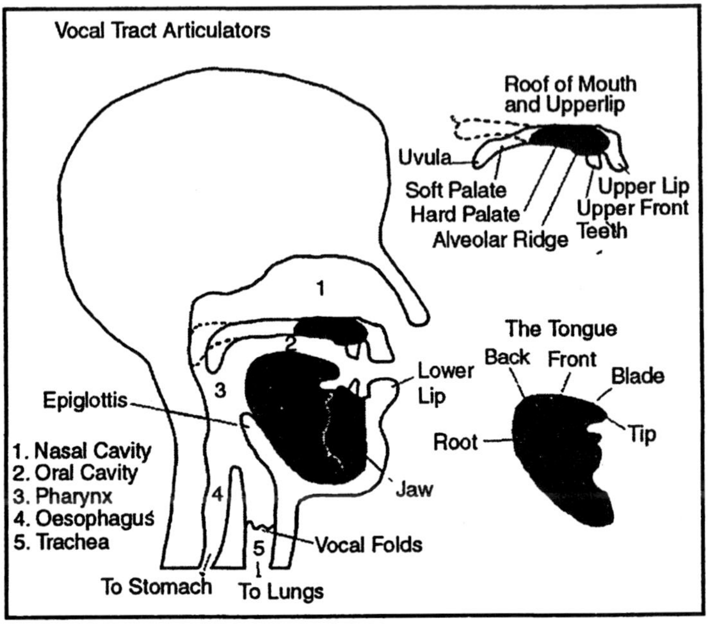

Fig. Vocal Tract Articulators

Chapter 3

Consonants and Vowels

CONSONANTS AND VOWELS

The distinction between vowels and consonants is based on three main criteria:

1. *Physiological*: airflow/constriction
2. *Acoustic*: prominence
3. *Phonological*: syllabicity

Sometimes, it is necessary to rely on two or three of these criteria to decide whether a sound is a vowel or a consonant.

PHYSIOLOGICAL DISTINCTION

In general, consonants can be said to have a greater degree of constriction than vowels. This is obviously the case for oral and nasal stops, fricatives and affricates. The case for approximants is not so clear-cut as the semi-vowels /j/ and /w/ are very often indistinguishable from vowels in terms of their constriction.

ACOUSTIC DISTINCTION

In general, consonants can be said to be less prominent than vowels. This is usually manifested by vowels being more intense than the consonants that surround them. Sometimes, certain consonants can have a greater total intensity than adjacent vowels but vowels are almost always more intense at low frequencies than adjacent consonants.

PHONOLOGICAL DISTINCTION

Syllables usually consist of a vowel surrounded optionally

by a number of consonants. A single vowel forms the prominent nucleus of each syllable. There is only one peak of prominence per syllable and this is nearly always a vowel. The consonants form the less prominent valleys between the vowel peaks.

This tidy picture is disturbed by the existence of syllabic consonants. Syllabic consonants form the nucleus of a syllable that does not contain a vowel.

In English, syllabic consonants occur when an approximant or a nasal stop follows a homorganic (same place of articulation) oral stop (or occasionally a fricative) in words such as "bottle" or "button" /bʌtn)/.

The semi-vowels in English play the same phonological role as the other consonants even though they are vowel-like in many ways. The semi-vowels are found in syllable positions where stops, fricatives, etc. are found (eg. "pay", "may", and "say" versus "way").

CLASSIFYING CONSONANTS

Occasionally other features are required to classify consonants.

For example, airstream direction (egressive, ingressive) is necessary to separate ejectives and implosives. Sometimes it is also necessary to specify which part of the tongue is being used in an articulation (eg. "apical" and "laminal" (tongue blade) gestures are possible for dental, alveolar and palato-alveolar places of articulation).

STRICTURE

Stricture is the extent to which the oral tract is constricted. The following diagram is ordered with the greatest "degree" (or "rank order") of stricture at the top and the least degree of stricture at the bottom. The greatest degree of stricture is the "stop" with complete closure or constriction of the oral cavity at some point.

Note that stricture specifically relates to oral cavity constriction and ignores the state of the nasal cavity (ie. whether the velum is open or closed).

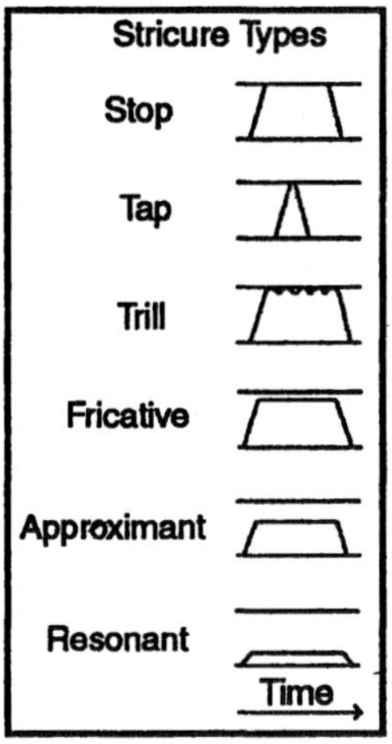

Fig. Stricture types: Degree of Closure as a Function of time.

Stop and Tap Stricture

Stop stricture is complete closure followed by release. At the release of an oral stop there is a brief burst of noise which may be followed by a period of aspiration.

Note that tap stricture is really a special case of stop stricture. A tap is an extremely brief stop.

Trill Stricture

A trill consists of a series of taps interspersed by narrow openings of a similar cross-sectional area to a fricative.

Fricative Stricture

Fricative stricture consists of a very narrow opening that has a small enough cross-sectional area to cause the air to flow turbulently. Turbulent air flow generates random or aperiodic sound that characterises fricatives.

Approximant Stricture

Approximant stricture consists of a opening with a greater cross-sectional area than a fricative but the opening is narrower than that of a vowel. The opening is greater than that which would produce turbulent air flow and aperiodic noise.

Resonant Stricture

This is stricture typical of vowels. Semi-vowels are also often produced with resonant stricture.

MANNER OF ARTICULATION

Consonant Manner of Articulation

There is considerable variation in the names applied to manners of articulation in the literature. In some cases different names are applied to the same manner of articulation, whilst in other cases labels divided up consonants in different ways.

In the present course we will mostly use the following labels for place or articulation:-

Oral Stops

Oral stops have stop stricture and have a closed velum (ie. no nasal airflow). Oral stops are sometimes referred to as "plosives" or simply as "stops". Be warned that in the literature the term "stop" can refer specifically to oral stops, to oral stops and nasal stops collectively, or to stop stricture.

Nasal Stops

Nasal stops have stop stricture and have an open velum (ie. nasal airflow and nasal resonance). Nasal stops are very often referred to simply as "nasals".

Fricatives

Fricatives are consonants with fricative stricture. Many systems include central and lateral fricatives in the same manner category (but the IPA Pulmonic Consonant chart and the chart below separates them). In most of the course notes for this subject the central and lateral fricatives are included in a single manner category. Fricatives are sometimes referred to as "spirants" but this term is now considered obsolete. The strong fricatives [s ʃ z '] are often termed "sibilant" fricatives.

Affricates

Affricates are commonly described as a complex

combination of stop plus fricative. Affricates can also be considered to represent one extreme end of a continuum of stop aspiration.

Approximants

Approximants are consonants with approximant stricture, although some approximants also commonly display resonant stricture. It is very easy to become confused about the terminology used in the literature when referring to this class of consonants.

Very often approximants are divided into the following two sub-classes:

1. Liquids (e.g. English, [y] and [l])
2. Semi-vowels (e.g. English, [w] and [j]) - also known as "glides"

When this system is used, liquids are effectively those approximants that are not classified as semi-vowels. Semi-vowels are those consonants that are most like vowels in their acoustic and articulatory characteristics and the semi-vowels often exhibit resonant stricture. Very often semi-vowels are only distinguishable from vowels using phonological criteria

Rhotics

Sometimes this further class of consonants is defined, but it is not strictly a manner of articulation. The rhotic sounds are the so-called r-like sounds and include the alveolar and retroflex approximants and the alveolar and uvular trills. In this course the term "rhotic" is used when dealing with the consonants of Australian Aboriginal languages. In many Australian languages there are two consonants in the rhotic class, the alveolar trill [r] and the alveolar or post-alveolar approximant[y]. Also, the term "rhotic" is also used when referring to the "rhotic" (eg. American) and "non-rhotic" (eg. Australian) dialects of English.

Obstruents Versus Sonorants

Sometimes you will see consonants classified as "obstruents" or "sonorants". Obstruents include the oral stops, the affricates and the fricatives. Sonorants include the nasal stops, approximants and the vowels.

MANNER OF ARTICULATION

Manner of articulation can be described in terms of Laterality, Nasality and Stricture. The following diagram shows how the various manners of articulation can be defined in terms of their laterality, nasality and stricture features.

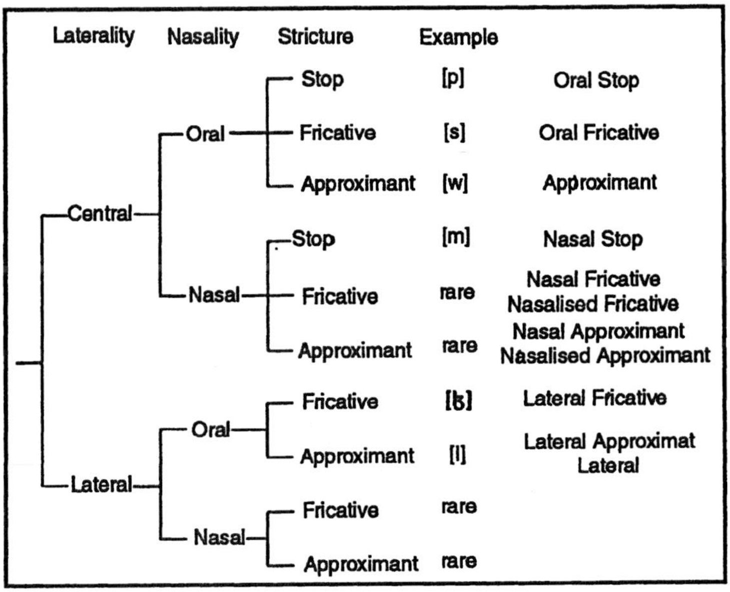

Fig. Relationship between Manner of Articulation and Laterality, Nasality and Stricture.

Note that there can be no lateral (oral or nasal) stops; lateral requires the air to be directed around the sides of the tongue, stop requires the air to be totally obstructed in the mouth. The features are therefore incompatible.

PLACE OF ARTICULATION

Place of articulation is defined in terms of the the articulators involved in the speech gesture. It is common to refer to a speech gesture in terms of an active articulator and a passive articulator.

Active Articulators

An active articulator is the articulator that does all or most of the moving during a speech gesture. The active articulator is usually the lower lip or some part of the tongue. These active articulators are attached to the jaw which is relatively free to move when compared to parts of the vocal tract connected directly to the greater mass of the skull.

Passive Articulators

A passive articulator is the articulator that makes little or no movement during a speech gesture. The active articulator moves towards the relatively immobile passive articulator. Passive articulators are often directly connected to the skull. Passive articulators include the upper lip, the upper teeth, the various parts of the upper surface of the oral cavity, and the back wall of the pharynx.

Naming Place of Articulation

The place of articulation of a consonant is generally named for the passive articulator. Sometimes the active articulator is also explicitly included in the name of a place of articulation by use of the prefixes "apico-" and "lamino-".

Illustrations of Place of Articulation in English

The following links lead to diagrams that illustrate place of articulation in English. These diagrams are applicable to most dialects of English. The possible exception is the diagram for /r/ which may be articulated differently in some dialects of English.

- Oral Stop Articulation
- Nasal Stop Articulation
- Fricative Articulation
- Approximant Articulation

Table of Possible and Impossible Articulations

The following table makes a distinction between articulations that are actually used contrastively in the world's languages, articulations that are not used but are possible, and articulations that are impossible.

INTERNATIONAL PHONETIC ALPHABET

Pulmonic Consonants

Pulmonic consonants are consonants that depend upon an egressive (outward-flowing) air stream originating in the lungs. The following table contains all of the single-articulation pulmonic consonants listed in the 1993 International Phonetic Alphabet. The aspirated stops and the voiceless alveolar trill don't actually belong in this table as they are combinations of existing consonant symbols plus diacritics.

The column titles are abbreviations of the place of articulation of the consonants in that column. For a key to the place-of-articulation abbreviations, see the table immediately below this table. The row titles indicate the manner of articulation of the sounds in that row. In this table, whenever two symbols appear in the same cell, the upper symbol is voiceless and the lower symbol is voiced. The third symbol in the oral stop cells is the voiceless aspirated stop. For information on voicing and aspiration in oral stops (voice onset time).

	BL	LD	D	AL	PAL	R	PL	V	U	PH	G
Oral Stop	p b pʰ			t d tʰ		ʈ ɖ ʈʰ	c ɟ cʰ	k g kʰ	q G qʰ		ʔ
Nasal Stop	m	ɱ		n		ɳ	ɲ	ŋ	N		
Trill	B			r̥ r					R		
Tap or Flap				ɾ		ɽ					
Fricative	ɸ β	f v	θ ð	s z	ʃ ʒ	ʂ ʐ	ç ʝ	x ɣ	χ ʁ	ħ ʕ	h ɦ
Lateral Fricative				ɬ ɮ							
Approximate		ʋ		ɹ		ɻ	j	ɰ			
Lateral Apprioximant				l		ɭ	ʎ	L			

Recorded examples (CV context with a following [P] vowel) have been supplied for each of the symbols in red.

Table. Of Place of Articulation Codes Used in the Pulmonic Consonant Table

BL	Bilabial	PL	Palatal
LD	Labiodental	V	Velar
D	Dental	U	Uvular
AL	Alveolar	PH	Pharyngeal
P-AL	Post-alveolar	G	Glottal
R	Retroflex		

Notes:

1) Note that the post-alveolar fricative symbols [ʃ] and [Á] are sometimes referred to in the literature as "palato-alveolar" fricatives. This implies a primary alveolar fricative articulation with a secondary palatal approximant articulation. The term "post-alveolar" implies a single fricative articulation just behind the alveolar ridge. For this course the term "post-alveolar" is preferred.
2) The retroflex sounds are sometimes referred to as "post-alveolar". Retroflex sounds can be post-alveolar or palatal, but they are distinguished from those sounds in their use of the tongue tip as the active articulator (that is they are "apico-" articulations). The tip of the tongue curls back towards these places of articulation. The post-alveolar consonants use the blade of the tongue whilst the palatal consonants use the front of the tongue.

Non-Pulmonic Consonants

These non-pulmonic consonants don't use pulmonic airflow. Instead they use velaric airflow or glottalic airflow (implosives and ejectives).

Clicks		Implosives		Ejectives	
ʘ	Bilabial	ɓ	Bilabial	p'	Bilabial
|	Dental	ɗ	Dental/Alveolar	t'	Dental/Alveolar
!	(Post) alveolar	ʄ	Palatal	k'	Velar
ǂ	Palatoalveolar	ɠ	Velar	s'	Alveolar Fricative
ǁ	Alveolar Lateral	ʛ	Uvular		

Recorded examples (CV context with a following [P] vowel) have been supplied for each of the symbols in red.

Complex Articulations

The following table is a list of some of the complex consonants that have either double articulation (both places of articulation with the same degree of stricture) or secondary articulation (a primary articulation coupled with a secondary articulation with a lesser degree of stricture) that also have their own single IPA symbol.

Most other double articulations are represented by two IPA symbols tied together by a ligature (for example kap for a double bilabial-velar stop). Most other secondary articulations are indicated by the addition of a diacritic to the symbol for the primary articulation (for example dafor a voiced velarised alveolar stop).

In the following table, [w] is the lip-rounded counterpart of the approximant [p] and [m] is the lip-rounded counterpart of the approximant [j]. Note that the labial-velar and labial-palatal approximants are not "labialised" as both the labial articulation and the velar or palatal articulation have approximant stricture. (This is also true for [M] except that the two articulations have fricative stricture) Since both articulations have the same stricture these sounds are double articulations and so take the place-of-articulation labels "labial-velar" and "labial-palatal".

The last two symbols on this table have a primary palatal articulation with fricative stricture and a secondary alveolar articulation with approximant stricture (note, however, that usage of these two symbols varies in the literature and they are sometimes confused with [ʃ] and [']).

Voiced Labial-velar Approximant	w
Voiced Labial-palatal Approximant	ɥ
Voiceless Labial-velar Fricative	ʍ
Voiceless Alveolo-palatal Fricative	ɕ
Voiced Alveolo-palatal Fricative	ʑ

Recorded examples (CV context with a following [P] vowel) have been supplied for each of the symbols in red.

VOWELS

In this topic we examine vowel articulation. We will focus on tongue position (vowel height and fronting), lip posture (spread, neutral and rounded), nasalisation, retroflexion, and duration. We will also examine the distinction between monophthongs and diphthongs.

VOWEL ARTICULATION

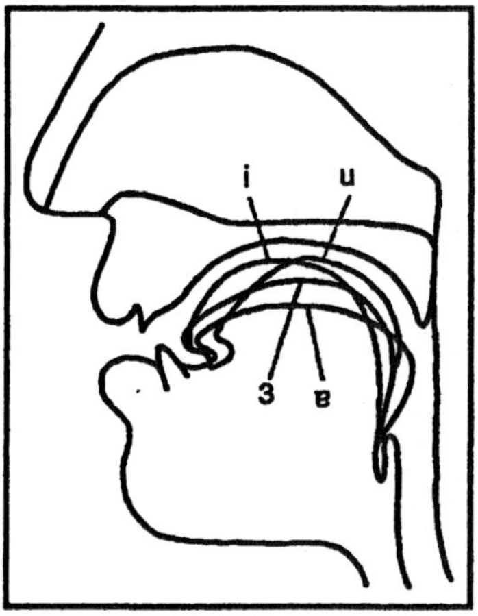

Fig. Approximate Tongue Positions for Four Vowel

The tongue position for the "neutral vowel" [\] is indicated on the above diagram by the black line. This tongue position creates an approximately constant cross-sectional vocal tract area from the glottis to the lips.

This results in a vowel spectrum which has uniformly spaced spectral peaks. Changing the shape of the vocal tract by raising, lowering, fronting or retracting the tongue results in vowel spectra of different patterns and this in turn is responsible for the different perceived quality of the various vowels.

Shown in this diagram, contrasted with [3], is a low vowel [P] a high front vowel [i] and a high back vowel [u].

VOWEL LIP POSTURES

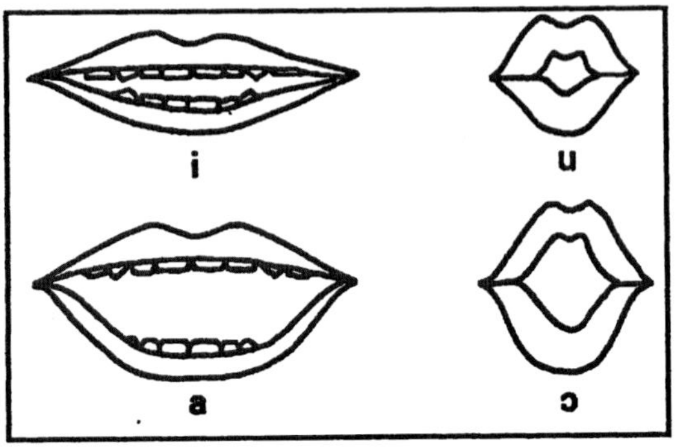

Fig. Approximate lip Postures for Four Vowels

This diagram displays the two extreme lip postures and two intermediate lip postures. The high front cardinal vowel [i] has a very spread lip posture. The high back cardinal vowel [u] has a very tightly rounded lip posture. The low front cardinal vowel [a] has a spread lip posture but this is a more neutral posture than for [i] because the lower jaw position for this vowel causes the lips to be more open. The half-open back cardinal vowel [T] has a rounded lip posture but the lips are more open then for [u] because of the lower jaw position.

The actual lip posture for vowels in any particular language may be similar to that of the closest cardinal vowel with the same lip posture feature, but often speakers of many languages adopt a more neutral posture than would be indicated by these cardinal vowels. Languages that have lip posture contrasts are more likely to adopt the more extreme lip posture to emphasise those contrasts.

For example, a language with the vowel phonemes /i/ and /y/ (such as French) tend to have a strongly spread /i/ and a strongly rounded /y/ to maximise their difference perceptually. Languages without rounding contrasts, such as English, may relax the degree of rounding of rounded vowels and the degree of spreading of spread vowels. In English the extent to which this is true varies from dialect to dialect. For example, Australian English is often described as having rounded vowels which are spoken by many speakers with less rounding than similar vowels in some other dialects of English. This impression may be due, however, to the observation that in English is less rounded. This difference in degree of rounding may simply be due to the fact that the American phoneme is a high back vowel and the Australian phoneme is a high central vowel. There is a tendency for front vowels to be less rounded than back vowels in the absence of a rounding contrast.

COMPLEX VOWEL ARTICULATIONS

Diphthongisation

Diphthongs are essentially single vowel phonemes that consist of two pure vowel targets in sequence. In diphthongs it is often assumed that both targets have equal importance and one does not dominate the other in determining the identity of the vowel.

When an initial brief vowel gesture is dominated by a following full target the initial gesture is referred to as an onglide. When a final brief vowel gesture is dominated by a preceding vowel target the brief final gesture is referred to as an offglide. Sometimes diphthongisation can be extended to three vowel targets intriphthongs.

Two identical sequences can be identified as a single diphthong phoneme in one language and as a monophthong phoneme plus a semi-vowel phoneme in another language.

Transcription

Diphthongs are ideally transcribed as a sequence of two vowel symbols that represent, as closely as possible, the pronunciation of each of the two targets.

eg. /aI//eI//æT/

Onglides are usually indicated by a preceding superscript and offglides by a following superscript of a symbol appropriate to the pronunciation of the glide gesture. Such glides are very often schwas, but this is certainly not always the case.

eg. [^{Y}i] [T^{Y}]

Examples: See the topic "The Vowels of Australian English and Other English Dialects" for examples of diphthongs from Australian English and other English dialects.

Nasalisation of Vowels

In the lecture on vowels we have already dealt briefly with nasalised vowels. This vowel nasalisation is a complex articulation and is an example of simultaneous nasalisation. Such contrastive simultaneous nasalisation must not be confused with contextual and pervasive nasality.

Contextual nasality occurs in vowels, as well as approximants and fricatives, when they are adjacent to nasal stops. Pervasive nasality is nasality that occurs throughout a person's speech as a result of habit, dialect or pathology. Simultaneous nasalisation of consonants is very rare as a contrastive feature in languages.

Transcription: Simultaneous nasalisation is transcribed by placing the "tilde" symbol ⊖over the symbol for the sound being nasalised.

eg. [e⊖], [æ⊖], [P⊖]

Vowel Retroflexion

Vowel retroflexion introduces an r-colouration to a vowel, usually by curling the tongue tip up and back from its normal position, but without moving the tongue body from it normal position for that vowel. Such vowels are often called "rhoticised" vowels. This vowel feature is commonly found in the speech of many American and Irish speakers of English. It occurs in the environment of a following [y] but in some cases the rhoticised vowel is all that remains of a deleted following[y] or alternatively the vowel is completely deleted and the [y] becomes syllabic.

Transcription

In the past vowel retroflexion was sometimes indicated by a following superscript "y" as in [Y^y]. The current IPA standard recommends instead the following transcription: eg. [a⊖] [T⊖] [Y⊖] (ie. the affected vowel followed by the diacritic ⊖)

Examples

Badaga (Dravidian Language, India) has two degrees of vowel retroflexion (but the intermediate contrast is disappearing)					
[be]	"mouth"	[be˞]	"bangle"	[be˞˞]	"crop"
[kaːsu]	"coin"	[ka˞ːsu]	"spread out"	[ka˞˞ːsu]	"remove "

PHARYNGEALISATION

Secondary pharyngealisation appears to be always simultaneous with lingual primary articulations and involves an adjustment of the tongue body. Only simultaneous secondary pharyngealisation appears to be used contrastively in human language.

It may be possible, however, for co-articulatory forces to result in transitional pharyngealisation of a bilabial such as [b] when followed (probably across a word or syllable boundary) by the pharyngeal fricative [•] in a language such as Arabic.

Transcription

The IPA standard recommends a superscript "•" following the symbol of the sound being pharyngealised.

eg. [sÁ] [tÁ] [dÁ]

Examples

Arabic has a number of normal and pharyngealised ("emphatic") consonant pairs (nb. for some Arabic dialects the secondary articulation is velar). The consonant pairs are [s, sˤ], [z, zˤ], [t, tˤ], [d, dˤ]. Below are examples for [s, sˤ] only.			
[sad]	"to prevail"	[sˤ]	name of the letter

Even (Siberia) has pharyngealised vowels			
[isli]	"plucked"	[iˤsliˤ]	"reached"
[us]	"weapons"	[uˤs]	"guilt"

CO-ORDINATE OR DOUBLE ARTICULATION

Co-ordinate or double articulations occur when two simultaneous articulations of the same stricture occur simultaneously.

Double articulations are most commonly double stops (both double oral stops and double nasal stops), typically involving a simultaneous lingual and a non-lingual stop articulation.

There are also some (very rare) examples of double fricative articulations. One could also call the very common labial-velar approximant [w] a double articulation, in this case a double approximant, as the labial and the velar articulations both have the same stricture, approximant stricture.

Naming Double Articulations

Since double articulations consist of two primary articulations it is not appropriate to talk of "labialised velar stops" or "velarised labial stops" when talking of a double labial and velar stop.

The normal name for such a double stop would be a "labial-velar stop". You will sometimes see a term like "labio-velar stop".

Such a name appears to be too similar to names like "apico-dental" where the first part of the name refers to the active articulator and the second part of the name refers to the passive articulator of a single primary articulation. The term "labio-velar" might, therefore, be seen to imply an impossible combination of active and passive articulators.

Transcription

Since the two articulations are of the same rank order of stricture, that is they are both primary articulations, neither symbol is subscripted or superscripted, but both are tied together by a ligature.

Usually the lingual articulation symbol is placed before the non-lingual symbol.

eg. [kp] [ab] [Km] [ta"]

Examples

Idoma (West Africa) has three bilabial-velar double articulations					
[ak͡pa]	"bridge"	[àg͡ba]	"jaw"	[àŋ͡màà]	"body painting"
Eggon (West Africa?) has single stops, double stops and pairs of single and double stops in sequence, all contrasting					
Single Segments					
[pom]	"pound (v.)"	[abu]	"dog"	[aku]	"room"
[gom]	"break"	[k͡pu]	"die"	[g͡bu]	"arrive"
Sequences					
[kba]	"dig"	[g͡bga]	"grind"	[ak͡pki]	"stomac h"
[bga]	"beat, kill"	[kpu]	"kneel"	[gba]	"divide "

SePedi (Northern Sotho, Africa) has three double fricatives (but acoustic analysis suggests that they may actually be fricative sequences)					
[βof͡sa]	"youth"	[lef͡ʃeːra]	"coward"	[β͡ʒalwa]	"beer"

AFFRICATION

An affricate is a stop with an extended and controlled fricative phase following the occlusion. The stop and aspiration or fricative phase are homorganic (same place of articulation).

Affricates form one extreme of the following continuum:

- Unaspirated stop
- Aspirated stop
- Affricated stop
- Affricate

In this continuum the stops have increasing strength and duration of aspiration, with an affricate effectively being a single phoneme with clear stop and fricative stages.

The affricate [tʃ] is very common, being found in about 45% of the world's languages. Dental and alveolar affricates are also very common.

Transcription

Affricates are very often written with a ligature tying together the symbol for the stop and fricative, but sometimes it is customary to write the two symbols without the ligature as is often the case for [tʃ] and [d'] in English.

eg. [tʃ], [dʒ], [ts]   (or [tʃ], [dʒ], [ts])

Affricated stops have been traditionally written in the form [t^{s}] but this does not appear to be supported by the current IPA standard.

Examples

Mandarin Chinese (Tones are omitted in the examples, below) ([ɕ] is a voiceless alveolo-palatal fricative)					
[tsa]	"to smack lips"	[tʂa]	"to pierce"	[tɕa]	"to add"
[ts^{h}a]	"to wipe"	[tʂ^{h}a]	"to stick in"	[tɕ^{h}a]	"to pinch tightly"

FOOTNOTES

- A context where a contrast is neutralised is one where a normal contrast on a particular language does not apply. For example, in English /p/ and /b/ contrast with respect to voicing (well, actually VOT). In the context /sp.../at the beginning of a syllable the contrast is neutralised. That is the sequences /sp.../ and /sb.../never contrast at the beginning of a syllable in English. The same is also true for the alveolar and velar oral stops. It can be said that in English the voicing contrast for oral stops is neutralised in this context.

MODULES OF VOWELS

VOWEL SYSTEMS

Types of Vowel Systems

This topic illustrates a number of possible types of vowel systems with examples from various languages. The vowel symbols used do not necessarily represent the exact pronunciation of the vowels of each of the sample languages but are intended to illustrate the types of vowel patterns that can be found. The systems are built up from a number of vowel features. All vowel systems have at least twoheight and two fronting contrasts. Further contrasts are built up from the features length (also known as lax/tense), nasality, and lip rounding. Some extra, less common, features that define vowel systems also exist and will be dealt with elsewhere.

In the following examples only monophthongs will be examined since the more complex diphthongs are difficult to categorise in terms of their place of articulation (having a separate place of articulation for each target).

The examples are mostly from Lass,

HIGH-LOW SYSTEMS

Languages with minimal vowel systems typically have three vowel phonemes: one high front, one high back, and one low vowel with no length contrast.

Aleut		Moroccan Arabic	
i	u	i	u
ɐ		a	

In other words there is a maximum dispersal of vowel quality towards the far corners of the vowel space.

Length contrast,

Alaskan Eskimo

i	u	iː	uː
ɐ		ɐː	

Some languages are based on this basic system but have in addition the added dimension of vowel length.

HIGH-MID-LOW SYSTEMS

No Length Contrast,

Ainu		Yiddish	
i	u	I	ʊ
ɛ	o	ɛ	ɔ
ɐ		ɐ	

Length Contrast,

Hawaiin

i	u	iː	uː
ɛ	o	ɛː	oː
ɐ		ɐː	

Australin English

i:	ʉ:		ɪ		ʊ
		o:			
	ɜ:		e		
					ɔ
	ɐ:		æ	ɐ	

Note that this table for Australian English does not imply that there are intermediate levels between mid and either high or low. The intermediate positions for /oÐ/ and /T/ merely indicate indecision about whether to make /oÐ/ mid or high and whether to make /T/ mid or low.

Nasal and Length Contrast,

Beembe

i		u	i:		u:	ĩ		ũ
ɛ		o	ɛ:		o:	ɛ̃		õ
	ɐ			ɐ:			ɐ̃	

Rounding Contrast,

Chuvash

i	y	ɯ	u
ɛ			ɒ

Four Height Contrasts

Rounding and Nasal contrast,

French

i	y	u			
e	ø	o			
ɛ	œ	ɔ	ɛ̃	œ̃	ɔ̃
a		ɒ			ɒ̃

The upper limit is about 21 monophthong phonemes (eg. Swiss German and Alsatian German with length and rounding contrasts).

Vowels of Australian English

Prior to the advent of modern acoustic analysis techniques, and overlapping with acoustic studies during the early years of acoustic phonetics, phonetic analysis was "impressionistic" and was carried out by phoneticians trained in auditory and transcription skills. For an overview of impressionistics studies of Australian English read:-

Acoustic Studies of Australian English Vowels

Until recently, most Australian phoneticians used the symbols originally used by Mitchell to make broad (or phonemic) transcriptions of Australian English vowels. Clark proposed a new system which more accurately represents the actual pronunciations of an "average" speaker of general Australian English. Clark's vowel symbols are an attempt to relate the actual pronunciation of each vowel by an average speaker of General Australian English (averaged across > 60 speakers) to the closest cardinal vowel. These pronunciations are derived from an acoustic study which will be dealt with in a separate course on Acoustic Phonetics. Cox, Harrington, Cox and Evans examined further detailed acoustic data of Australian English vowels spoken by both adolescents and adults. The conclusions of those studies resulted in a further revision of Clark's proposals for the transcription of Australian English vowels. This new system is contrasted with that of Mitchell and Delbridge in the table below.

Table. The Vowel Symbols Utilised by Mitchell and Delbridge and Harrington, Cox and Evans.

Mitchell	Harrington, Cox & Evans	Example word
i	iː	heed
ɪ	ɪ	hid
ɛ	e	head
æ	æ	had
a	ɐː	hard
ʌ	ɐ	hut
ɒ	ɔ	hot
ɔ	oː	horde
ʊ	ʊ	hood
u	ʉː	shoot

ɜ	ɜː	heard
ə	ə	suppose
eɪ	æɪ	hate
aɪ	ɑe	hide
aʊ	æɔ	howl
oʊ	əʉ	hope
ɔɪ	oɪ	hoist
ɪə	ɪə	hear
ɛə	eː	hair
ʊə	ʊə	tour

Very Important Note: Unless specifically told otherwise, when doing a broad transcription of Australian English for assessment in this course you must use the Harrington, Cox and Evans (HCE) vowel set.

Vowel Systems of Four English Dialects

The links at the bottom of this section are to diagrams of acoustic data plotted onto cardinal vowel charts. The data for Australian English is for General Australian English.

To work out a reasonably descriptive system of transcription for a dialect, simply use the closest cardinal vowel, or other IPA vowel symbol, to each vowel. For diphthongs, select the symbols nearest to the beginning and end of the arrow that describes the diphthong targets. The General Australian English data, when analysed in this way, should give you the symbols that we use in this course for the broad transcription of Australian English vowels.

Centring Diphthongs and Non-Rhotic Dialects of English

In the above diagrams the centring diphthongs of Australian English, British RP English and New Zealand English have been omitted. These diphthongs only occur in non-rhotic dialects of English. These are dialects that don't pronounce the /r/ consonant at the end of a syllable when there is a following pause or consonant. These diphthongs occur as a result of the /r/ phoneme being reduced to a schwa offglide in these contexts. These diphthongs include /Iə,eə,ʊə/ but their realisation in most dialects is evolving and there is evidence that some centring diphthongs may be disappearing (or in the case of Australian English, changing to monophthongs eg. /eə/>/eÐ/).

AIRSTREAM AND LARYNGEAL FEATURES IN SPEECH

AIRSTREAM

Source of Power	Direction of Airflow
pulmonic (lung action)	egressive
glottalic (larynx action)	egressive or ingressive
velaric (tongue action)	ingressive

PULMONIC AIRSTREAM

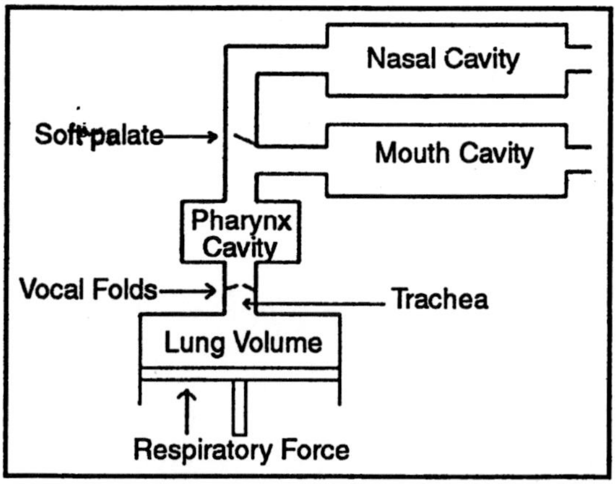

A simplified diagram of the vocal tract showing the energy generation function of the lungs. Above the vocal folds are the various cavities that can be modified in size and shape to cause changes in the sound quality of the speech sounds.

Expanding the thoracic cavity by expanding the rib cage (raising the ribs) and by lowering the diaphragm increases lung volume, decreases air pressure in the lungs and so air is drawn in from the from the outside to equalise pressure. Contracting the thoracic cavity by contracting the rib cage (lowering the ribs) and by raising the diaphragm decreases lung volume, increases air pressure in the lungs and so air is expelled from the lungs to equalise pressure with the outside air.

COMPLEX CONSONANT ARTICULATIONS

DEFINITION

For the purposes of this course, complex articulations can be considered to belong to two categories:

- Simultaneous articulations (double articulation or secondary articulation)
- Sequence of two (or more) gestures within the same phoneme

In reality, all speech is complex, involving the coordination of the movement of numerous articulators. The articulatory movements of the various articulators can be assumed to be attempting to reach particular articulatory targets for each phoneme in a sequence of speech sounds. The articulatory gestures belonging to one phoneme overlap with the articulatory gestures of other phonemes as each of the articulators attempts to reach its target positions. Because some articulators move slower than others these movements are not synchronised.

The key to this concept of "complex articulation" revolves around the notion of the "articulatory target" for each articulator.

To determine whether a sound is a complex articulation you should ask the following questions:

- Does the phoneme have more than one articulatory target (simultaneous or in sequence)?
- If yes, is more than one of these targets contrastive?

The second question is essential as all phonemes involve more than one articulator with its own particular articulatory target. For example, a low vowel has both a low tongue target position and a low jaw target position. The jaw target articulation does not add to the phonological contrastiveness of the vowel, however, as the low tongue position alone is sufficient to identify this vowel sound as a low vowel.

On the other hand, the contrast between /i/ and /y/ in a language such as French depends upon both the target articulation of the tongue (high, front) and the target articulation of the lips (spread or rounded). Changing either target articulation will change the phonemic identity of the sound. In other words the two targets (lingual and labial) are both contrastive.

We can now reduce the two questions, above, to a single question:

- Does the phoneme have more than one contrastive articulatory target (simultaneous or in sequence)?

If the answer to this question is yes then we can conclude that we have a complex articulation.

MAIN TYPES OF COMPLEX ARTICULATION

It is useful to divide Complex articulations into three main types:

1. Simultaneous Articulations
   a. Secondary Articulations
   b. Co-ordinate or Double Articulations
2. Transitional or Sequential Complex Articulations

Simultaneous Articulations

Primary and Secondary Articulations

Complex simultaneous articulations are usually described in terms of primary and secondary articulations. The primary articulation is the articulation with the greater degree or rank order of stricture. Stricture order, from highest to lowest, is stop, trill, fricative, approximant, resonant. Secondary articulations very often have approximant stricture, especially when the primary and secondary articulators are different parts of the tongue.

Lingual (of the tongue) articulations sometimes take precedence over nasal articulations of the same degree of stricture so that the lingual articulation would be primary and the nasal articulation would be secondary. This means that lingual articulations would be considered primary when the other contrastive articulation is nasal. For this reason we have nasalised vowels in numerous languages and contrastive nasalised approximants and fricatives in a small number of languages.

CO-ordinate or Double Articulation

When a sound has two simultaneous contrastive articulations and these articulations are of the same rank order of stricture (eg. both have stop stricture or both have fricative stricture) then it is not possible to distinguish between primary and secondary articulations. Both articulations in such a case are considered to be primary and the sound is said to be produced by a co-ordinate or double articulation.

The most common double articulations are stop-stop double articulations although fricative-fricative double articulations also exist. Another very common double articulation is the labial-velar approximant-approximant double articulation/w/.

Transitional (Sequential) Complex Articulations

This type of complex articulation involves "...separate and successive articulatory activities which together can be identified as a single segment". Such segments include affricates and diphthongs as well as a number of other classes of segment.

Co-articulation

It will quickly become clear in the discussion below that many cases of complex articulations are not contrastive but are the result of the modification of the articulation of a particular sound as a consequence of the influence of an adjacent sound.

When the pronunciation of a sound is influenced by another sound, co-articulation is said to have occurred. Such co-articulation involves the modification of a particular articulator's gesture so that it is more like the influencing sound. These modifications are usually to non-contrastive gestures as there is a linguistic need to maintain phonological contrasts so that the word can be understood. For this reason, vowels are nasalised when adjacent to nasal consonants and this nasalisation is greatest in languages which do not have an oral-nasal vowel contrast. Co-articulation occurs very strongly for non-contrastive articulators and gestures and is the main contributor to the allophonic richness of many phonemes.

When a contrastive gesture is modified this often results in a change in the phoneme. Such changes are usually referred to as assimilation. These assimilations can potentially change the meaning of a word.

There are, however, many contexts in English, for example, where such phoneme-changing assimilation does not result in communicative difficulty. These are typically highly predictable contexts, contexts in which the contrast is neutralised, or contexts in which the listener can be reasonably expected to rely upon linguistic context to determine meaning.

Naming of Complex Articulations

When naming a complex simultaneous articulation, the primary articulation provides the main name of the sound and the secondary articulation usually acts as a pre-modifier of that name. As a consequence we have "labialised velar", "velarised alveolar", "nasalised labial", etc. Sometimes we split a secondary articulation into sub-categories and use those sub-category names as pre-modifiers, eg. "rounded high-front vowel" instead of "labialised high-front vowel".

To add a further complication, when the primary articulator is the tongue then the name of the articulation is most often taken from the passive articulator that the tongue articulates with (eg. alveolar, velar, etc). Sometimes the name of the articulation is modified by the part of the tongue being used (eg. "apico-dental" versus "lamino-dental"), but only when that extra information is necessary. This means that we could potentially talk about complex articulations with names like "pharyngealised apico-dental".

Types of Complex Articulation Nasalisation

Simultaneous Nasalisation

Simultaneous nasalisation of consonants is very rare as a contrastive feature in languages but is very common in vowels. See the topic "vowel nasalisation".

Prenasaliastion

Prenasalisation most commonly occurs in prenasalised stops where the initial part of the occlusion phase of the oral stops involves nasal output.

Transcription: Prenasalisation is transcribed by placing the appropriate nasal stop symbol before the oral stop symbol (generally with a ligature tying them together).

eg. [mab] [nad] [Kak]

For weaker prenasalisation it has been customary for the nasal symbol to precede the stop symbol as a superscript (eg. [^{m}b] [^{n}d]). Note that the latest IPA standard does not appear to support the preceding superscripted forms and so only transcriptions of the type [mb] and[nd] will be used in this course.

Examples:

Margi (Northern Nigeria) (Note also the four pre-nasalised affricates)			
[mpà]	"fight"	[mbà]	"tie"
[ntà]	"split"	[ndàl]	"throw"
[ntsàntsà]	"shouted"	[ndzə̀ndzəʔbʊ]	"covered"
[ntʃà]	"point at"	[ndʒà]	"open wide"
[ɲcàhʊ]	"break"	[ɲɟárì]	"leave"

Postnsalisation

Postnasalisation is effectively the reverse of prenasalisation and most commonly occurs in nasally released oral stops. During the occlusion both the oral cavity and the velum are closed. Release occurs initially into the nasal cavity by the opening of the velum a short time before the opening of the oral cavity.

Transcription

Postnasalisation can be transcribed by placing the appropriate nasal stop symbol after the oral stop symbol (generally with a ligature tying them together).

eg. [bm] [dn]

The latest IPA standard recommends the use of a superscripted "n" following the oral stop symbol to indicate nasal release of any oral stop. [b^{m}] and [d^{n}] have been used traditionally, but the IPA standard appears to be recommending [b^{n}] and [d^{n}]. In other words ^{n} is used for all nasal release regardless of the place of articulation.

eg. [b^{n}] [d^{n}]

Examples:

Arrernte (Northern Australia) This language has both pre-nasalised and post-nasalised stops					
[anəmə]	"sitting"	[amp͡əɻə]	"knee"	[ap͡məɻə]	"camp"
[mwarə]	"good"	[mp͡waɻə]	"make"	[p͡mwaɻə]	"coolamon "
[aɳə]	"tree"	[aɳʈ͡əmə]	"aching"	[kəʈ͡ɳə]	"top"
[aməŋə]	"fly"	[aŋk͡əmə]	"speaks"	[ak͡ŋə]	"carry"

Simulataneous Labialisation

Simultaneous labialisation is the protrusion or rounding of the lips at the same time as the primary articulation. This may be used phonemically when it contrasts with a neutral or spread lip posture which would be the normal or default posture for this type of primary sound. Simultaneous labialisation can be used contrastively or may be only contextual labialisation. For example, consonants adjacent to rounded vowels may be rounded through coarticulation with the lip posture of that sound. For example, in English [s] will most often be labialised [s^{w}] when surrounded by rounded vowels (eg. [‰Đ]) in sequences such as "two suits".

Transcription

Simultaneous labialisation is transcribed by placing a superscript "w" symbol ^{w} to the right of the sound being labialised.

eg. [s^{w}], [k^{w}], [l^{w}]

Some phoneticians have used a "w" placed under the symbol of the sound being labialised. This does not appear to be supported by the latest IPA standard and will not be used in this course.

Transitional Labialisation

In transitional labialisation the lip rounding or protrusion only becomes evident in the later part of the sound being labialised. This phenomenon most commonly occurs when a sound is followed by a lip rounded or protruded sound (such as [w] or [u]) and occurs because of coarticulation with that sound. Such examples are generally not phonemic, but rather are allophones of the normally unlabialised phoneme.

Transcription

Transitional labialisation is transcribed by placing a superscript "w" symbol · To the right of the sound being labialised.

eg. [s^w], [k^w], [l^w]

Examples: The following examples are probably of simultaneous labialisation.

Kwakw'ala Labialised and non-labialised Velar and Uvular stops (nb. ˈ indicates that the following syllable is stressed, whilst ' indicates that the preceding stop is an ejective stop)			
Voiceless velar and uvular oral stops			
[ˈkasa]	"beat soft"	[k^weˈsa]	"splashing"
[qeˈsa]	"coiling"	[q^weˈsa]	"peeling"
Voiced velar and uvular oral stops			
[ˈgisgas]	"incest"	[g^weˈsu]	"pig"
[ˈɢaɢas]	"grandparent"	[ˈ$ɢ^w$alas]	"lizard"
Voiceless velar and uvular fricatives			
[xeˈsa]	"lost"	[ˈx^wasa]	"a dance"
[ˈχasa]	"rotten"	[ˈ$χ^w$at'a]	"sparrow"
Voiceless velar and uvular ejective stops			
[ˈk'ata]	"writing"	[k^w 'eˈsa]	"light (weight)"
[ˈq'asa]	"sea otter"	[ˈq^w 'asa]	"crying"

Palatalisation

Simultaneous Paltalisation

In simultaneous palatalisation the front of the tongue is raised to approximate the tongue position for the vowel [i] below the hard palate.

This is a secondary articulation for a sound which has a primary articulation anterior to the hard palate, such as alveolar, dental and labial articulations. Simultaneous palatalisation very often occurs as a result of co-articulation when a sound with an anterior primary articulation is uttered adjacent to palatal consonants such as [j] or high front vowels such as [i].

For example, in English, the [p] in the words "peel" (/piÐl/) and "pure" (/pjʊ ə/) can be pronounced with either simultaneous or transitional palatalisation. In English the consonant [l] is usually pronounced with palatalisation when it precedes a vowel at the beginning of a syllable (this is generally referred to as the "clear l").

Transcription

Clark and Yallop show simultaneous palatalisation as being transcribed with a subscript "j" following the symbol of the primary articulation, as in [l_j]. This does not appear to be supported by the recent IPA standards and will not be used in this course. Instead, the IPA recommended superscript "j" will be used to indicate both simultaneous and transitional palatalisation, as follows:-

eg. [l^j] [p^j]

Transitional Palatalisation

Transitional palatalisation is most often seen as a palatal feature in the transition to the next segment. If the next feature is a palatal sound then this feature may be merely a non-contrastive co-articulatory anticipation. Transitional palatalisation can also be used contrastively and is produced in such cases independently of the nature of the following sound.

TRANSCRIPTION

The IPA standard recommends a superscript "j" following the symbol of the sound being palatalised. This is identical to the transcription of simultaneous palatalisation.

eg. [lʲ] [pʲ] [k²]

Examples: The following examples may involve either simultaneous or transitional palatalisation. No distinction is made in these examples between simultaneous and transitional palatalisation.

Russian Contrasting plain and palatalised bilabial stops (and also a [pj] sequence) as well as giving two examples of palatalised [rʲ]					
[pot]	"sweat"	[pʲotr]	"Peter"	[pjot]	"drink"
[rʲab̥]	"pock-marked"	[rʲab̥ʲ]	"ripples"		

Velarisation: It is possible to imagine co-articulatory influences resulting in a transitionally velarised labial sound into a following velar consonant (such as [...apxa...]). Only simultaneous velarisation is possible for sounds with lingual primary articulations as velarisation involves an adjustment of the entire tongue body. Contrastive velarisations are always simultaneous.

Transcription

The IPA standard recommends a superscript"?" following the symbol of the sound being velarised.

eg. [sa] [ta] [da]

Also, a tilde character "~" is sometimes placed through another symbol to indicate velarisation or pharyngealisation. This is traditionally done most often to indicate a "dark" or velarised [l].

eg.[?]

Examples:

Marshallese (North Pacific) Normal and velarised bilabial nasal stop					
[matʲ]	"eye"	[mˠatʲ]	"eel, worm"		
Normal and velarised lateral approximant					
[lale]	"check"	[ɫaɫ]	"knock"	[laɫ]	"earth"

COARTICULATION AND ASSIMILATION

ACTIVE AND PASSIVE ARTICULATORS

Active articulators are those moveable parts of the vocal tract that participate in the production of speech. They do this by moving towards or away from passive articulators (other active articulators).

Passive articulators are relatively stationary parts of the vocal tract.

GESTURE AND CONSTRICTION

The goal of active articulator gestures is to produce certain degrees of stricture (opening/closure) at certain points in the vocal tract.

A speech gesture is the coordinated movement of one or more articulators to achieve a desired constriction.

Constriction involves the following degrees of stricture:

Vowel	minimal stricture
Approximant	medium degree of stricture
Fricative	open but high degree of stricture
Stop	total stricture

ARTICULATORY PHONOLOGY

Articulatory Phonology is a phonological theory that regards gestures as the basic units of phonological contrast. This system of gestures is based on constrictions involving the lips, tongue tip, tongue body, velum and glottis.

Articulatory Phonology describes 8 tract variables:

1	LP	lip protrusion
2	LA	lip aperture
3	TTCL	tongue tip constriction location
4	TTCD	tongue tip constriction degree
5	TBCL	tongue body constriction location
6	TBCD	tongue body constriction degree
7	VEL	velic aperture
8	GLO	glottal aperture

Lip protrusion (LP) accounts for rounding and spreading whilst lip aperture (LA) accounts for differences in degree of constriction (eg. vowel rounding-[u] or spreading [i], approximant [w], fricative [v] and stop [b] articulations). Three articulators are involved in LP and LA: upper lips (mostly for protrusion), lower lips (protrusion and stricture), jaw (assists stricture). The tongue tip can move partly independently of the tongue body. Three articulators are involved in tongue tip constriction location (TTCL) and degree (TTCD). They are the tongue tip, tongue body (tongue body movement can assist tongue tip placement), and jaw (its easier to reach the roof of the mouth if the jaw isn't too low).

Tongue body constriction degree (TBCD) and location (TBCL) is important for all vowels, and for palatal, velar, uvular and pharyngeal consonant place of articulation (for approximants, fricatives and stops). Articulators involved in TBCD and TBCL are the tongue body and the jaw (which assists in raising the tongue for some articulations).

Velic aperture (VEL) must not be confused with tongue body articulations (TBCL and TBCD) in which the velum acts as a passive articulator for a tongue gesture. VEL refers to velum opening and closing. The velum must be open for nasal stops, must be closed for oral stops and fricatives, and its opening for other sounds is language dependent.

Glottal aperture (GLO) relates to voicing. GLO is closed for normal voicing, and partly open (slightly open at the back of the glottis) for breathy voicing. GLO is wide open for voiceless stops and voiceless fricatives (excluding the glottal stop closure and the glottal/h/fricative). GLO opening and closing is subject to complex language specific timing patterns in oral stops. This relates to differences in voice onset time (VOT). GLO is closed for ejectives and implosives and is also subject to important timing constraints in these sounds.

Gestures overlap in an utterance. The relative timing of gestures can be extremely important.

Differing patterns of overlapping gestures distinguish phonemes, syllables and larger speech units (eg. polysyllabic words, phrases).

THE SYLLABLE

Two major theories of speech perception regard the syllable as the minimal unit of speech perception. In these theories, speech perception is the perception of gestures.

These theories are:

- Motor theory of speech perception.
- Direct-realist theory of speech perception.

There is a very large, and growing, body of research that suggests that the syllable is the most basic unit of articulatory planning in the brain.

Gestures interact with each other to a greater extent within syllable boundaries than they do across syllable boundaries.

PHONEMES IN CONNECTED SPEECH

Phonemes rarely occur in isolation. In English this only occurs in the citation (isolated word) utterance of the words "I"/"eye"/"aye", "owe"/"oh" and "a" (also "air", "ear", "are", "oar"/"or"/"ore", "err" in non-rhotic dialects such as Australian English) plus the interjections "eh" and "oi"/"oy" (note that they are all long vowels or diphthongs).

Phonemes are articulated as part of a syllable and each syllable is normally part of a longer sequence of speech. The majority of syllables consist of more than one phoneme and most syllables are made up of one vowel and one or more consonants.

ARTICULATORY TARGETS

In simple models of articulatory planning, each phoneme has a single ideal articulatory target for each contrastive articulator. At the most abstract level of motor planning each articulator might be thought of as having a target position that it must try to achieve for each phoneme. That is the idealised target for a phoneme is invariant. Differences in actual articulations occur as a consequence of physics and timing.

In the following diagram we can see two ideal (and entirely abstract) targets for a particular articulator in two adjacent phonemes. The blue lines represent idealised phoneme boundaries.

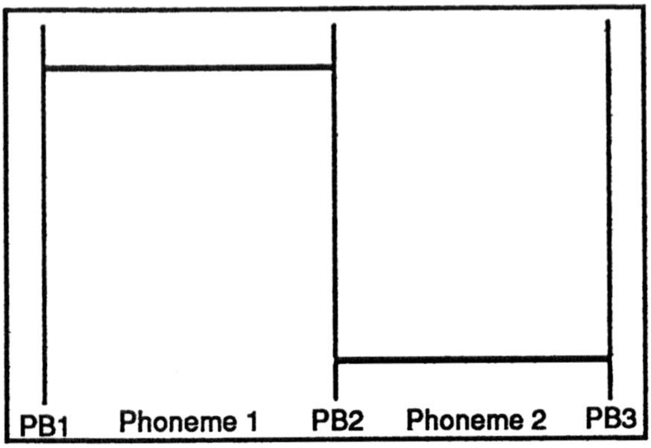

Fig. Two Ideal Articulatory Targets for a Single Articulator and two Adjacent phonemes. PB1, PB2 and PB3 are the Idealised Phoneme Boundaries for Phoneme 1 and Phoneme 2.

There are no readily definable articulatory or acoustic boundaries between phonemes in continuous speech, except at certain phrase boundaries which are characterised by pauses.

When we talk about boundaries between phonemes we are only referring to an approximate boundary at some point in the transition between the two phonemes. True acoustic and articulatory boundaries between phonemes don't exist. What we are referring to when we talk about (or plot) phoneme boundaries is a point between two phoneme targets where the two phonemes contribute approximately equally to the articulatory or acoustic pattern.

The cortical centres that plan articulatory movements during speech production can be understood as producing a series of increasingly more concrete specifications for articulator muscle movement. At the most abstract level of motor planning each articulator might be thought of as having a target position that it must attempt to achieve for each phoneme. Such a target would be the ideal target for each phoneme and would depend upon an individual's physiology and linguistic experience. This model of articulatory planning assumes a fixed ideal articulatory target for each contrastive articulator.

ARTICULATORY TRANSITIONS

Phonemes are best described in terms of target positions with articulatory (and resulting acoustic) transitions between the two targets. These transitions share the characteristics of the two targets.

A "transition" in speech is caused by the movement of articulators between phoneme targets. Phonemes can be defined in terms of one or more idealised articulatory targets. For example, a monophthong vowel is defined as having one target whilst a diphthong vowel is defined as having two targets. There are transitions between the targets of two adjacent phonemes as well as between the multiple targets within a single phoneme.

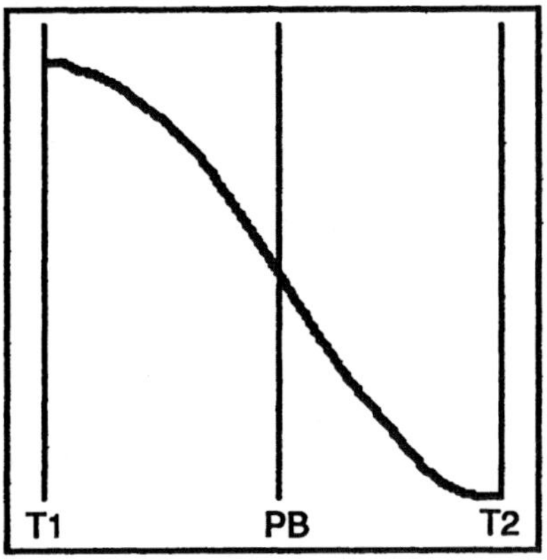

Fig. An Idealised Articulatory Transition from the Target of one Phoneme (T1) to the Target of Another Phoneme (T2). PB Represents the Approximate Position of the Phoneme "Boundary".

The transition between two phonemes shares the articulatory and acoustic characteristics of both phonemes but gradually changes from being predominantly like the first phoneme target to predominantly like the second phoneme target.

CONTRASTIVE ARTICULATORS

A contrastive articulator is an articulator whose configuration (shape, constriction) or position (place) is important to the accurate transmission of the intended phoneme to a listener. The listener ideally shares the same language or dialect and therefore the same expectations for the articulatory, acoustic and auditory characteristics of each phoneme.

Which articulators are contrastive may vary from phoneme to phoneme. An articulator that is contrastive in one language for a certain class of sounds may not be contrastive for another language.

Velum opening is always contrastive for oral stops (closed) and nasal stops (open), in all languages that have these classes of sound.

Velum opening is contrastive for certain (but not all) vowels in French (distinct nasal and non-nasal vowel phonemes), but is not contrastive for English vowels (nasality does not change vowel phonemes).

For the vast majority of languages (possibly only one exception), the position of the tongue body in the front-back and the high-low dimensions are contrastive for vowels and so the tongue body constriction location (TBCL) is a contrastive for vowels.

In English the configuration of the lips (rounded, neutral, spread) is not contrastive for vowels (no pair of vowels is contrasted solely on the basis of lip shape) and so the lips are not contrastive articulators for English vowels (but are for certain pairs of French vowels). This lack of contrastiveness does not mean that there are not characteristic lip shapes for English vowels but such lip shapes are redundant as they can be predicted from tongue position. That is, in English high front vowels are always lip spread, high back vowels are always rounded and low vowels tend to have a neutral lip shape.

When an articulator is not contrastive in a phoneme that is surrounded by two other phonemes for which that articulator is contrastive then the articulator is free to move slowly (or not at all) within that central phoneme. A good example in English is nasality, or velum opening. In English velum opening is contrastive for both oral stops (must be closed) and for nasal stops (must be open) but it is not contrastive for vowels. Vowels are identified as the same phoneme regardless of whether the velum is open or closed (but recall that this is not true for languages such as French). A vowel between two oral stops has a closed velum whilst a vowel between two nasal stops has a significantly open velum and the vowel is said to be nasalised.

ARTICULATOR INERTIA

Inertia is the tendency of a stationary body to resist movement or for a moving body to resist changes in its rate or direction of movement. The more massive (ie. bigger and heavier) an articulator is the greater its inertia or resistance to movement.

The tongue body is more massive than the tongue tip and so it moves more slowly than the tongue tip. The jaw is even more massive and so it moves even more slowly.

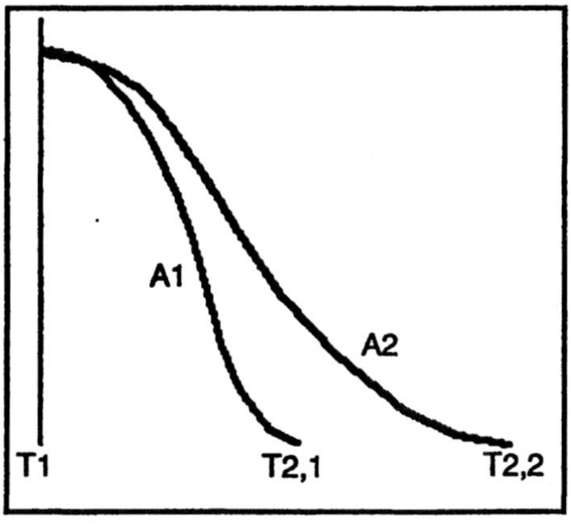

Fig. Two Articulators with Different Degrees of Inertia will take a Different times to move the same Distance. Articulator 1 (A1) has less Inertia than Articulator 2 (A2). Therefore, artiCulator 1 (A1) can Move from its first Target (T1) to its second target (T2,1) in much less time than Articulator 2 (A2) can move the same Distance to its target 2 (T2,2).

The maximum distance that an articulator can move in a given time depends upon its inertia.

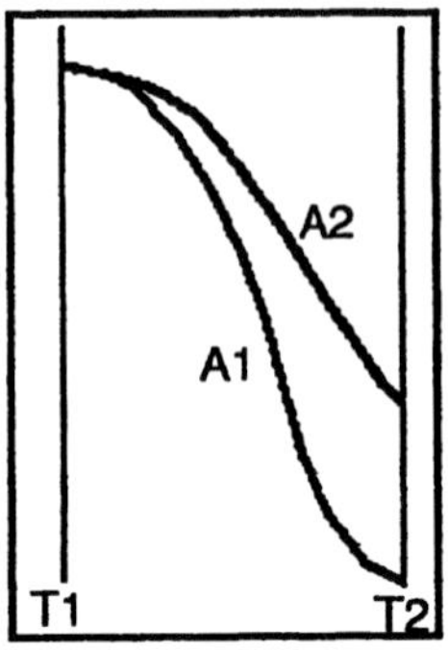

Fig. Two Articulators with Different Degrees of Inertia can move Different Maximum Distances in the same time. Articulator 1 (A1) has less Inertia than Articulator 2 (A2). Therefore, Articulator 1 (A1) can move a greater Distance from its first Target (T1) to its Second target (T2) than can Articulator 2 (A2).

ARTICULATOR AGILITY

Articulators with low inertia, such as the tongue tip, can be manoeuvered rapidly. Another variable that affects articulator agility is the extent to which it is controlled neurally. An articulator with a larger proportion of nerve fibres per unit mass has fewer muscle fibres per nerve fibre. A nerve fibre and its associated muscle fibres is known as a motor unit and each motor unit can potentially be controlled individually. The larger the number of motor units in an articulator the more controllable its movement is.

The tongue tip and the velum have similar mass but the tongue tip has smaller and more numerous motor units. This means that the tongue tip is more manoeuvrable than the velum in spite of their similar mass.

The high degree of innervation and the larger number of motor units in the tongue tip doesn't mean that as a whole it moves faster. This is limited by inertia and therefore by its overall mass. The greater degree of innervation does, however, make it possible to semi-independently move sub-structures in the tongue tip (eg. to permit such things as tongue tip grooving). These sub-structures are limited in their independent movement by their elastic linkage to the rest of the tongue tip, but being sub-structures (rather than the whole structure) of the tongue tip they have lower mass and therefore they have less inertia than the whole structure.

TARGET UNDERSHOOT

Target undershoot occurs when there is insufficient time for an articulator to reach its target position. The articulator has too much inertia to move between two targets in the available time so it doesn't travel as far as it would if there was more time. Target undershoot can occur in both vowels and consonants.

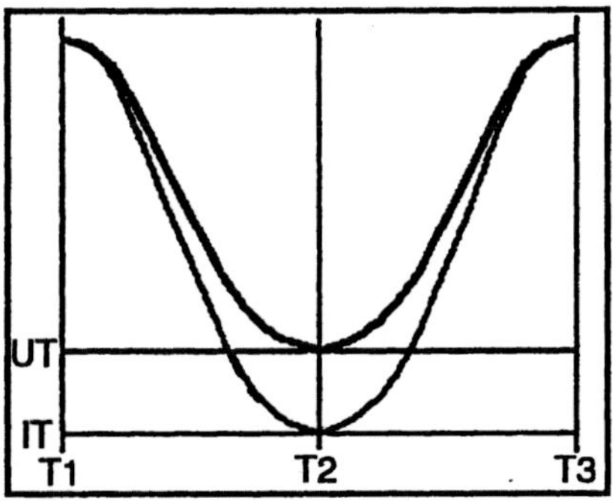

Fig. This Figure Illustrates Target Undershoot. In this example the Ideal Target of Phoneme 2 (T2) is Represented by the Articulator position value IT whilst UT Represents the Undershot target value. This would be Typical of an Unaccented short low vowel between two Alveolar or velar stops, for Example.

OVERLAPPING GESTURES

A "gesture" is the movement of one articulator, such as the lower lip, the tongue tip or the tongue body, from an articulatory position characteristic of one speech sound to an articulatory position characteristic of the next speech sound.

Articulatory gestures overlap. This means that the movement of each articulator occurs at the same time as the movements of all the other articulators. These overlapping gestures may not be synchronised because of sequencing requirements, articulator contrastiveness and articulator inertia.

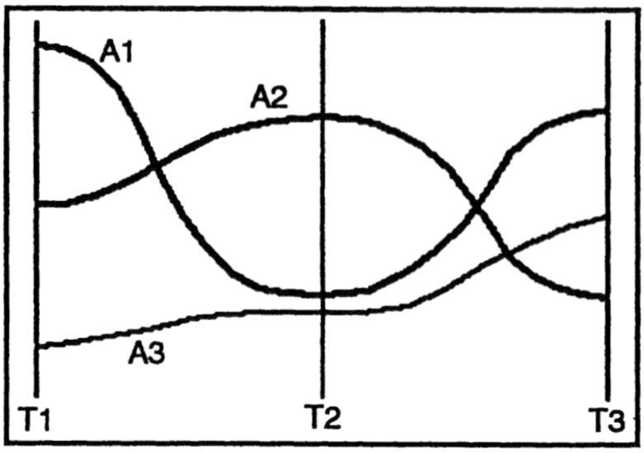

Fig. The Gestures of three Articulators (A1, A2, A3) Overlap in time as they Pass Through three Idealised Phoneme targets (T1, T2, T3).

COARTICULATION

Coarticulation tends to be stronger within syllables rather than across syllable boundaries. This greater coarticulation within syllables is evidence for the cognitive existence of the syllable as a fundamental unit of articulatory organisation.

Greater degrees of coarticulation between the phonemes in a syllable increase the perceptual integration of syllables. That is, greater degrees of coarticulation increase the perception that the phonemes in a syllable are connected.

We perceive speech by recognising the (auditorily-transformed) acoustic patterns of syllables. These patterns consist of targets (or rather the effect of coarticulation on the realisation of those targets) and the transitions between targets.

COARTICULATION BETWEEN CONSONANTS AND VOWELS

Vowels affect the articulation of adjacent consonants (and adjacent vowels). Consonants affect the articulation of adjacent vowels (and other adjacent consonants).

Some sounds are more resistant to coarticulation than other sounds. This may be due to differences in phoneme duration, differences in the inertia of contrastive articulators, differences in articulator movement distances or it may be due to the phoneme inventory effect.

Coarticulation is greatest (for a given phoneme duration) when there is the greatest articulator movement (ie. greatest distance) between phonemes.

Many consonants have a high tongue position (eg. [k]) and so they are more likely to cause target undershoot in low vowels than in high vowels. This is because there is a longer distance to travel from a high consonant tongue position to a low vowel tongue position than there is to a high vowel tongue position.

Long vowels are more resistant to target undershoot than are short vowels as there is more time for the articulator to reach its target. Accented and stressed vowels are more resistant to undershoot than are unstressed vowels as they are even longer.

In other words (when adjacent to consonants with high tongue body articulations):

- Accented high long monophthongal vowels are the most resistant vowels to target undershoot.
- Unstressed low vowels and particularly unaccented short low vowels are most affected by target undershoot.

Schwa is not realised by a defined target. It is usually very short and is therefore greatly affected by coarticulation with adjacent consonants but since it doesn't have a defined target it can't be said to have target undershoot.

PHONEME INVENTORY EFFECTS

Coarticulation is resisted (reduced in degree) when it will result in perceptual confusion. The chances of perceptual confusion occurring is greatest in languages that have a large number of phonemes of a particular class. The greater the number of members of a class of speech sounds the greater the chance that adjacent phonemes will be close together.

Vowels coarticulate most in languages with a small number of vowels. Some languages have three (or even fewer) phonological vowels. Vowel fronting and height is free to vary considerably in such languages without a vowel phoneme being confused for an adjacent phoneme.

Consonants coarticulate most in languages with a small number of places of articulation. For example, in English there are only three places of oral stop articulation and only one place of articulation that uses the tongue body. Vowel articulations are also tongue body articulations. Australian aboriginal languages, with both a palatal and a velar oral stop, can't afford to have velar stop phonemes moving too far forward as they would be confused with the palatal stop phoneme. Arabic, with both a uvular and a velar oral stop, can't afford to have velar stop phonemes moving too far back as they would be confused with the uvular stop phoneme.

COARTICULATION AND ASSIMILATION

Coarticulation is the way in which the movements of different articulators affect each other and the ways in which preceding and following articulations of an individual articulator affect its current articulation. Articulatory planning in the brain takes these affects into account when producing a sequence of speech sounds. Some of these effects are very slight whilst some are quite strong.

Coarticulation always occurs in all languages for all sequences of sounds not separated by pauses. Speakers have no choice - they must coarticulate adjacent sounds. Without appropriate coarticulation (eg. in poor synthetic speech) the resulting speech sounds unnatural and is hard to understand.

Two opposing forces are at work in speech production and perception.

- There is a tendency to simplify speech patterns to increase ease of articulation as simpler speech is easier to produce.
- This is opposed by the competing need ("constraint") to maintain phonological distinctiveness in speech perception.

One of the reasons why we accent certain words (eg. words containing new information) is so that we can increase their duration, and therefore can avoid undershoot (ie. more time to reach targets).

- Accented words are the words for which we most need to maintain maximum perceptual distinctiveness as we can't rely on context to perceive them. (constraints maximised)
- We tend to not accent words representing given information. We don't require maximum perceptual distinctiveness as word identification is assisted by context. (constraints reduced)
- Function words carry very little of the semantic load and so they are often reduced as there is no need to maintain their perceptual distinctiveness. (constraints almost absent)

These patterns of accenting certain words (new information) and reducing the other words (given information) in a sentence, provides a pattern of timing that results in the greatest time to reach articulatory targets in accented words and much greater chance of undershoot for other words (especially function words).

If we always attempted to maximise phonological distinctiveness in speech perception (without the opposing tendency towards ease of production) then we could perhaps predict the degree to which targets are achieved or undershot from articulator inertia and the timing of each syllable in each accented or unaccented word. However, this isn't always possible.

We vary in the extent to which we maximise distinctiveness from one phonetic context to another. This variation may be language, dialect, local speech community and individual specific. That is, there are different constraints on the extent to which we can relax perceptual distinctiveness and increase ease of articulation. Assimilation is a language (or speech community) specific and also a phonetic context specific relaxation of these constraints. Assimilation constraints may allow some allophones in certain contexts but disallow other allophones in other contexts.

In some cases it may even be possible to increase ease of articulation to a point where a sound assimilates to such a great extent that it becomes more like another phoneme.

Examples:

- In Australian English, alveolar consonants (especially alveolar oral and nasal stops) readily assimilate to the place of articulation of a following consonant.
- Sometimes this results in an allophonic change (eg. to dental) and sometimes a phonemic change (eg. to velar or bilabial)

This change in Australian English alveolar stops (particularly the phonemic assimilations) also happens in other, but not all, English dialects. It isn't permitted in many other languages.

The extent or degree of such assimilations may vary between discourse contexts (eg. formal vs. informal)

Even where such a relaxation of constraints is permitted, we often find different degrees of assimilation for different speakers or different groups of speakers. (eg. some speakers of Australian English exhibit greater degrees of contextual nasality than do others).

Careful physiological analysis of alveolar to bilabial or velar phonemic assimilations appears to indicate that some aspect of the alveolar articulation is still present. eg. in alveolar to bilabial assimilation there is a clear primary bilabial articulation but often a secondary tongue tip gesture can also be detected.

Assimilation is a language (or dialect or speech community) specific relaxation in constraints that maintain a certain degree of balance between perceptual distinctiveness and ease of articulation. In other words, assimilation could be regarded as a language (or dialect) specific enhancement of the degree of coarticulation.

In the topic "Phonemic (Broad) Transcription of Australian English" there are numerous examples of assimilation where the identity of the phoneme is changed by adopting an articulatory strategy that simplifies articulatory effort. Most of these examples involve the conversion of an alveolar consonant (oral stop or nasal stop or fricative) into the same place of articulation as the following consonant (in these cases alveolar oral and nasal stops become bilabial or velar and alveolar fricatives become palato-alveolar fricatives). There is not a clear case for considering this to be driven strongly by coarticulation as the tongue tip is the most rapidly moveable of all articulators. The reverse seems to be the case. In order to prevent the adjacent sound from being affected by coarticulation (ie. slower lip or velar movements) the intervening alveolar phoneme is substituted for a homorganic phoneme. This seems to be an articulatory or phonological choice made in either the higher levels of articulatory planning or at the even more abstract level of phonological specification.

On the other hand, in the topic "Phonetic (Narrow) Transcription of Australian English" oral and nasal stops are assimilated to the place of articulation of the following labiodental, dental or postalveolar consonants. This can't occur at the level of phonological specification as there is no change of phoneme involved so this suggests a habitual choice made at the higher levels of articulatory planning. It seems best to treat these two types of assimilation (those that change phoneme and those that don't) as being equivalent and therefore not specified at a phonological level but at an articulatory planning level. The fact that this is possible in English without confusion is that there are very few contexts where this would create ambiguity. Such a processes are prohibited in Australian Aboriginal languages which have up to six places of stop articulation. This process tends to be language-specific.

STUDIES OF ENGLISH PHONETICS

COMMENTS ABOUT THIS TOPIC

Most of this topic is provided as background reading only. The discussion on early attempts at descriptions of Australian English, up to and including Sidney Baker, should be considered to be non-assessable historical background. The studies by Mitchell and Delbridge are more relevant to the content of this subject. The material on nasality, assimilation, deletion and intonation is also only provided as non-assessable background material. The focus of the module to which this material belongs is the vowel system of Australian English and students should focus particularly on the vowels when reading this material.

What you should understand from this material is:

- The nature of Impressionistic Phonetics and its strengths and shortcomings
- The general findings regarding the nature of Australian English vowels (particularly the six vowels that differ greatly between varieties of Australian English)
- The historical background behind the symbols traditionally used for the phonemic (broad) transcription of Australian vowels
- The division of Australian English into Broad, General and Cultivated varieties. You should understand that these "varieties" are not distinct and separate but represent an arbitrary division of a dialect continuum.

A.E. PRONUNCIATION

Attempts at the deciphering of early comments and descriptions of Australian English are fraught with many problems. Many non-linguists made comments about the pronunciation of the inhabitants of the distant colonies in Australia and these were often written up in various publications devoted to the impressions and experiences of travellers. For the most part, the comments of travellers about A.E. speech tended to be uncomplimentary and often included various unfounded notions about the nature or causes of the A.E. pronunciation that persist in the popular mythology to this day. It was often noted that A.E. speech tended to be "slovenly", poorly articulated, "nasal", etc. and such afflictions were variously ascribed to the climate, excessive pollen in the air, alleged laziness of the people, inferiority complexes, social inhibition, etc.

Another possible source of information might be expected to be found in the works of various fiction writers (eg. Henry Lawson) who attempted to capture the Australian vernacular language in the orthography. Of course, such attempts persist up to this day (eg. "Let Stalk Strine" by Afferbek Lauder) and it is not difficult to see that these attempts vary from writer to writer, are extremely difficult to interpret phonetically, and usually do little more than highlight the alleged non-standard nature of the pronunciations they attempt to mimic.

Another source of information about early A.E. pronunciation is denied us because English spelling had been standardised well before the advent of the British invasion of Australia. Because of this, letters, diary accounts etc. cannot be utilised since those who were literate were generally scrupulous in their attempts to spell correctly and so their spelling can't throw much light on their pronunciations as similar sources often do for far more ancient languages (eg. Greek, Latin, Old English).

IMPRESSIONISTIC PHONETICS

Before a description of the pronunciation of a language or dialect can be carried out there is a need for a consistent system of symbols to represent that speech. Ideally, such a system would have one (and only one) symbol for each sound and one sound to each symbol. It takes only a little reflection to realise that such systems are many in number and have been in existence for a very long time. The earliest forms of alphabet were probably designed with this goal in mind. Unfortunately, such systems have a tendency to become conservative and often do not keep up with actual pronunciation and phonological changes in a language. Quite often this means that new sounds incorporated into a language are represented by a symbol that already belongs to another sound.

A further problem arises when spelling itself becomes fossilised and no longer represents the current pronunciation of a word but rather that of an archaic pronunciation. In English, much of this standardisation of spelling had occurred between the times of Chaucer and Shakespeare. In Arabic, spelling had standardised at the time of the writing of the Qur'an in the 8th century A.D. Some languages maintain a fairly "phonetic" orthography, but very often the orthography has only an approximate match to the sound structure of a language or dialect. Further, no orthography is equipped to represent slight interpersonal variation, regional variation, and the complete picture of the language's allophonic variation. system that attempts to represent all of the sounds that are utilised in all human languages in either a contrastive or a non-contrastive manner. In the European tradition there have been several attempts to devise such a system with varying success and this culminated in the development of the International Phonetic Alphabet (IPA) in the late 19th century. The refinement of IPA continues to this day. A particularly useful idea was the development of a system of standard reference vowels which could be used to define the quality of any vowel. Vowels occupy a continuum of possible articulations and using such a standard system it is possible to locate any vowel relative to the closest standard vowel. The best known such system today is Daniel Jones' system of "cardinal vowels".

Impressionistic phonetics, to be practiced successfully, requires that the intending practitioner be thoroughly trained by a teacher already skilled in transcription. Ideally the practitioner must not only be able to hear the sounds but also to pronounce them as well. It is extremely undesirable to try to learn such a system from a book without the aid of at least some sort of recorded version of the sound to which each symbol refers. Instructions such as "similar to the French vowel in the second syllable of... " are really not adequate guides to the accurate acquisition of transcription skills. In spite of this the first two attempts at description of Australian English were by authors who had learnt phonetic transcription from books. As will be seen below, only one of these two attempts could be considered to be reasonably successful.

Impressionistic phonetics is predominantly an auditory skill requiring the practitioner to listen carefully to the utterance to be transcribed and then to record the utterance using an appropriate phonetic script. Additionally, the impressionistic phonetician may use sight to confirm auditory impressions (eg. lip posture). The transcription is only as good as the phonetician's skill and the only way a reader has of determining the extent of that skill is through awareness of reputation, comparisons with the transcriptions of other phoneticians etc. For this reason most phoneticians tend to be wary of transcriptions made by people not trained by an established institution or scholar.

The chief disadvantage of impressionistic phonetics (ie. compared to instrumental phonetics) is this element of potential unreliability. It tends to lack objectivity. An instrumental (acoustic) study by Ladefoged of the production of cardinal vowels by 11 highly trained phoneticians showed considerable variation between their attempts and even overlap between adjacent cardinals. This is in spite of the fact that all the measured vowels were judged by Daniel Jones (the originator of the most commonly used cardinal vowel system) to be good productions of the target vowel. This may be due, at least in part, to the complex nature of speech perception, and especially to the apparent ability of a listener to "normalise" a speaker's vowels (which will differ with different vocal tract dimensions) to fit into a standard template (mental representation) in which the effects of differing vocal tract dimensions have been removed. An informal study (ca. early to mid 1990s) by the present author of the production of an Australian phonetician of the cardinal vowels may suggest a further process at work. The speaker produced several sets of cardinal vowels and he and two other trained and experienced phoneticians then selected from these the best attempts or if unsatisfied requested further recordings. It was particularly interesting to note the relative position of the third cardinal. This was found to be significantly higher than that of the British phoneticians. This allowed the A.E. /æ/ vowel to fit between cardinal 3 and 4. When this AE vowel is mapped onto the cardinal vowel productions of Daniel Jones it is found to very close to his version of cardinal 3. When it is considered that, for many speakers, the A.E. /æ/ is higher than the British /æ/ the possibility arises that even trained phoneticians are not immune from the influences of their own dialects when it comes to the learning of the cardinal vowels. We are told that /æ/ is to be found between cardinal 3 and 4 (as it is in British

English) and so we oblige by shifting our cardinal 3 upwards so that /æ/ can fit below it. In more recent years the /æ/ vowel has moved progressively downwards, towards cardinal 4, for many speakers (especially younger speakers) of Australian English so it might be perdicted that this raising of cardinal 3 for Australian English phoneticians will have disappeared.

The main advantage of impressionistic phonetics is that of data compression. The human ear is able to reduce an extremely complex acoustic signal into a series of discrete symbols. An acoustic analysis, on the other hand, produces a vast amount of data which ultimately needs to be much reduced before its significance can be grasped by a human mind. Further, it is sometimes stated by phoneticians that the "auditory world" is really quite different to that of the "acoustic world". If we want to study the information presented to the linguistic processing systems in the brain then the only way to do that accurately is to listen. This position becomes weaker as it becomes possible to more adequately model the effects of the auditory system on the acoustic waveforms. Before impressionistic phonetics can be finally laid to rest however, it will also be necessary to also accurately model the processes of speech perception. We do not, at this stage, even remotely approach this position.

SAMUEL MCBURNEY

This study (quoted in Ellis (1889)) was the first systematic characterisation of AE. McBurney was a Scottish school teacher who lived and taught in Australia for several years and who traveled widely in Australia and New Zealand recording the pronunciations of the local people. He was phonetically self-trained and made all of his transcriptions in Ellis' "glossic" script (nb. this was later converted to another script "palaeotype" by Ellis before publication). He recorded the pronunciations of school children in Victoria, Tasmania, Sydney, Brisbane and New Zealand and further indicated the frequency of usage of each type and, if relevant, preferences by boys and girls. This suggests either that these variations in /iÐ/ did not exist then, or, that McBurney may simply have missed them because all of the AE variants may have not seemed strange to his ears. In other words, it may be that he was only prompted to record those AE sounds that varied from his own experience in the British Isles. McBurney's account, for the most part, can be considered most perceptive.

Table. Transcriptions of 6 key Vowels as Described by Samuel McBurney (1887).

/iː/	ii
/ʉː/	u, uu, ə'uu
/æɪ/	ee, éei, éi, ææ'i
/əʉ/	oo, á'u
/ɑe/	i, A'i, 'i
/æɔ/	éeu, ææ'u, áa'u, u, 'u

In this table, the doubling of a symbol is used to denote longer duration. Most of the symbols have similar values to the modern IPA values. [A] is most likely similar to the low-central vowel [P].

SIDNEY J. BAKER

Baker devoted a chapter of his book "The Australian Language" to a phonetic description of Australian English. His description, although rather amateurish, wasn't entirely inaccurate. He was clearly well read in the available literature of the time and highly critical of the many myths that had been perpetuated about AE, and yet he still persisted in using adjectives such as "slovenly" in his descriptions of certain varieties of the dialect. He had obviously studied Daniel Jones' cardinal vowels, and for the most part used them reasonably well, but he managed to record three and four target allophones of some vowels that can only be described as ludicrous.

eg. /iĐ/ = [ij, Yj, iY, ji, eji, ejij]

The allophones containing [j] are certainly out of line with modern ideas of the nature (consonants) and distribution (non-post-vocalic) of semi-vowels. Further, the [e-j-i] transitions are overstated as a transition from [e] to [i] in AE passes directly through the [j] position, and further, these sequences are probably an attempt at transcribing the very common schwa-[i] glide or diphthong (ie. [ᵊi, ə i]) so common in broad AE.

He quite correctly contrasted AE with Cockney, whilst many earlier writers, including McBurney, tended to at least partially equate the two dialects. He also described three versions of AE which are similar to Mitchell's two, and later three categories of AE. In a later edition he strongly criticised Mitchell for having taken twenty years to give up the notion of two varieties in favour of three. "In the long interval... his phonetics students had been misled as to the nature of Australian speech". He failed to see the division of AE into two, three or however many varieties as no more than a convenient dividing up of a continuum and not the identification of three separate and separable varieties.

A.G. MITCHELL

Mitchell is the first comprehensive phonetic description of AE by a professionally trained phonetician. Like Baker, he used Jones' cardinal vowel diagram on which to plot his AE vowels, but unlike Baker, he was trained in its use and familiar with Jones' actual pronunciation of the cardinal vowels.

/æɪ/	[eɪ ~ ʌɪ]
/ɑe/	[aɪ ~ ɒɪ]
/æɔ/	[aʊ ~ æʊ]
/əʉ/	[oʊ ~ ʌʊ]

Often, the broad realisation of one phoneme overlaps with the educated realisation of another phoneme.

A.G. MITCHELL AND ARTHUR DELBRIDGE

This survey of the speech habits of young Australians has sometimes been described as the outstanding achievement of impressionistic phonetics in Australia and undoubtedly, in some respects at least, it deserves this description. It had by far the largest number of subjects (>7000) of any impressionistic study (or any other type for that matter) of AE and drew these samples from six states. The subjects included both males

(47%) and females (53%) and were each identified using a wide range of social parametres. All of the speech parametres were assessed impressionistically by the authors and included variety of AE spoken, use of weak consonants, elision or assimilation, type of intonation (normal or restricted), speed of speech and nasality (normal, pervasive or contextual). The only other impressionistic study of AE to go to the trouble of collecting samples several states and to indicate the frequencies of occurrence was McBurney. The survey was a collection of tape recordings by teachers from the 309 participating schools, and because of this, both the quality of the recording and the quality of the interview varied greatly.

One of the analysis methods was the analysis of the six vowels identified by Mitchell as being the main indicators of AE variety being used. For the most part subjects used all the sounds in a particular set (i, ii, or iii), although a significant minority used vowels from more than one set.

Set	Name	/iː/	/ʉː/	/æɪ/	/əʉ/	/ɑe/	/æɔ/	% of sample
i)	Cultivated	[ɪi]	[ʊu]	[ɛɪ/eɪ]	[oʊ]	[aɪ]	[aʊ]	11%
ii)	General	[əɪ]	[əʊ]	[ʌɪ]	[ʌʊ]	[ɒɪ]	[æʊ]	55%
iii)	Broad	[ə̹ˑɪ]	[ə̹ˑʊ]	[ʌ̹ˑɪ]	[ʌ̹ˑʊ]	[ɒˑɪ]	[æ̹ˑʊ]	34%

Sets i and ii conformed to Mitchell's early values for educated and broad and set iii largely conformed to the earlier notion that broader speakers had longer slower glides in their closing diphthongs. It is at this point that Mitchell and Delbridge settled on the new groupings "Cultivated", "General" and "Broad".

Further tests indicated that the Broad speakers demonstrated a greater tendency for syllable assimilation and consonant elision, were more likely to use weak consonants or restricted intonation (narrow pitch range), were more likely to speak slowly (drawl), and further, showed a greater tendency to exhibit pervasive nasality. For none of these parametres, however, was the tendency >30%, meaning that at least 70% of Broad speakers did not show these features (ie. each feature taken separately), and suggesting that the usually popular characterisations of AE are in no way representative of the way most Broad speakers speak. The enormous size and geographical scope of this project probably ensures that it will never be surpassed in breadth, and anyhow, future studies are more likely to be instrumental rather than impressionistic. The advantage of the impressionistic method for this kind of study means that each utterance can be reduced to a minimum number of variables (ie. to a series of narrow phonetic transcriptions determined according to the judgment of the researcher). An acoustic study, on the other hand, produces an increase in parametric detail by several orders of magnitude and is therefore likely to require a much smaller sample of subjects than in the present study. The major disadvantage of an impressionistic study is the degree of subjective disagreement between workers (nb. 25% disagreement on assignment of speaker category in this study) and this disagreement increases if the workers have trained under different traditions etc.

Table. Percentage of Broad, General and Cultivated subjects, by Sex and region

	Broad	General	Cultivated	Total
Sex				
Males	24	22	1	47%
Females	10	33.5	9.5	53%
Region				
Capital Cities	11	27	9	47
Other Centres	23	28	2	53%

Table. Degree of Assimilation and Elision by Dialect Variety and Sex)

	Assimilation and Elision	
	Normal	Excessive
Broad	71	29
General	91	9
Cultivated	99	1
Male	75	25
Female	94	6

Table. Intonation Type by Dialect Variety and Sex. Restricted Intonation is a Flat or Monotonous Intonation.

	Intonation	
	Normal	Restricted
Broad	95	5
General	98	2
Cultivated	100	0
Male	97	3
Female	98	2

Table. Degree or Type of Audible "Nasality" by Dialect Variety and Sex

	Nasality		
	Normal	Pervasive	Contextual
Broad	73	13	14
General	92	3	5
Cultivated	98	1	1
Male	78	10	12
Female	93	3	4

Table. Rate of Utterance by Dialect Variety and Sex

	Fast	Normal	Slow ("drawl")
Broad	3	89	8
General	5	93	2
Cultivated	3	96	2
Male	4	92	4
Female	4	92	4

GENERAL PHONETICS EXERCISES

The following exercises are provided to test your knowledge of the concepts dealt with in lecture topics 1-4 and 6 as well as the tutorial topic on the International Phonetic Alphabet. An answer sheet is also provided.

- *What are the active and passive articulators in the following*:

- Velar nasal stop
- Central uvular fricative
- Alveolar lateral approximant
- Velar ejective
- Retroflex approximant

- Provide phonetic notation for any three sounds produced on an ingressive airstream.
- Provide phonetic notation for any five front vowels.
- Provide phonetic notation for any three open (low) vowels.
- Provide phonetic notation for any two different lateral consonants.
- Circle the place(s) of articulation at which lateral consonants can be produced.
  bilabial labiodental alveolar uvular
- Provide phonetic notation for any four sounds whose active articulator is the back of the tongue.
- Which of the following combinations are not possible?

Active articulator	Passive articulator
lower lip	upper teeth
back of tongue	alveolar ridge
back of tongue	upper lip
back of tongue	uvula
tongue tip	hard palate
tongue blade	uvula

- Which of the following productions are not possible?
  - Central nasal oral fricative
  - Central lateral nasal stop
  - Oral approximant
  - Lateral approximant
  - Lateral fricative
  - Lateral nasal stop
- Which vocal organ provides the main source of power in producing ejectives and implosives?
- Briefly describe the production of clicks.
- Define secondary articulation.

- What diacritic is added when transcribing labialised sounds?
- Circle the sounds that are produced with nasal airflow:
  I G w v m T! 6K
- Circle the labial sounds:
  v n d² y· u w
- Circle the sounds in which the passive articulator is the uvular:
  k × n u
- Circle the sounds that are produced with complete closure at the alveolar ridge:
  s W ~ t° ′ n o n
- Provide phonetic names for the feature classes Laryngeal, Airstream, Place, Nasality, Stricture for the speech sounds listed below.
  i. m
  ii. z²
  iii. W
  iv. a
  v. ●
  vi. ′ ˋ
- *Give phonetic notation for the following speech sounds*:
  i. breathy alveolar lateral approximant
  ii. voiced retroflex oral stop
  iii. voiceless lateral fricative
  iv. creaky alveolar fricative
  v. alveolar lateral click
- In a certain language, consonants are palatalised before close (high) front vowels and velarised before close (high) back vowels. Make any changes to the consonants on the left that precede the vowels on the right in accordance with this rule. If no change is necessary, write NC.
  i. t y
  ii. f o
  iii. k i
- In a certain language, close (high) vowels become

glides (maintaining their fronting and rounding features) when they precede other close vowels. Make any changes to the vowels on the left that precede the vowels on the right in accordance with this rule. If no change is necessary, write NC.

i. u y
ii. ø ø
iii. i i
iv. i y
v. o u

- What features do the groups of sounds have in common?
  i. m,b,x voiceless lateral bilabial approximant egressive
  ii. 3, j breathy retroflex pulmonic palatal nasal
  iii. r,ʘ voiced egressive trill tap fricative
  iv. z,n,l,z^2 alveolar voiced nasal pulmonic fricative
  v. y, n,ø,v,T front half-open close rounded voiced
- *Convert the following sounds into equivalent laterals:*
  i. z
  ii. s
- *Convert the following sounds into equivalent fricatives:*
  i. t
  ii. d
  iii. l
- *Convert the following into equivalent sounds produced with lip-rounding:*
  i. θ
  ii. j
- *Briefly explain why the following notation is not possible:*
  i. u^w
  ii. d'
  iii. m^h
- Give a brief definition of what is meant by the following labels:
  i. glottalic
  ii. breathy

iii. velarised
iv. ingressive

- *Provide phonetic notation for any two speech sounds that conform to the following description:*
  i. The soft-palate is lowered; the airstream mechanism is velaric
  ii. The vocal folds are completely closed at some stage during the production of the sound
  iii. The tip of the tongue makes a complete closure against the alveolar ridge
  iv. The blade of the tongue is raised towards the hard-palate but without making a complete closure
- Define a diphthong
- Give three criteria for distinguishing consonants from vowels

ANSWER SHEET

- *What are the active and passive articulators in the following:*

		Active	Passive
i.	Velar nasal stop	back of tongue	soft palate
ii.	Central uvular fricative	back of tongue	uvula
iii.	Alveolar lateral approximant	tongue tip	alveolar ridge
iv.	Velar ejective	back of tongue	soft palate
v.	Retroflex approximant	tongue tip	hard palate

- Provide phonetic notation for any three sounds produced on an ingressive airstream.
  S W A Á Γ ÀK etc.
- Provide phonetic notation for any five front vowels.
  i e [a y ø œ
- Provide phonetic notation for any three open (low) vowels.
  a Q R œ

- Provide phonetic notation for any two different lateral consonants.
  l n l
- Circle the place(s) of articulation at which lateral consonants can be produced.
  alveolar
- Provide phonetic notation for any four sounds whose active articulator is the back of the tongue.
  k a q b K k¼ etc.
- Which of the following combinations are not possible?

active articulator	passive articulator
back of tongue	alveolar ridge
back of tongue	upper lip
tongue blade	uvula

- Which of the following productions are not possible?
  - Central nasal oral fricative
  - Central lateral nasal stop
  - Lateral nasal stop
- Which vocal organ provides the main source of power in producing ejectives and implosives?
  - larynx
- Briefly describe the production of clicks.
  - Complete closure achieved at the soft palate
  - Another closure in front of velar occlusion
  - Posterior occlusion slides back towards uvular
  - Air pressure reduced between the two occlusions
  - Release of alveolar constriction
  - Inflow of air to equalise pressure
- *Define secondary articulation*: Simultaneous bilabial, palatal or velar approximant produced at the same time as a primary articulation which has a higher degree of stricture (usually stop stricture, occasionally fricative stricture) and which is produced at another place of articulation.
- What diacritic is added when transcribing labialised sounds?

·*The diacritic [ʷ] superscripted to the symbol of the primary articulation:*

- Circle the sounds that are produced with nasal airflow.
  m T⊖ ÁK
- *Circle the labial sounds:*
  v r^w u w
- *Circle the sounds in which the passive articulator is the uvular:*
  ×
- *Circle the sounds that are produced with complete closure at the alveolar ridge:*
  W ~ t^h n
- Provide phonetic names for the feature classes Laryngeal, Airstream, Place, Nasality, Stricture for the speech sounds listed below.

		Laryngeal	Airstream	Place	Nasality	Stricture
i.	m	voiced	pulmonic	bilabial	nasal	stop
ii.	z^j	voiced	pulmonic	palatalised alveolar	oral	fricative
iii.	ɗ	voiced	glottalic	alveolar	oral	stop
iv.	g	voiced	pulmonic	velar	oral	stop
v.	ʁ	voiced	pulmonic	uvular	oral	fricative
vi.	ʒ	voiced	pulmonic	palato-alveolar	oral	fricative

- *Give phonetic notation for the following speech sounds:*

i.	breathy alveolar lateral approximant	l̤
ii.	voiced retroflex oral stop	ɖ
iii.	voiceless lateral fricative	ɬ
iv.	creaky alveolar fricative	z̰
v.	alveolar lateral click	ǁorǁŋ

- In a certain language, consonants are palatalised before close (high) front vowels and velarised before close (high) back vowels. Make any changes to the consonants on the left that precede the vowels on the right in accordance with this rule. If no change is necessary, write NC.

i.	t	y	→	t^j
ii.	f	ɯ	→	f^{γ}
iii.	k	i	→	k^j or c

- In a certain language, close (high) vowels become glides (maintaining their fronting and rounding features) when they precede other close vowels. Make any changes to the vowels on the left that precede the vowels on the right in accordance with this rule. If no change is necessary, write NC.

i.	u	y	→	w
ii.	ø	ø	→	NC
iii.	i	i	→	j
iv.	i	y	→	j
v.	ɯ	u	→	ɰ

- What features do the groups of sounds have in common?

i.	m,b,ɸ	bilabial egressive
ii.	ç,j	pulmonic palatal
iii.	r,ʁ	voiced egressive
iv.	z,n,l,z^j	pulmonic voiced alveolar
v.	y, n, ø, œ,ɔ	voiced

- *Convert the following sounds into equivalent laterals:*

i.	z	→	ɮ
ii.	s	→	ɬ

- *Convert the following sounds into equivalent fricatives:*

i.	t	→	s
ii.	d	→	z
iii.	l	→	ɮ

- Convert the following into equivalent sounds produced with lip-rounding

i.	θ	⟶	$θ^w$
ii.	j	⟶	ɥ

- *Briefly explain why the following notation is not possible:*

i.	u^w	u is already labialised
ii.	d'	ejectives cannot be voiced
iii.	m^h	only oral sounds can be aspirated

- *Give a brief definition of what is meant by the following labels:*

i.	glottalic	airstream involving laryngeal power source
ii.	breathy	inefficient vocal fold vibration allowing escape of air
iii.	velarised	secondary articulation involving raising the back of the tongue
iv.	ingressive	inflowing air

- *Provide phonetic notation for any two speech sounds that conform to the following description:*

i.	the soft-palate is lowered; the airstream mechanism is velaric	ǀŋ̇ ǁŋ ǃŋ
ii.	the vocal folds are completely closed at some stage during the production of the sound	ʔ p' t' k'
iii.	the tip of the tongue makes a complete closure against the alveolar ridge	t d n
iv.	the blade of the tongue is raised towards the hard-palate but without making a complete closure	j ç

- Define a diphthong
  - When two vowels occur in a single syllable
- Give three criteria for distinguishing consonants from vowels

i.	acoustic	-	loudness
ii.	physiological	-	oral impedance
iii.	phonological	-	syllabic position

TRANSCRIPTION

INTERNATIONAL PHONETIC ALPHABET

"The aim of the International Phonetic Association is to

promote the study of the science of phonetics and the various practical applications of that science. For both these it is desirable to have a consistent way of representing the sounds of language in written form.

From its foundation in 1886 the Association has been concerned to develop a set of symbols which would be convenient to use, but comprehensive enough to cope with the wide variety of sounds found in the languages of the world; and to encourage the use of this notation as widely as possible among those concerned with language.

The system is generally known as the International Phonetic Alphabet. Both the Association and its Alphabet are widely referred to by the abbreviation IPA.... The IPA is based on the Roman alphabet, which has the advantage of being widely familiar, but also includes letters and additional symbols from a variety of other sources. These additions are necessary because the variety of sounds in languages is much greater than the number of letters in the Roman alphabet. The use of sequences of phonetic symbols to represent speech is known as transcription."

AIMS

- To introduce students to the transcription of the languages of the world using the IPA. Given the short time allocated to this task in the current course, students are only expected to gain a very basic skill level. LING210 students will be assessed on their acquisition of this basic skill level and are expected to be able to transcribe simple syllables containing the vowel and consonant symbols shown in red on the IPA tables.
- To introduce students to all of the vowel, consonant and diacritic symbols used in this course. Students in all courses are expected to learn all of the symbols (both black and red symbols) on the IPA tables. Students are also expected to be able to associate with those symbols their various phonetic features. LING210 students will be assessed by examination

on this knowledge whilst LING901 and SLP801 students will be assessed by assignment.

INTERNATIONAL PHONETIC ALPHABET (IPA)

IPA Vowel Symbols

The following table shows most of the vowel symbols defined in the current version of the International Phonetic Alphabet. This table represents the vowels symbols that you will need to know for this course. In this table the "vowel quadrilateral" roughly represents tongue position, with positions to the left of the diagram representing vowels produced with the tongue moved towards the front of the mouth and with positions to the right of the diagram representing vowels produced with the tongue moved towards the back of the mouth. Similarly, high positions on the table represent vowels produced with a high tongue position and low positions on the table represent vowels produced with a low tongue position. The third dimension on this table (represented implicitly by the paired vowels) represents lip posture. Four IPA vowel symbols have been omitted. *The missing vowels are*:

1. [Y], the rounded version of [I]
2. Three central vowels, including the rounded version of [ɛ]

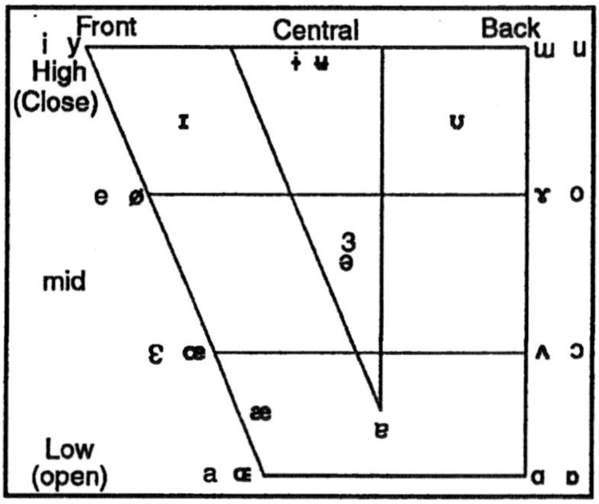

Fig. Recorded Examples have been Supplied for each of the Symbols in Red.

Rounded ans Uurounded Vowels

In this diagram, whenever there is a pair of symbols together, the sounds only differ with respect to lip posture, with the left symbol being unrounded and the right symbol being rounded.

Rounded Vowels

The rounded vowels on the above diagram are:

[yø œ Œ R T o Ʊ u ‰]

Unrounded Vowels

The unrounded vowels on the above diagram are:

[i I ε æ a P Q Λ d o h \ ə]

Cardinal Vowels

The 16 cardinal vowels are sub-divided into 8 primary and 8 secondary cardinal vowels. The first five primary cardinal vowels are unrounded and the last three are rounded. The first five secondary cardinal vowels are rounded and the last three are unrounded.

The primary cardinal vowels (1 -8) *are:*

[i e ε a Q T o u]

The secondary cardinal vowels (9-16) *are:*

[yø œ v R Λ d o]

When you compare these symbols with their position on the diagram above, you will see that each set is a mixture of unrounded and rounded vowels and that the secondary set is identical with the primary set with the exception that the lip posture is reversed.

The primary cardinal vowels tend to be much more commonly found in the world's languages than the secondary cardinals but the three secondary cardinals highlighted in red are also very common. For this reason, sample recordings are provided for these 11 cardinals.

Position and Nature of Vowels [?] and [ə]

Note also that the true position of [\], according to the current version of the IPA, is about half way between where it is on this diagram and the position of the vowel [P]. In the

IPA the vowel[ə] is the true central or neutral vowel. The vowel [\ ] has been placed in the same position as[ə] because it is a convention in both Australian and British phonetics to use [\ ] as the long central vowel and [ə] to represent the unstressed, reduced schwa vowel.

Students should expect to find in American texts the symbol [ə] being used to represent the unreduced fully-realised central vowel.

IPA DIACRITICS

The diacritics in this table have been paired with an "×" in the first column to provide a consistent display context. You should understand that this does not necessarily imply that "×" can be paired with each of these diacritics. Phonetically sensible examples are displayed in the right-most column.

Note that the diacritics (5, 7, 8, 10) that can be placed beneath another character, can be placed above a character that has a descender (such as [g]). Note that this cannot be so for the creaky voice (11) and nasalisation (12) diacritics as that would result in confusion. Note that the syllabic diacritic (9) and the dental diacritic (18) are only found under the affected symbol.

Diacritic Font Problems

This table has been provided as a graphic image so that you have a reliable reference of the diacritic symbols. You should not interpret your ability to see the diacritic symbols on this table as proof that diacritics display accurately on your browser.

You should particularly check the topic "Complex Articulations" and ensure that the diacritics used on that page are correctly displayed.

From a font design perspective there are two types of diacritic:

1. Superscript and subscript characters that precede (1, 2) or follow (3, 4, 6, 13, 14, 15, 16, 19, 20, 21, 22). These characters, from a font design perspective, are no different from ordinary IPA characters and if your

system displays ordinary IPA characters it will have no trouble displaying these diacritic characters.

2. "Combining" characters are characters that "overstrike" a preceding character. That is they either go through (17), over or under (5, 7, 8, 9, 10, 11, 12, 18) the preceding character. Some browsers have trouble displaying these characters (especially some releases of Netscape) so you should be very careful to ensure that you can read these characters and that they look like they do on this table. People viewing the Unicode version of these pages (so far, only SLP801 students) may find that some of these characters are not properly displayed (the bottoms get cut off when using the Lucida Sans Unicode font).

1	ˈx	Primary stress	ˌfəʊnəˈtɪʃən
2	ˌx	Secondary stress	ˌfəʊnəˈtɪʃən
3	xː	Long	iː
4	xˑ	Half-long	iˑ
5	x̥	Voiceless	z̥ g̊
6	xʰ	Aspirated	pʰ
7	x̟	Advanced	k̟ ġ
8	x̠	Retracted	d̠ ḡ
9	x̩	Syllabic	beɪn̩
10	x̤	Breathy Voiced	a̤ ŋ̈
11	x̰	Creaky voiced	a̰
12	x̃	Nasalided	ẽ
13	xʷ	Labialised	tʷ
14	xʲ	Palatalised	tʲ
15	xˠ	Velarised	tˠ
16	xˤ	Pharyngealised	tˤ
17	x̴	Velarised or Pharyngealised	ɫ
18	x̪	Dental	n̪ d̪
19	xⁿ	Nasal Release	dⁿ
20	xˡ	Lateral Release	dˡ
21	x̚	No Audible Release	d̚
22	x˞	Rhoticity (Retroflexion)	ə˞

PHONOLOGY AND STRUCTURE OF LANGUAGE

STUDY OF SOUND STRUCTURE

If there were no structure, then:

- We would have to memorise lists of utterances.
- There would be no units into which utterances can be decomposed.
- Utterances would be unrelated to each other

What Kinds of Structure?

Units that are:

- Paradigmatically opposed to each.
- Syntagmatically related to each other.

PARADIGMATIC CONTRASTS

Units that are paradigmatically opposed to each other belong to different classes that function in different ways.

E.g. words belong to paradigmatically contrasting grammatical classes.

We know this by applying a substitution test.

I was happy to ________

learn/leave/wander/relax (verbs)

- Underneath/overhead
- Student/door/wanderer/relaxation
- Energetic/thoughtful/green/sad

SYNTAGMATIC RELATIONSHIPS

- The units can be parsed into higher order units in different ways
- The order of units matters
- There can be a multilevelled hierarchy
- There is headedness

Parsing Into Higher-Order Units

- "Australian boys and girls love to swim" *could be either*:
- [Australian boys] and girls love to swim

or:

- Australian [boys and girls] love to swim

Order Matters

- Australian boys and girls love to swim *Boys Australian and girls to swim love (*note*: "*" means that this is not possible)

Hierarchical Structure

A hierarchical structure means: there are units within units within units...

E.g. a *noun-phrase* is a unit, and so is a *verb-phrase*, but together they makeup another unit called a *sentence*:

[[Great truths]$_{NP}$ [were spoken]$_{VP}$]$_{S}$=

...and the unit, noun-phrase, is itself made up of two other units, an adjective and a noun

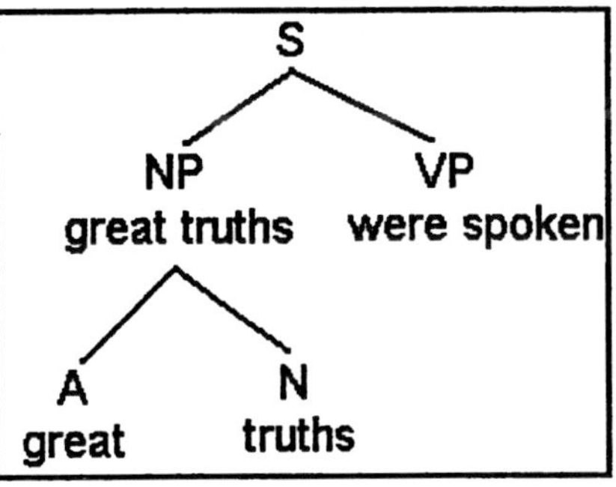

Headedness

Headedness means that one of the units that makes up a hierarchical unit is *obligatory*. This obligatory unit is the head of the hierarchy.

For example:

- exclamations aside, you can't usually form a sentence without a verb (so the verb is the head of the sentence)
- every noun-phrase must have a noun (so the noun is the head of the noun-phrase)

Phonology — if there is structure to sound then:

Are There Units

What's the evidence that:

- They are paradigmatically contrastive?
- They form syntagmatic relationships?

Phonology: Units

In each human language, there are a finite number of units called phonemes that a language uses to build its words.

Animal languages:

- They don't have phonemes (no 'building blocks' for words) and so there is a one-to-one relationship between meaning and sound.

Human languages:

- Phonemes are combined in different, productive ways to produce new meanings e.g.,/pIt/'!/tIp/
- The relationship between meaning and sound is arbitrary

Phonology: Paradigmatic Oppositions I

Words must sound sufficiently distinct (from each other) in order to be understood.

For this to be possible, phonemes have to be chosen from a number of dimensions, or *natural classes*, that have *contrastive values. Contrastive* is in an articulatory and/or acoustic sense. For example, phonemes are often chosen from the natural class **Stricture** which has contrastive articulatory values (stop/ fricative/approximant) which have different acoustic consequences (silence/aperiodicity/low frequency energy)

Phonology: Paradigmatic Opposition II

Languages tend to form phonemes out of natural classes *in a highly productive way.*

For example:

Nasality	oral vs. nasal (2)
Place	bilabial vs. alveolar vs. velar (3)
Maximum number of possible phonemes = 2 x 3 = 6	

	b	d	g	m	n	ŋ
Nasality	-nasal	-nasal	-nasal	+nasal	+nasal	+nasal
Place	bilabial	alveolar	velar	bilabial	alveolar	velar

This is one of the reasons why phonemes tend to form patterns:

Language A		
b	d	g
m	n	ŋ
f	s	

is much more probable than,

Language B				
b			g	
	n			
		ʃ		h

SYNTAGMATIC STRUCTURE

Is there syntagmatic structure in phonology?

- Can phonemes be grouped into superordinate units?
- Does order matter?
- Are there hierarchies? (units within units within units)?
- Is there headedness?

Superordinate Units

The simplest evidence that there are superordinate phonological units is that, in almost every language, phonemes are organised into syllables.

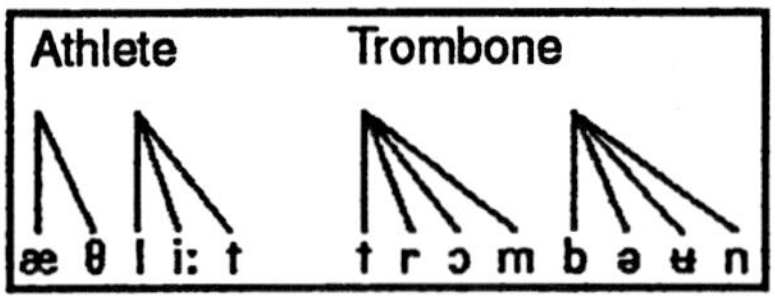

Order

In all languages, the order in which phonemes can occur in syllables is restricted.

For example:

In English, /k/ can be followed by /w j l r/ at the beginning of a syllable:

/kwiĐn/ ('queen'); /kj‰Đt/ ('cute'); /kliĐn/ ('clean'), / kriĐp/ ('creep').

But there are not many words in English that can begin with /pw/,/bw/,/tl/,/dl/. *And although approximants can follow some oral stops, /w r l/ can't follow nasals:*/nw/,/nl/,/nr/ don't occur.

Hierarchy

- Utterances are made up of one or more *intonational phrases*
  [When I get to Sydney] [I'll visit Emily]
- Every intonational phrase is made up of one or more *words*

You could have an intonational phrase as small as one word. For example:

[Stop!][Emily?] [Adelaide] [is in South Australia]

- Every word is made up of one or more *syllables*
- Every syllable is made up of one or more *phonemes*

Headedness

Is one of the units at each level of the hierarchy obligatory?

Intonational phrase: Every intonational phrase has to have a *tonic syllable.* The word containing the tonic syllable is often called the nuclear accented word.

Word: Every word has to have a *primary stressed syllable.*

Unstressed syllables are optional ('pat', 'John', 'said')

Secondary stressed syllables are possible ('imagination'), but optional ('America')

Syllable: Every syllable has to have a *nucleus* which is a vowel, or vowel-like sound,

Initial consonant(s) are optional ('opt', 'each', 'own')

Final consonant(s) are optional ('free', 'say', 'do')

CONCLUSIONS

There is structure to the sounds of language. In phonology, we want to find out what this structure looks like as well as how it differs across languages.

Evidence For Structure

There are units (phonemes, syllables, words, intonational phrases),

There is paradigmatic contrast (e.g. oral vs. nasal phonemes)

There is syntagmatic structure:

- Phonemes are sequentially grouped or parsed into syllables
- There are restrictions on the sequential order of phonemes in a syllable
- There are multiple hierarchies
- There is headedness

PHONEME AND ALLOPHONE

INTRODUCTION

It is the task of phonology to study which differences in sound are related to differences in meaning in a given language, in which way the discriminative elements... are related to each other, and the rules according to which they may be combined into words and sentences."

Linguistic **units** which cannot be substituted for each other without a change in meaning can be referred to as **linguistically contrastive** or significant units. Such units may be phonological, morphological, syntactic, semantic etc.

Logically, this takes the form:

	IF	unit X	in context A	GIVES meaning 1
	AND IF	unit Y	in context A	GIVES meaning 2
	THEN	unit X AND unit Y		belong to separate linguistic units
eg.	IF	sound [k]	in context [_æt]	GIVES meaning "cat"
	AND IF	sound [m]	in context [_æt]	GIVES meaning "mat"
	THEN	sound [k] and sound [m]		belong to separate linguistic units

PHONEMES

Phonemes are the linguistically contrastive or significant sounds (or sets of sounds) of a language. Such a contrast is usually demonstrated by the existence of **minimal pairs** or **contrast in identical environment (C.I.E)**. Minimal pairs are pairs of words which vary only by the identity of the **segment** (another word for a single speech sound) at a single location in the word (eg.[mæt] and [kæt]). If two segments contrast in identical environment then they must belong to different phonemes. A **paradigm** of minimal phonological contrasts is a set of words differing only by one speech sound. In most languages it is rare to find a paradigm that contrasts a complete **class** of phonemes (eg. all vowels, all consonants, all stops etc).

Sometimes it is not possible to find a minimal pair which would support the contrastiveness of two phonemes and it is necessary to resort to examples of **contrast in analogous environment (C.A.E)**. C.A.E. is almost a minimal pair, however the pair of words differs by more than just the pair of sounds in question. Preferably, the other points of variation in the pair of words are as remote as possible (and certainly never adjacent and preferably not in the same syllable) from the environment of the pairs of sounds being tested. eg. /ʃ/ vs /'/ in English are usually supported by examples of pairs such as "pressure" [preʃY] vs "treasure" [tre'Y], where only the initial consonants differ and are sufficiently remote from the opposition being examined to be considered unlikely to have any conditioning effect on the selection of phones.

A **syntagmatic** analysis of a speech sound, on the other hand, identifies a unit's identity within a language. In other words, it indicates all of the locations or contexts within the words of a particular language where the sound can be found.

For example, a syntagm of the phone [n] in English could be in the form:

(#CnV..., #nV......Vn#...VnC#...VnV..., etc)

whilst [K] in English would be:

(VK#...VKC#...VKV..., etc)

but would not include the word initial forms of the kind described for [n].

Note that in the above examples, "#" is used to represent a word or syllable boundary, "V" represents any vowel, and "C" represents another consonant.

For example, examples of the type "#CnV..." would include "snow" [snə ‰], "snort" [snoÐt]and "snooker" [sn‰kY]. In this case, the only consonant (for English) that can occupy the initial "C" slot is the phoneme/s/, and so the generalised pattern could be rewritten as "#snV...".

ALLOPHONES

Allophones are the linguistically non-significant variants of each phoneme. In other words a phoneme may be realised by more than one speech sound and the selection of each variant is usually conditioned by the phonetic environment of the phoneme. Occasionally allophone selection is not conditioned but may vary form person to person and occasion to occasion.

A phoneme is a set of allophones or individual non-contrastive speech segments. Allophones are sounds, whilst a phoneme is a set of such sounds.

Allophones are usually relatively similar sounds which are in **mutually exclusive or complementary distribution (C.D)**. The C.D. of two phonemes means that the two phonemes can never be found in the same environment (ie. the same environment in the senses of position in the word and the identity of adjacent phonemes). If two sounds are phonetically similar andthey are in C.D. then they can be assumed to be allophones of the same phoneme.

eg. in many languages voiced and voiceless stops with the same place of articulation do not contrast linguistically but are rather two phonetic realisations of a single phoneme (ie. /p/=[p,b],/t/=[t,d], and /k/=[k,a]). In other words, voicing is not contrastive (at least for stops) and the selection of the appropriate allophone is in some contexts fully conditioned by phonetic context (eg. word medially and depending upon the voicing of adjacent consonants), and is in some contexts either partially conditioned or even completely unconditioned (eg. word initially, where in some dialects of a language the voiceless allophone is preferred, in others the voiced allophone is preferred, and in others the choice of allophone is a matter of individual choice).

eg. Some French speakers choose to use the alveolar trill [r] when in the village and the more prestigious uvular trill [R] when in Paris. Such a choice is made for sociological reasons.

PHONETIC SIMILARITY

Allophones must be phonetically similar to each other. In analysis, this means you can assume that highly dissimilar sounds are separate phonemes (even if they are in complementary distribution). For this reason no attempt is made to find minimal pairs which contrast vowels with consonants. Exactly what can be considered phonetically similar may vary somewhat from language family to language family and so the notion of phonetic similarity can seem to be quite unclear at times. Sounds can be phonetically similar from both articulatory and auditory points of view and for this reason one often finds a pair of sounds that vary greatly in their place of articulation but are sufficiently similar auditorily to be considered phonetically similar (eg. and [3] are voiceless fricatives which are distant in terms of glottal and palatal places of articulation, but which nevertheless are sufficiently similar auditorily to be allophones of a single phoneme in some languages such as Japanese).

eg. In English, /h/ and /K/ are in complementary distribution. /h/ only ever occurs at the beginning of a syllable (head, heart, enhance, perhaps) whilst /K/ only ever occurs at the end of a syllable. They are, however, so dissimilar that no one regards them as allophones of the one phoneme. They vary in place and manner of articulation, as well as voicing. Further the places of articulation (velar vs glottal) are quite remote from each other and /h/ is oral whilst /K/ is nasal.

According to Hockett if a and b are members of one phoneme, they share one or more features. Phonetic similarity is therefore based on the notion of shared features. Such judgments of similarity will vary from language to language and there are no universal criteria of similarity.

The following pairs of sounds might be considered to be similar:

- *Two sounds differing only in voicing:*
  [pb] [td] [ka] [ɸβ] [θð] [sz] [ʃ′] [×c] etc...
- Two sounds differing in manner of articulation only as plosive vs fricative. The sibilant or grooved fricatives [s,z,ʃ,′] are excluded from this category as they are quite different auditorily from the other ("central") fricatives.
  [pɸ] [k×] [bβ] [ac] etc...
- Any pairs of consonants close in place of articulation and differing in no other contrastive feature:
  [sʃ] [z′] [nrK] [lm] [lŽ] [mq], etc...
- Any other pairs of consonants which are close in articulation and differ by one other feature but are nevertheless frequently members of the same phoneme
  [ly] [ca] [tɸ] [ˈdð]
  In languages where voicing is non-contrastive, two phones differing in voicing and only slightly in place of articulation might be considered similar eg. [ca] etc)
  Further, for the purposes of this type of analysis, the place of articulation of the apicodental fricatives [ɸ,ð] is considered to be close enough to that of the alveolar stops [t,d] to be considered phonetically similar.
- Any two vowels differing in only one feature or articulated with adjacent tongue positions
  [æ P] [i I] [PĐ P] [i y] [Q Q⊖]

Although it is implied above that the notion of "phonetic similarity" is in some way less linguistically abstract (more phonetic?) than the notion of complementary distribution, it is, nevertheless, a quite abstract concept. The are no obvious and consistent acoustic, auditory or articulatory criteria for phonetic similarity. Furtheı, since a notion of similarity implies a continuum the following question must be asked of two phones in complementary distribution. How similar must they be before they are to be considered members of the same phoneme?

There are many examples of very similar phones which are perceived by native speakers to belong to separate phonemes. In English, for example, a word terminal voiceless stop may be either released and aspirated or unreleased. The homorganic [1] voiced stop may also be released or unreleased. Often the unreleased voiced and voiceless stops may actually be identical in every way except that the preceding vowel is lengthened before the phonologically voiced stop. In terms of phonetic similarity, the two unreleased stops may actually be identical and yet be perceived by native speakers to belong to different phonemes.

For example:

/kPp/'![kPp°] ... [kPp]

/kPb/'![kPÑb] ... [kPÑb] ... [kPÑp]

(nb. " " means unreleased stop and " Ñ " means partially lengthened vowel)

Conversely, phones which are very dissimilar (at least from certain perspectives) may be felt by native speakers to belong to a single phoneme.

eg.	Japanese[2]	/h/	→	[ɸ] before /u/	eg.[ɸuku] "luck"
			→	[ç] before /i/	eg.[çito] "man"
			→	[h] before /e,a,o/	eg.[hana]

From an articulatory perspective, these phones seem very dissimilar (bilabial, palatal, and glottal) being produced at the extreme ends of the vocal tract. They are, however, relatively similar acoustically and auditorily (they are all relatively weak voiceless fricatives). This kind of phonetic similarity is listener orientated rather than speaker orientated.

eg.	English	/t/	→	[ʔ] medially and finally in some dialects eg. Cockney - "butter", "wait"
			→	[t] initially
nb.		/k/	→	[k,ʔ] does not occur although they are articulatorily closer

PHONEMIC PATTERN

A pair of phones in complementary distribution may sometimes be classified into separate phonemes on the basis of phonemic pattern. In other words, is there a group of phonemes which exhibit a similar pattern of distribution (eg. clustering behaviour, morphology, etc) to one of the phones being examined? In the case of the pair , [K] there are some similarities in patterning between and certain fricatives, and between [K] and the nasals.

For example, there is a suffix which when placed before a word commencing with a stop has the effect of negating the original meaning. The suffix has the form /I/ plus the nasal homorganic with the stop.

ie.	"impossible"	[ɪmp...]
	"intolerable"	[ɪnt...]
	"incalculable"	[ɪŋk...] or [ɪnk...]
		(free variation in citation form, but homorganic predominating in rapid speech)

Clearly, this pattern suggests that [K] behaves in some instances with the same phonological pattern as the other nasals. It does in fact raise the question of [K] being an allophone of /n/. This was indeed the case until the 1600's, but now there are quite a few minimal pairs which have since crept into the language. ("sin"/"sing", "run"/"rung").

PHONOLOGICAL SPACE

The greater the distance between a phoneme and its nearest neighbours, the greater the scope for allophonic variation. In other words, the larger the number of redundant features (ie. features which when changed will not create another phoneme) the greater the number of allophones which can actually occur.

eg.	English	/p/	→	[-voice]
				[+bilabial]
				[+stop]
				[+/-aspirated]

(nb. + indicates that a feature is present, - indicates that a feature is absent, +/- indicates that a feature is optional)

Changing the feature [-voice] to [+voice] will create /b/, changing the feature [bilabial] will create /t,k/ (or potential allophones of them) and changing the feature [stop] will create/ w,f,m/.

The only feature with complete freedom of movement is aspiration, and variation of this feature does indeed create the main pair of allophones of this phoneme in English.

eg.	English	/r/	→	[ɹ]	alveolar approximant
				[ɹ̥]	voiceless alveolar approximant (after voiceless sounds)
				[ɻ]	retroflex approximant (West England)
				[ɾ]	alveolar flap (Scottish) eg. [gɾɪn]
				[ʁ]	uvular fricative (Tyneside)

The possible varieties of /r/ seem to include variations of manner, place and voicing. The only restrictions are that its allophones may not overlap with those of /l/ and /w/.

PREMISES OF PRACTICAL PHONEMICS

This section examines some of the basic assumptions behind phonemic analysis. The first four premises are particularly important to remember during the process of phonemic analysis.

"Phonemic analysis cannot be made with phonetic data alone; it must be made with phonetic data plus a series of phonemic premises and procedures"

"Phonemic procedures... must be founded upon premises concerning the underlying universal characteristics of languages of the world...."

- "Sounds tend to be modified by their environments" (coarticulation, producing allophones)
  The actual details of these processes vary from language to language.
- "Sound systems have a tendency towards phonetic symmetry"

eg.IF unequivocal evidence that [p] vs [b] and [k] vs [a] are separate phonemes then it is likely that [t] vs [d] are separate phonemes:

- "Sounds tend to fluctuate"
  Free variation of allophones, eg. sometimes /tas/ = [tas] and sometimes /tas/ =[das]
- "Characteristic sequences of sounds exert structural pressure on the phonemic interpretation of suspicious segments or suspicious sequences of segments"

For example, in the interpretation of syllable structure:

eg1.	[ma]	"cat"
	[bo]	"to run"
	[su]	"sky"
	[sa]	"leaf"
	[ia]	"moon"
	[tsa]	"ten"

If in all non-suspicious words the syllable structure was found to be CV then:

[ia]	→	/ja/
[tsa]	→	/tasa/

which would agree with the CV structure.

eg2.	[maba]	"dog"
	[nasaa]	"elephant"
	[saplam]	"egg"
	[pasak]	"to eat"

All clear syllable initials are found at the start of the words and are always $CV.... All clear syllable finals are found at the end of words and are either..VC$ or..V$. There are no unambiguous examples of CC clusters at the start or end of a syllable therefore the most likely analysis would be to place the syllable boundary in [saplam] thus /sap$lam/. In the cases of[maba],[nasaa] and [pasak] the most satisfactory syllabification would be to place the medial consonant in the second syllable (placing at the end of the first syllable would require an additional syllable initial $V... which is not unambiguously attested (ie. no words begin with a vowel)).

Some extra premises (Pike lists more but these are the most important):

- "Every language has consonants and vowels"
- "Certain kinds of segments may be vowels in one language but consonants in another."
  eg. [ia] →/ia/ in language 1 (L1) but [ia] = /ja/ in language 2 (L2)
- "The dichotomy between vowel and consonant is not strictly an articulatory one but is in part based on distributional characteristics."
- "A long vowel or consonant may in some languages constitute two phonemes."
  eg. [aÐ] →/a/ in L1 and /aa/ in L2
- "A sequence of two segments may in some languages constitute a single phonetically complex phoneme."
  eg. [atsa] →/at$sa/ in L1 and /atsa/ in L2 (nb. $ = syllable boundary)
  It may be that L2 only allows open syllables (V and CV) and so the L1 form would be illegal.
- "Some segments may be non-significant transition sounds"
  eg. in English /ea/ may be ["ea], where the glottal stop is phonemically non-significant.
- "If two segments are sub-members of a single phoneme, the NORM of the phoneme is that sub-member [allophone] which is least limited in its distribution and least modified by its environments."
  eg. /n/"! [K]/__ {k/a} and [n] elsewhere (here, [K] is clearly an environmental modification)
- "In order to be considered sub-members of a single phoneme, two segments must be
  - Phonetically similar
  - Mutually exclusive as to the environments in which they occur."
- "When two phonemic conclusions each appear to be justifiable by the other premises, and each seems to account for all the available facts of all types, that conclusion is assumed to be correct

- Which is the least complex,
- Which gives to suspicious data an analysis parallel with analogous non-suspicious data,
- Which appears most plausible in terms of alleged [coarticulations in] specific environments.

THE SYLLABLE AND THE FOOT

THE SYLLABLE

Aspects of phonology above the segmental level comprise units of greater length than the segment. These are referred to as suprasegmental features.

Suprasegmental aspects of language encode rhythm and melody and thereby contribute to meaning and give a language its characteristic cadence. Suprasegmental constituent structure is considered hierarchical with the phonological phrase (ϕ) dominating the phonological word (ω) which in turn dominates the foot (F), the superior constituent to the syllable (σ).

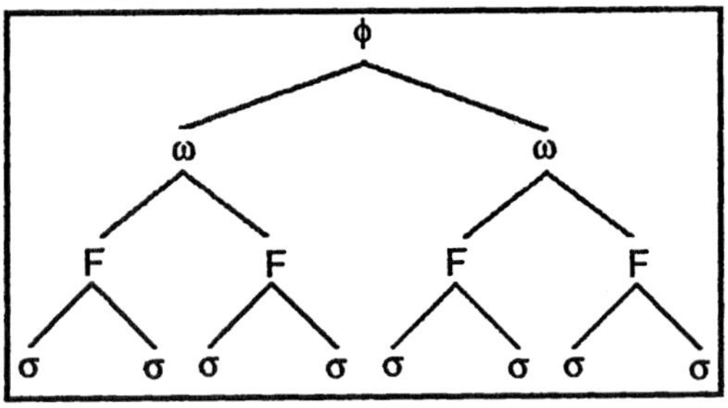

The syllable is the most basic element in this constituent structure. It has psychological reality as a unit that speakers of a language can identify. Speakers are able to count the number of syllables in a word and can often tell where one syllable ends and the next begins.

Phonetically, it is claimed that when identifying syllables, listeners are responding to sonority. Sonority is the relative loudness of a segments compared with others. Each syllable has a single sonority peak.

What is a syllable? There is no definition of the syllable that phoneticians or phonologists currently agree upon yet the notion of a unit at a higher level than that of the phoneme has existed since ancient times.

The various definitions have a number of commonalities that relate to properties of sound and properties of speakers:

- Sonority or prominence: this is where some sounds are said to have greater prominence than others and these form the basis of syllables. Syllable boundaries fall at points of weak prominence.
- Speaker awareness: this relies on the intuition of the speaker to define syllables. People without any linguistic knowledge are capable of dividing words into syllables. Children can clap syllables before they can read. People who have not been exposed to alphabetic writing systems have greater difficulty segmenting utterances into phonemic units than identifying syllables. Many writing systems are syllabic where each symbol represents a syllable. Japanese is an example

The CV (consonant followed by vowel) structure has been suggested as a basic phonological unit.

What's the evidence that a CV sequence is a phonological unit?

- Almost all languages have CVCV or CV words.
- If a language has CCV words, it also has CV words.
- Hardly any language has V or VC words without CV ones. One of the rare exception to this is the Arrandic group of Aboriginal languages
- The first systematic utterances of children are usually of this form regardless of language type.

The syllable is seen as a unit of neural programming rather than primarily muscular or acoustic events. If an error is made in the duration of a phoneme, the error is compensated for within the syllabic unit suggesting that articulatory events are programmed in terms of higher-level articulatory units rather than single phonemes. Other evidence for neural programming comes from speech errors such as slips of the tongue. When spoonerisms occur, for instance, and one consonant is substituted for another, this only occurs in same syllable position. eg initial consonants are swapped for initial consonants and final consonants for final consonants. eg beas and peans, or else whole syllables are switched "drugtator dic Baron". Errors do not involve random switching between segments.

The syllable is a structural unit and within that structure we can identify a sequence of consonants (C) and vowels (V). Just as in grammar we can parse a grammatical structure, in phonology we can parse syllabic structure.

Grammatical category is signaled not just by paradigmatically different classes but also by their sequential arrangement from which we parse a superordinate NP structure (in this example).	So too in phonology: we parse a hierarchical syllable structure from a sequential arrangement of C's and V's
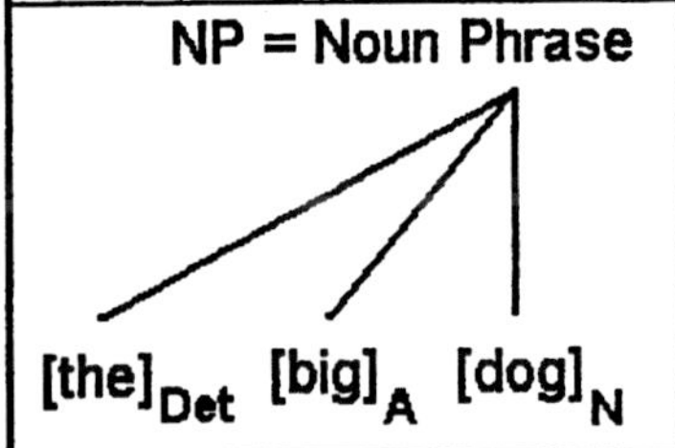	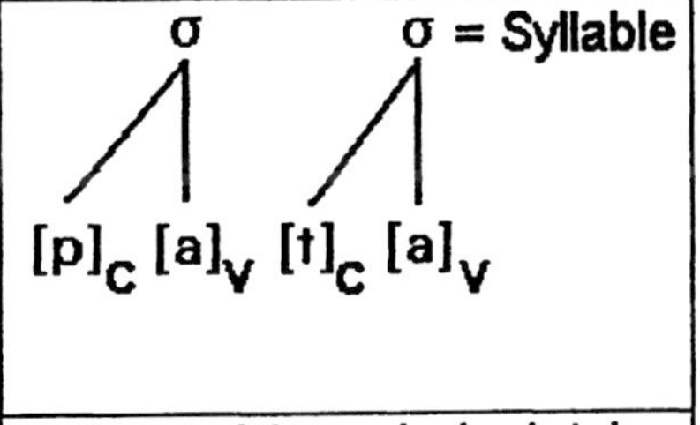
[big]A means: 'big' belongs to the grammatical category Adjective	[p]c means: /p/ belongs to the phonological category Consonant.

Syllables:

- Most syllables have a single vowel plus zero or more consonants (occasional syllables have a syllabic consonant rather than a vowel).
- No syllable has more than one vowel. Vowel-like sequences in a single syllable are interpreted as diphthongs or semi-vowel plus vowel sequences.
- Depending upon language-specific rules, syllables have certain numbers of consonants before and after the vowel.

Open and Closed Sykkabkes

Closed syllables are syllables that have at least one consonant following the vowel. The most common closed syllable is the CVC syllable. Open syllables are syllables that end in a vowel. The most common open syllable is the CV syllable.

English Monosyllabic Words

English has a large number of monosyllabic words. All monosyllabic words in English have a single vowel. By examining the legal consonant+vowel sequences in English monosyllabic words we can get a good idea of what types of syllable structure are legal in English.

a) Open syllables,

V	"I"	/ɑe/
CV	"me"	/mi:/
CCV	"spy"	/spɑe/
CCCV	"spray"	/spræe/

b) Closed syllables,

VC	"am"	/æm/
VCC	"ant"	/ænt/
VCCC	"ants"	/ænts/
CVC	"man"	/mæn/
CVCC	"bond"	/bɔnd/
CVCCC	"bands"	/bændz/
CVCCCC	"sixths"	/sɪksθs/
CCVC	"brag"	/bræg/
CCVCC	"brags"	/brægz/
CCVCCC	"plants"	/plænts/
CCCVC	"spring"	/sprɪŋ/
CCCVCC	"springs"	/sprɪŋz/
CCCVCCC	"splints"	/splɪnts/

It is clear from this list that English has a very flexible syllable structure. There are languages at the opposite extreme that have only CV syllables.

It should be noted, however, that there are nevertheless considerable constraints on which phoneme sequences are permissible. Such constraints are called phonotactic constraints and these constraints are very language-specific. Nevertheless, there is a universal tendency for phonotactic constraints to conform mostly to sonority profile constraints.Phonotactic constraints and sonority are dealt with in another section.

SYLLABLE STRUCTURE

The syllable can be structured hierarchically into the following components:

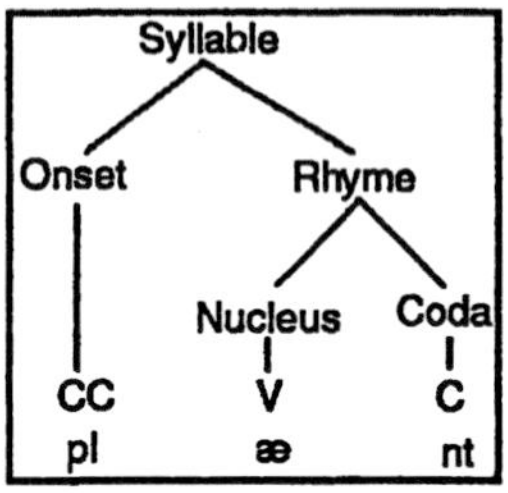

The rhyme has been further divided into the nucleus, which in the vast majority of syllables is a vowel (the exceptions are syllabic consonants) and the coda, which are any consonants following the nucleus.

Some other examples:

flounce:	onset = /fl/ rhyme = /aʊns/ nucleus = /aʊ/ coda = /ns/
free:	onset /fr/ rhyme = /iː/ nucleus = /iː/ coda zero
each:	onset zero rhyme = /iːtʃ/ nucleus = /iː/ coda = /tʃ/

The Rhyme

The rhyme is the vowel plus any following consonants. 'plant'. Syllable is composed of an Onset = /pl/and a Rhyme = /ænt/(the rhyme is obligatory = the head of the syllable)

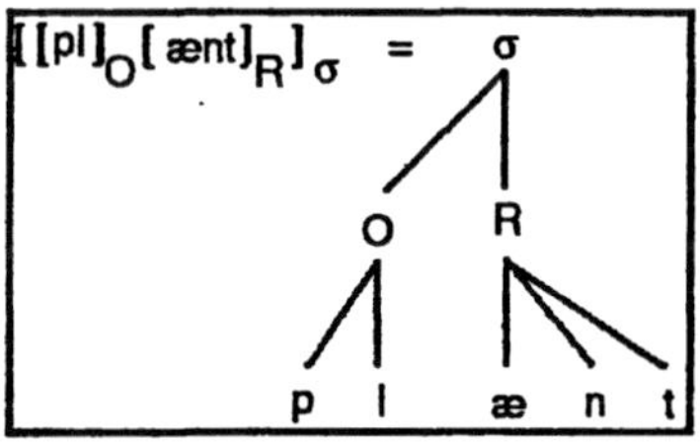

There is phonological evidence of at least two kinds to suggest that the vowel forms a unit (the rhyme) with the following consonants:

- Restrictions on phoneme combinations
- Sound change

Evidence For the Rhyme: Phoneme Combination

There are often restrictions *within* syllable units (within the Onset; within the Rhyme); but not many restrictions on phoneme combinations *between* syllable units (between the onset and the rhyme)

For example: There are few restrictions on what vowel can follow /fl/ (column 1) but many restrictions on the type of vowel that can precede /lf/ (column 2)

	/fl/+ vowel/	/vowel + /lf/
iː	fleece	*
ɪ	flip	sylph
ʉ	flew	*
e	fled	self
eɪ	flake	*
əʉ	flown	*
ɔ	flop	golf
ɐ	flood	gulf
oː	floor	*
æ	flack	Ralph
æɔ	flounce	*
ɑe	fly	*

* means — no word with this combination

Evidence for the Rhyme: Sound Change

A vowel and consonant in the rhyme are often merged historically resulting in a long vowel (known as compensatory lengthening).

This kind of merger hardly ever happens in a CV onset-rhyme.

Italian /ka:ne/	From Latin Kasnus (dog)		
V:	VC		
English "Five" < Old English /fi:f/	< Old Teutonic /fImf/	and Greek /Pente/	
V:C	VCC	VC	

SYLLABLE AND PHONOTACTIC CONSTRAINTS

Phonotactic Constraints

We have seen in the preceding section that all languages build their words from a finite set of phonemic units. It is also true that in all languages there are constraints on the way in which these phonemes can be arranged to form syllables. These constraints are sometimes known as*phonotactic* or *phoneme sequence constraints* and they severely limit the number of syllables that would be theoretically possible if phonemes could be combined in an unconstrained way.

Some simple examples of phonotactic constraints in English include: all three-consonant clusters at the beginning of a word start with /s/ ('sprint', 'squire', 'stew' etc); nasal consonants cannot occur as the second consonant in word-initial consonant clusters unless the first consonant is /s/ (e.g. there are no words in English than begin with /bm dn/ etc), although this is certainly possible in other languages (e.g. German which allows /kn/ in words like 'Knoten', meaning 'knot' - we can see from the spelling that English used to allow this sequence as well). Another important point about phonotactic constraints is that they vary from language to language, as this example of English and German has just shown.

We will consider firstly why languages have phonotactic constraints. The main reason is to do with the limits on the talker's ability to pronounce sequences of sounds as one syllable, and the listener's perception of how many syllables he or she hears from a given sequence of phonemes. Consider for example a sequence like /p●/ i.e. a voiceless bilabial followed by a voiced uvular fricative. Most of us with some training can produce this sequence (e.g. /p●a p●it/ etc) as*a* *monosyllabic* word even though it doesn't occur in English. Now try reversing the order of the cluster. With some phonetics training, you could almost certainly produce /●p/, but what is much harder (even for a trained phonetician) is to produce the sequence before a vowel such that the resulting sequence is monosyllabic. For example, try /●pi/ — even your best attempts at producing the /●/ followed by the /p/ will probably still lead to a percept of two syllables when/●p/ precedes a vowel.

One of the main reasons, then, why languages have phonotactic constraints is because their sequential arrangement is itself a cue to the number of syllables in a word. When we produce an English word like 'print' for example, we want to convey to the listener not only that this word is composed of a certain number and type of phonemes, but also that the word happens to be monosyllabic: and the listeners' perception of how many syllables there are in a word depends to a certain extent on the arrangement of phonemes in sequence, as we saw from the example of/p●/ and /●p/ that has just been given.

In order to explain why listeners hear e.g. /p●i/ as one syllable, but /●pi/ as two, we need to appeal to what has been called the syllable's *sonority profile.*

Sonority Profile

Sonority is an acoustic-perceptual term that depends on the ratio of energy in the low to the high part of the spectrum, but it is also closely linked with the extent to which the vocal tract is constricted. In general terms, open vowels like [a] have the highest sonority because the vocal tract is open and a large amount of acoustic energy radiates from the vocal tract. At the other extreme, voiceless oral stops have least sonority because there is no acoustic energy during the closure in which the vocal tract is constricted.

Languages prefer to build syllables with the most vowel-like sounds nearer the middle, and the least vowel like sounds (=oral stops, voiceless fricatives) near the edge(s). Syllable structured in this way are said to conform to the *sonority profile.*

Oral Stops	Fricatives	Nasal Stops	Liquids*	Glides	Vowels

Low Sonority ←→ High Sonority

Low Sonority	High Sonority
Constricted Vocal Tract	Unconstricted Vocal Tract
Low in Acoustic Enegrgy	High in Acoustic Energy
Acoustically Aperiodic	Acoustically Periodic

* Liquid =/l/ and /r/ Sounds

i.e. oral stops are less sonorous than fricatives which are less sonorous than nasals etc.

If they conform to the sonority profile, consonants sequences in syllable onsets increase in sonority from left to right and consonant sequences in syllable codas decrease in sonority from left to right. From this we can predict which consonant sequences are more probable for syllable onsets and codas.

probable	less probable	Why? The syllables on the right
/pla fni lju sma pfle/	/lpa nfi jlu lfpe/	have two sonority peaks -- and so it's much more difficult to produce them *so that they sound like one syllable*...for example:
/alp ims ort/	/apl ism otr/	

So a language is more likely to build monosyllabic words from the combination of phonemes on the left than on the right.

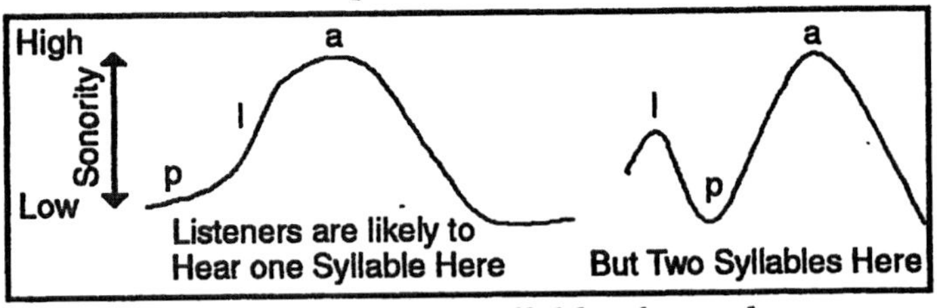

Languages prefer to build syllables from phonemes such that the sonority rises from the left syllable edge, then reaches a peak (at the vowel), and then falls. Therefore, a language is more likely to have a syllable like /pla/ than /lpa/, because in /pla/ the sonority rises from its lowest value for /p/, increasing for /l/, and reaching a peak with /a/. Similarly, a language is more likely to have /amp/ than /apm/. We can now see why listeners might hear two syllables in /•pa/ even if a talker intends only one: because the sonority is higher for /•/(since it is a fricative), then falls for /p/, then rises again for /a/ (and the condition to hear one syllable would be that there is a progressive rise in sonority from the syllable's left edge).

It must be recognised that there is only a *tendency* for syllables to conform to the sonority profile. So while most syllables do conform to the sonority profile in English, many syllables that contain a consonantal cluster with /s/ do not. An example of a syllable that *does* conform to the sonority profile is 'flounce', phonemically /flæTns/ in (Australian) English. In the initial consonant cluster, /f/ is less sonorous than /l/ which is less sonorous than the diphthong; in the final consonant cluster, the diphthong is more sonorous than /n/ which is more sonorous than /s/and so the sonority rises from the left edge of the syllable, reaches a peak at the diphthong, and then falls over the final cluster. But a word like 'spin' violates the sonority profile (because /s/ is more sonorous than /p/) and so does 'act' (because /k/ and /t/ are equally sonorous). The sonority profile is therefore a general tendency which determines many, but by no means, all phonotactic constraints.

Phonotactic Constraints: Syllable Onset, Coda and Rhyme

When discussing phonotactic constraints, it is helpful to structure the syllable hierarchically in terms of an *onset* and a *rhyme*, and sometimes also the syllable *coda*.

We can then discuss phonotactic constraints:

- Within the onset
- Within the coda
- Within the rhyme

The most extreme phonotactic constraints (extreme in terms of the greatest restrictions in the sequential arrangement of phonemes) are in the onset. For example, in English:/f/can only be followed by approximants (as in 'fly'), there are no consonant phonemes that can follow affricates etc.

The phonotactic restrictions in the coda in English are often (but not always) a mirror-image of those in the onset (as you'd expect if the syllable's legal phoneme sequences are strongly influenced by the sonority profile). For example,

English allows /pl/ in the onset ('play') and/lp/ in the coda ('help'); it allows /fr/ in the onset ('free') and, for rhotic dialects (e.g. Gen. American English), /rf/ in the coda ('surf'). But there are also many permissible coda sequences that are allowed whose mirror-image is disallowed in the onset (e.g. /mp/ as in 'lamp', but no/pm/ in the onset).

Finally, there are far fewer restrictions in the rhyme – these are to do with the restrictions on nucleus-coda combinations. But as an example of a rhyme constraint, there are no long vowel +/K/ sequences (no words like 'seeng', 'flowng', although the onomatopoeic 'boing!' is allowed).

Language-Specific Constraints

Languages differ in the kinds of onsets they allow:

	/kn/	/skw/	/sb/	/vr/
English	no	yes	no	no
German	yes	no	no	no
French	no	no	no	yes
Italian	no	no	yes	no

In English the maximum number of consonants that can make up the syllabic onset at the beginning of an isolated word is three. The first can only be /s/, the second has to be/p, t, k/, and the third has to be an approximant /w, j, r, l/.

eg.	splayed	strayed	scrape
	spew	stewed	skewed
	squish	squawk	squeal

These are all CCCVC

When the third consonant is /w/ then the first two must be /sk/Whilst /spr/ and /str/ are permitted syllable-initially, / spw/ and /stw/ are not permitted syllable-initially in English.

Most languages do not allow as many as three consonants in the syllabic onset however there are some that allow up to six.

Restrictions in the coda are often the mirror image of those in the onset, eg pl ~ lp due to the sonority principle. However there are many exceptions eg /nd/ in "end" but not /dn/.

The number of final consonants in an English rhyme can range from one to four.

eg. /sIk/ sick, /sIks/ six, /siksθ/ sixth, /siksθs/ sixths

Languages differ in the structures that they permit. English permits complex codas and onsets. Languages like Hawaiian, for instance, only allow a single consonant in the onset and none in the coda, so every syllable ends in a vowel. Standard Chinese allows only nasal consonants in the coda, so syllables are either open or closed with a nasal.

Phonotactic Constraints: Combinatory and Distributional

Some Combinatory Constraints in English:

- /K/ cannot be preceded by long vowels or diphthongs
- /tf, d', ð, z/ do not cluster
- /r, w, l/ only occur alone or as non initial elements in clusters
- /r, h, w, j/ do not occur in final position in Australian English, but /r/ can occur in final position in rhotic dialects such as American English.
- in final position only /l/ can occur before non-syllabic /m/ and /n/.

Some Distributional Constraints in English:

- /K/ cannot occur word initially
- /e, æ, P, Š, T/ cannot occur word finally
- /Ʊ/ cannot occur initially
- /'/ only occurs initially before /j, iÐ, æ, T/ in foreign words such as genre.

Defining NonON-Words Using Phonotactic Constraints

We can define two kinds of nonword monosyllables:

Accidental gaps: These are phonotactically legal word-like sequences, but happen not to occur in that language eg. /stremp/ in English is an accidental gap because /str/ is legal (as in "string"),/emp/ is legal (as in "hemp"), but /stremp/ happens not to be a word.

Illegal Syllables: These violate a phonotactic constraint in that language.

eg. /knep/ is illegal in English because no words can start with /kn/. In German, this would be an accidental gap since /kn/ does occur ('Knoten', 'Kneipe' etc).

Maximum Onset Principle

Phonotactic constraints in the onset are sometimes used to syllabify polysyllabic words under an algorithm known as the *maximum onset principle*. The problem is as follows. If we have a word like 'athlete', which we know consists of two syllables, where does the syllable boundary occur? The maximum onset principle algorithm works on the basis that as many consonants should be syllabified with a following vowel, providing that the resulting sequence is phonotactically legal. In this case, we have to decide whether /θl/ belongs with the first syllable, the second, or whether/θ/ goes with the first, and /l/ with the second etc.

Based on the maximum onset principle, we would ask:

- Are there any words in English that can begin with / l/?

  Yes, e.g. 'leaf', 'lot' etc.

  Then assign/l/to the second syllable.
- Now move one slot to the left: are there any syllables that can begin with /θl/?

No. Therefore, the syllable boundary goes after /θ/ i.e. the word has two syllables, the first of which is /æθ/, and the second of which is /liÐt/.

Another example. Syllabify 'constrain' based on the maximum onset principle. Here we have to decide how to break up the medial consonantal cluster /nstr/.

- Are there any words that begin with/r/?
  - Yes, 'red', 'range' etc.
- Are there any words that begin with /tr/?
  - Yes, 'train', 'try' etc.
- Are there any words that can begin with /str/?
  - Yes, 'string', 'strike' etc.
- Are there any words that can begin with /nstr/?

No. Therefore, syllabify the word as /kYn.streIn/, where the full stop marks the syllable boundary.

It must be understood that syllable structure is required to satisfy the maximum onset principle only within the limits set by the syntactic, morphological and phonotactic constraints of the language.

THE FOOT AND WORD STRESS

Word Stress

In almost all languages, there is a variation in the relative prominence of syllables. This prominence is a function of loudness, pitch, and duration and it is often the change in pitch along with the other factors that is most important. The prominence of syllables is referred to as stress.

Different languages allow for different types of stress patterns. In English the stress pattern of words is fixed to the extent that we can't arbitrarily shift stress around without compromising meaning. The accent falls on the same syllable of the word whenever it occurs (excepting when affixes are added). However, stress placement is also free in that different words can have different stress patterns. This is in contrast to languages like Turkish which has stress on the final syllable of all root forms or Finnish where stress is always on the first syllable. In English, the main accent can be on the first syllable in "answer, sweater, finish, student, photograph", the second in "result, above, around, behind", the third in "understand, politician" or later in words like "articulation, rhoticisation, characteristic".

Word Stress and Perception

Strong syllables are generally more important for distinguishing between words. For example:

Only 5 out of the 20 Australian English vowel phonemes (/ə, iÐ, I, ‰Ð, ə ‰/) can occur in weak syllables and of these, schwa occurs with by far the greatest frequency. Therefore, the extent to which unstressed syllables distinguish meaning is considerably reduced compared with stressed syllables.

Compatibly, there is psycholinguistic evidence to show that listeners are much more attuned to/aware of strong syllables (presumably because they are so much more important for understanding what is being said).

Evidence: In reaction time experiments, listeners' responses are much faster to strong syllables.

Word Stress and the Metrical Foot

Words are made up of rhythmic units called feet and these comprise one or more syllables. Feet represent the rhythmic structure of the word and are the units that allow us to describe stress patterns.

In each foot, one of the syllables is more prominent or stronger than the other syllable(s) and it is called the strong syllable. It is the head of the syllable. The other syllables in the foot are the weak syllables. In "party", the first syllable is strong and the second syllable is weak.

There are two kinds of feet; left-dominant and right-dominant. Languages use either one or the other type:

- Left-dominant feet have a strong first syllable with the following syllables weak.
- Right-dominant feet have a strong final syllable with preceding syllables weak.

English is a left-dominant language. For example, "consultation" has two feet, /kTn.sYl/ and/tæj.ʃYn/. In each of these feet, the first or left-most syllable is strong and the second is weak, that is, left-dominant.

In each word, one of the feet is stronger than the other feet. Its head is more prominent because it is assigned intonational tone or extra length. This strong syllable has primary word stress and the heads of the other feet have secondary stress.

In "escalator" /eskYlæjtY/, there are two left-dominant feet and the first has primary stress. The first syllable of the second foot carries secondary stress. The weak syllables are unstressed.

In English there is a tendency for the first syllable of words to be strong and for words not to have adjacent strong syllables. For example, words like "lantern" (s w) and "halogen" (s w w) are far more common than "arise" (w s) or "apex" (s s). So within feet we can identify a distinction between strong and weak syllables, and within a word across feet we can identify primary, secondary stress and unstressed syllables. Metrical theory is principally concerned with the parametres that determine the position of stressed syllables in words. Stress is seen as a strength relationship between different syllables.

Building Feet into Words

English Words are built from three types of feet:

1. Binary (trochaic) containing a strong then a weak syllable, eg "elbow"
2. Ternary containing a strong followed by two weak syllables, eg "oxygen"
3. Non-branching containing a single strong syllable, eg "cat"

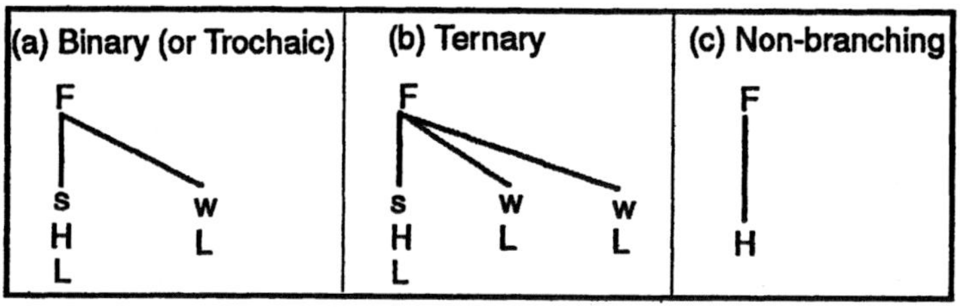

Most words in English have one foot. Obviously all monosyllables are one-footed, but so are also the large majority of two syllable ('pattern') and three-syllable ('Pamela') and even many four-syllable words ('America'). However, many words also have two feet: for example, 'imagination', 'orthodox', 'altitude'.

One of these feet is always stronger relative to the other and is marked *Fs*(strong foot) as opposed to *Fw* (weak foot). The strong foot always includes the primary stressed syllable while the other weak foot (or feet) includes the syllable(s) with secondary stress.

In bipedal words, the order of the feet can be either Fs Fw (i.e., with the strong foot first): these include e.g. 'altitude' and 'orthodox') or they can be Fw Fs (e.g., 'chimpanzee', 'latex'; 'imagination'). There are a few long words with three or more feet: these always have the strongest foot as the last foot (e.g., 'reconciliation' which is Fw ('recon'), followed by Fw ('cili') followed by Fs (ation).

There are more than a few words in English that begin with a weak syllable. Since feet are left-dominant, and since every foot has to begin with a strong syllable, this will mean that and word-initial weak syllable is unfooted (not associated with a foot).

Examples of such initial weak syllables occur in e.g. the first syllable of 'America', 'medicinal', 'pedestrian').

Words can be built by combining sequentially the above feet, or indeed the feet with themselves. For example, we can have two binary feet ('imagination'), a ternary foot followed by a binary foot ('abracadabra'), a binary foot followed by a non-branching foot ('lemonade'), two non-branching feet ('latex') and so on.

For example (where "(a)" = binary, "(b)" = ternary, and "(c)" = non-branching):

(a) + (a)	"economics"
(b) + (a)	"abracadabra"
(a) + (c)	"mātador"
(c) + (a)	rare, but possible: "Nintendo"
(c) + (b)	very rare
(c) + (c) + (c)	impossible

Because of these constraints and the preference for (a)+(a), strong and weak syllables tend to nearly alternate in English.

This near-alternation of s and w is the basis for our perception of rhythm in English.

Natural speech is highly rhythmic, it tends to have a regular beat. But different languages have different rhythms. In English all feet tend to be of roughly the same length so that feet with more syllables will have relatively shorter syllables than those with fewer syllables. eg abracadabra 2 feet, 1 with three syllables and 1 with 2 but approximately equal duration.

Antidisestablishmentarianism:				
5 feet, 12 syllables				
an-ti	dis-est	ab-lish-ment	a-ri-an	is-m
s w	s w	s w w	s w w	s w

Having said this, its important to note that the stress pattern of natural spoken English is not based on words at all. Phrases like "my dog, the chair, love it", pattern like single words with just one prominent syllable.

There is no difference in stress between pairs of words like "arise, a rise" or "ago, a go". Words that begin with unstressed syllables like "above" may have initial unstressed syllable allocated to a preceding foot. eg/IT was a/SIGN from a/BOVE

Stress patterns associated with the foot determine the characteristic rhythm of spoken English. A foot can comprise just a single word or a group of words. In English there are some words that are generally unstressed. They are high frequency, usually monosyllabic function words like "the, a, is, to, and, that".

These words can in exceptional circumstances be stressed for particular semantic intent but generally speaking they remain unstressed.

The foot is analogous to the bar in music and spoken utterances consist of a succession of feet in the same way that music consists of a succession of bars. The first syllable of each foot is always strong.

Quantity-Sensitive Feet

In some languages, the choice of primary stress is related to the number and type of segments in the syllable rhyme and this is called quantity-sensitivity. Syllables are considered to be either heavy or light depending on the segmental constituents of the rhyme.

Heavy and Light Syllables

A light syllable is defined as any (C)V syllable where (C) is zero or more consonants, and where the V is one of /I e æ P

Ʊ T/ (as in 'hid', 'head', 'had', 'hud', 'hood', 'hod') or /ə/. (The simplest way to remember these vowels is to ask yourself whether there are any open monosyllables with such vowels in English - they are also phonetically quite short). A light syllable also includes (C)VC syllables in word-final position - so the last syllable of 'imagine' is light.

All other types of syllables - that is (C)VC syllables which are not word-final, (C)VCC syllables, (C)V: syllables where V: is any other vowel or diphthong not listed above, or (C)V:C syllables all count as heavy.

What Kinds of Syllables are Metrically Weak

In order to be able to work out the prosodic tree structure for any word, it's obviously important to be able to identify which syllables are strong and weak.

This is fact quite easy because, apart from all weak syllables necessarily being Light, the very large majority of weak syllables have a /ə/ vowel, or a vowel that can reduce to schwa (for example, the second syllable of 'minimum' which can be either /I/ or /ə/). There are a few other kinds of weak syllables that don't have a /ə/ as their vowel.

These are listed below:

- /iÐ/ in 'city', 'happy', 'very'. These are metrically weak because in many accents (not Australian) they can be reduced to quite a central vowel. But a clearer indication is given by the realisation of /t/ in words like 'city': certainly in American English, and increasingly in Australian English, it can be produced as an alveolar flap which is voiced and unaspirated (and weakly contacted with the roof of the mouth). And since alveolar flaps can only ever occur in unstressed syllables in English, the syllable in these words is likely to be metrically weak.
- /ə ‰/ in words like 'rainbow', 'shadow', 'window'. Word-final /ə ‰/is metricallyweak for the same reason as the /iÐ/ in words like 'city' and 'happy' above. /ə ‰/ is often reduced to a centralised

monophthong and /t/ can be produced as a flap preceding word final /ə ‰/ in words like 'ditto' and 'potato' in some accents.

- /iÐ/ or /I/ when it precedes /ə/ in words like 'Daniel', 'pedestrian'. This is certainly metrically weak both because it is quite short in duration, and because it can often be produced as a glide /j/, thus, /dænjəl/ is certainly a possible two-syllable production of this word.
- /‰Ð/ or /Ʊ/ when it precedes /ə/in words like 'annual' and for the same reason as above: these vowels are very short in duration and can even be deleted resulting in a range of productions from three-syllable /ænj‰Ðəl/ to two syllable /ænjəl/.

English words of Latin origin (and Latin and Germanic languages) have quantity-sensitive feet. i.e. The phonemic structure of the rhyme contributes to the determination of stress.

For English, non-final syllables with heavy rhymes prefer to be strong:

- *Non-final*: the syllable is not at the end of the word
- *Heavy rhyme*: a VC (short vowel + consonant) or V: (long vowel) rhyme
- *Light rhyme*: a V (short vowel)

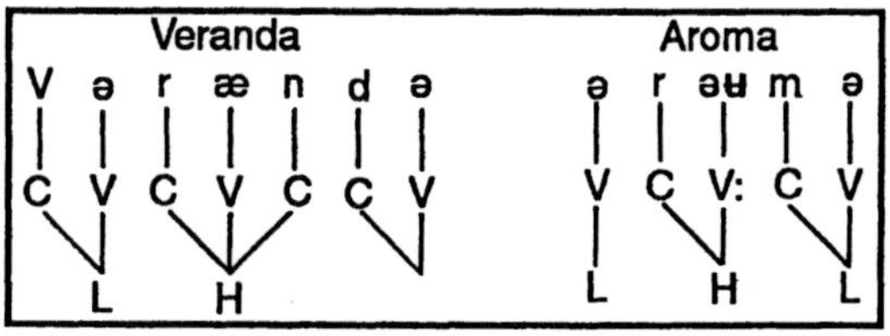

Fig. These (H) are Non-Final Heavy Rhymes and they are Strong

Morphology and Word Stress

English word stress is dependent on:

- Origin (Latin and Greek origin have different stress patterns)

- Rhythmic factors (as we have seen: In Latin base words non-final heavy syllables like to be strong)

Morphological Factors

The position of lexical stress serves to distinguish noun from verb in words like conduct, insert, reject, abstract, convict, object, subject. Stress is on the first syllable of the noun and the second of the verb. For some words stress can also be said to fall on the root word despite the addition of suffixes and prefixes. Board, aboard, boarder; rise, arise, arisen.

However, some suffixes shift stress. Consider:

president	presi den tial	presi den ti a lity
w	s w	s w s w w

The suffixes -ion, -ity, -ic, -ify, -ible, -igible, -ish, require stress to be on the preceding syllable:

- 'Edit, e'dition ('nation, 'ration, ma'gician)
- 'Quality, natio'nality
- 'Drama, dra'matic, (em'phatic, pho'netic)
- 'Terrify, 'justify, i'dentify
- In'credible, 'terrible
- 'Negligible, in'telligible
- 'Publish, 'finish,'flourish

Words of three or more syllables ending in -ate throw the main accent back 2 syllables eg negotiate, indicate dedicate, whereas words of two syllables ending in ate place the accent on -ate eg translate, dictate, debate.

English Word Stress Parametres: Summary

Adequate accounts of English word stress must recognise three relevant factors:

- Is largely trochaic (left-dominant) feet
- Is quantity-sensitive ie is influenced by the phonemic structure of the rhyme
- Is influenced by morphology

There can also be:

- Languages with iambic (right-dominant) feet. The w syllable leads: e.g. an American Indian language Seminole = w s w s, two iambic feet

- Many quantity-insensitive languages. E.g., Warlpiri, an indigenous Australian language, takes no account of whether the rhyme is heavy or light in assigning stress
- Languages like French in which morphology does not influence stress.

Building a Prosodic Word Tree

Here are two examples of how to build a prosodic word for the words 'Turramurra' and 'pedestrian'.

Example 1: "Turramurra"

(1) Begin by identifying whether there are any syllables that are schwa vowels, or which can reduce to schwa, because these have to be metrically weak: for this word, this applies to the second and fourth syllables. Confirm that the other syllables cannot reduce to schwa. If this is the case, they are likely to be metrically strong. We therefore have four syllables which are s w s w.

(2) *Join a foot node to each strong syllable. This gives:*

(3) *Associate any weak syllables with the foot that precedes them. As a result of this, we get two binary feet:*

(4) If there is more than one syllable, one of the feet has to marked strong, and the other(s) as weak. The foot that is marked strong is the one that dominates the primary stressed syllable (the third syllable in this example). So the first foot is weak.

We therefore arrive at:

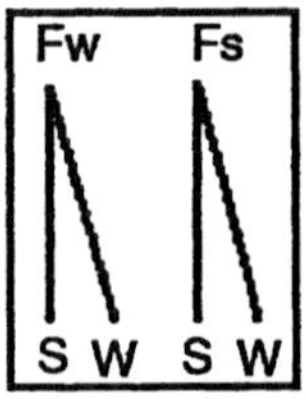

(5) Join up the feet to form *word tree*. If there is an initial weak syllable (doesn't apply in this case, but it would in e.g. 'asparagus') join that to the word level. We therefore have the following with the transcription included:

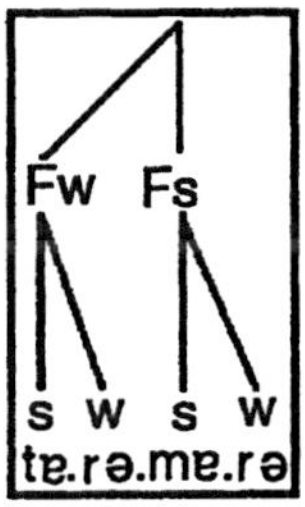

Example 2: "Pedestrian"

Draw a prosodic word tree for 'pedestrian'. Following through the above five steps.

(1) 'pedestrian' = w s w w

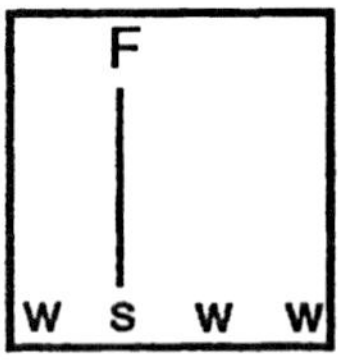

(2)

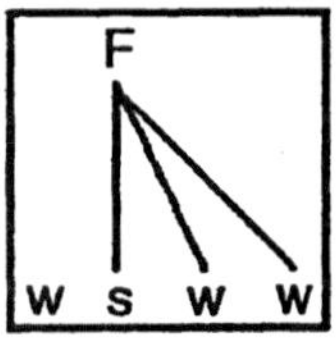

(3) (i.e. a ternary foot)

(4) This won't apply because there's only one foot.

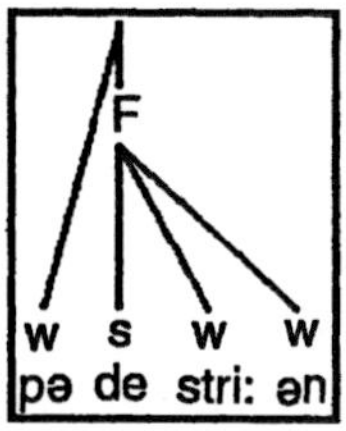

SUMMARY

Sequences of segments in language are organised into syllables based on the sonority principle. Syllables may be either weak or strong depending on their prominence relative to other syllables in an utterance. Prominence is a product of duration, loudness, vowel quality and pitch change. A syllable contains an onset and a rhyme made up of a peak and coda. The peak is the most sonorous sound in the string and is usually a vowel.

Syllables are organised according to the sonority principle with most sonorous components at the centre and least sonorous components at the syllable margins. Syllables join together sequentially to form feet. A foot is a rhythmical unit usually containing two syllables, one weak and one strong (the head). English is a left-dominant language where the left-most syllable of a foot is usually strong and the following syllable(s) are weak. Feet can be monosyllabic eg "dog" (s), disyllabic (sw) eg "city" or ternary (sww) eg "oxygen". Longer words are constructed from combinations of these three foot types.

Words are made up of feet. A word can have one or more feet. If a word has a single foot its strong will have primary word stress in citation form. If a word has more than one foot, the strong syllable of one of the feet will have primary stress and the strong syllable of the other feet will have secondary stress.

The choice of syllable for stress attachment will depend on the individual rules of the language but some languages such as English are quantity sensitive in that the number of elements in the rhyme help to determine which syllable will be stressed. If a rhyme has a short vowel + consonant or a long vowel the rhyme is said to be heavy. If the rhyme has just a short vowel, the rhyme is said to be light. In English non-final syllables with heavy rhymes prefer to be strong. However, the origin of a word and also its morphology are important factors in determining stress placement in English.

DISTINCTIVE FEATURES

Up until now we have mainly examined phonological units at the level of the single phoneme, syllable or word. In this topic we will examine units below the level of the phoneme. We call this type of unit a feature. A phoneme can be described in terms of a matrix of features. If we start with a single phoneme and substitute one of its features for another we might end up with a different feature.

We will begin by looking at some ideas that form the basis for a theory of phonological features. You should note that we are referring to phonological features and not to phonetic features. Traditionally, phonological and phonetic features are quite distinct, with phonological features being more abstract and phonetic features being concrete and often measurable (eg. acoustically or physiologically). We will particularly focus on a model of phonological features known as distinctive features. This was developed by Jakobson and his colleagues and further elaborated by Chomsky and Halle in their very influential book the *Sound Pattern of English* (Chomsky and Halle, 1968). The set of features that we will be using are based on Chomsky and Halle's features but will incorporate subsequent suggested modifications by a number of phonologists and phoneticians. We will conclude by briefly considering articulatory phonology which describes phonemes in terms of explicitly (and exclusively) articulatory features.

FERDINAND DE SAUSSURE

Saussure made distinctions between signified and signifier and between form and substance. For example, in his theory the word "dog" (its external spoken and written versions and mental representations of the word's morphology, spelling and pronunciation) is a signifier that relates to our concept of a dog (not to an actual physical dog, but to our idea of what a dog is). In other words, the word "dog" is a **signifier** and its *signified* is our concept of what a dog is. The details of this aspect of his theory are better dealt with in a course on semantics (ie. generally about meaning in language) or semiotics (ie. about meaning but from the perspective of the concepts signified and signifier). What interests us here are his ideas about form and substance.

- *Form*: an abstract formal set of relations
- *Substance*: sounds (phonemes) or written symbols (graphemes)
- *Word*: the union of signified and signifier

Phonetic segments (speech sounds) are elements that have no meaning in themselves. They have, however, non-semantic and non-grammatical rules of combination etc.

Meaningless elements (phonetic segments) can combine to form meaningful entities. ie. words, which are combinations of phonetic segments (or of phonemes) are meaningful.

There is an arbitrary relationship between the Meaningless and the Meaningful. For example, the relationships between the meaningless elements (phonetic segments or written symbols) and meaningful combinations of those elements (words) are arbitrary.

Each language has its own set of distinct rules for the combination of sounds, or **phonotactic rules**. The need to find ways of expressing such rules in a simple manner motivated the development of the idea of phonological features.

NIKOLAI TRUBETZKOY

Nikolai Trubetzkoy was a core member of the Prague school of linguistics which was highly influential in developing some areas of linguistic theory (including phonology), particularly in the 1930s. His most influential work was published posthumously in 1939, shortly after his death. One aspect of Trubetzkoy's work examines the idea of different types of "oppositions" in phonology. These oppositions are based on phonetic (or phonological) features. We won't look at all of the types of oppositions that he described, but only a few that are of particular relevance to this topic. That is, we will examine types of opposition that are relevant to the definition of phonological features.

a) Bilateral Oppositions

A bilateral opposition refers to a pair sounds that share a set of features which no other sound shares fully. For example, voiceless labial obstruents = /p,f/. Note that obstruents are defined as having a degree of stricture greater than that of approximants (that is, stops and fricatives).

b) Multilateral Oppositions

A group of more than 2 sounds which share common features. For example, labial obstruents,/p,b,f,v/, are both labial and obstruents, so they share two features.

c) Privative (Binary) Oppositions

One member of a pair of sounds possesses a mark, or feature, which the other lacks. Such features are also known as **binary** features which a sound either possesses or lacks. Voicing is such a feature. A sound is voiced or NOT voiced. The sound which possesses that feature is said to be **marked** (eg **[+voice]**) whilst the sound lacking the feature is **unmarked** (eg. **[-voice]**).

d) Gradual Oppositions

The members of a class of sounds possess different degrees or gradations of a feature or property. For example, the three short front unrounded vowels in English /j, e, æ/ which are distinguished only by their height. In this system height would be a single feature with two or more degrees of height.

e) Equipollent Oppositions

The relationship between two members of an opposition are considered to be logically equivalent. Consonant place of articulation can be seen in this sense. Changes in place involve not just degree of fronting but also involve other articulator changes.

ROMAN JAKOBSON ET AL

Roman Jakobson was also a member of the Prague school of linguistics and worked closely with Trubetzkoy. Distinctive feature theory, based on his own work and the work of Trubetzkoy, was first formalised by Roman Jakobson in 1941 and remains one of the most significant contributions to phonology.

Briefly, Jakobson's original formulation of distinctive feature theory was based on the following ideas:

- All features are privative (ie. binary). This means that a phoneme either has the feature eg. [+VOICE] or it doesn't have the feature eg. [-VOICE]
- There is a difference between PHONETIC and PHONOLOGICAL FEATURES
  - Distinctive Features are Phonological Features.
  - Phonetics Features are surface realisations of underlying Phonological Features.
  - A phonological feature may be realised by more than one phonetic feature, eg. [flat] is realised by labialisation, velarisation and pharyngealisation
- A small set of features is able to differentiate between the phonemes of any single language
- Distinctive features may be defined in terms of articulatory or acoustic features, but Jakobson's features are primarily based on acoustic descriptions

Jakobson and colleagues (Jakobson, Fant and Halle, 1952, Jakobson and Halle, 1956) devised a set of 13 distinctive features. They are not reproduced here, but they represent a starting point for the set defined by Chomsky and Halle.

CHOMSKY AND HALLE

Distinctive feature theory was first formalised by Roman Jakobson. There have been numerous refinements to Jakobson's set of features, most notably with the development of Generative Phonology.

In recent years, there have also been proposals that features should themselves be hierarchically structured and arranged on separate levels or tiers which is consistent with the developments in autosegmental phonology since the publication of the *Sound Pattern of English.*

Regardless of the many differences and controversies, the various kinds of feature systems share the following characteristics.

a) Features establish natural classes

Using distinctive features, phonemes are broken down into smaller components. For example, a nasal phoneme/m/ might be represented as a feature matrix [+ sonorant, -continuant, +voice, +nasal, +labial] (nb. you will often see the features of the matrices arranged in columns in phonology books — this is exactly equivalent to the 'horizontal' representation used here).

By representing/m/in this way, we are saying both something about its phonetic characteristics (it's a sonorant because, like vowels, its acoustic waveform has low frequency periodic energy; it's a non-continuant because the airflow is totally interrupted in the oral cavity etc), but also importantly, the aim is to choose distinctive features that establish *natural classes* of phonemes.

For example, since all the other nasal consonants and nasalised vowels (if a language has them) have feature matrices that are defined as [+nasal], we can refer to all these segments in a single simple phonological by making the rule apply to [+nasal] segments.

Similarly, if we want our rules to refer to all the approximants and high vowels, we might define this natural class by [+sonorant, +high].

The advantage of this approach is readily apparent in writing phonological rules. For example, we might want a rule which makes approximants voiceless when they follow aspirated stops in English.

If we could not define phonemes in terms of distinctive features, we would have to have separate rules, such as [l] becomes voiceless after /k/ ('claim'), /r/ becomes voiceless after/k/ ('cry'), /w/ becomes voiceless after /k/ ('quite'), /j/ becomes voiceless after /k/('cute'), and then the same again for all the approximants that can follow /p/ and /t/. If we define phonemes as bundles of features, we can state the rule more succinctly as e.g. [+sonorant, -syllabic, +continuant] sounds (i.e. all approximants) become [+spread glottis] (aspirated) after sounds which are [+spread glottis] (aspirated).

If the features are well chosen, it should be possible to refer to natural classes of phonemes with a small number of features. For example, [p t k] form a natural class of voiceless stops in most languages: we can often refer to these and no others with just two features, [-continuant, -voiced].

On the other hand, [m] and [d] are a much less natural class (ie. few sound changes and few, if any, phonological rules, apply to them both and appropriately it is impossible in most feature systems to refer to these sounds and no others in a single feature matrix).

b) Economy

In phonology, and particularly in Generative Phonology, we are often concerned to eliminate redundancy from the sound pattern of a language or to explain it by rule. Distinctive features allow the possibility of writing rules using a considerably smaller number of units than the phonemes of a language.

Consider for example, a hypothetical language that has 12 consonant and 3 vowel phonemes:

p	t	k
b	d	g
m	n	ŋ
f	s	ç

i	u
ɑ	

We could refer to all these phonemes with perhaps just 6 distinctive features - a reduction of over half the number of phoneme units which also allows natural classes to be established amongst them:

[+voice]	b d g m n ŋ i u a
[+nasal]	m n ŋ
[+high]	i u k g ŋ ç
[+labial]	p m b u f
[+anterior]	p t b d m n f s
[+cont]	f s ç i u a

At the same time, each phoneme is uniquely represented, as shown by the distinctive feature matrix:

	voice	nasal	high	labial	anterior	continuant
p	-	-	-	+	+	-
b	+	-	-	+	+	-
t	-	-	-	-	+	-
d	+	-	-	-	+	-
k	-	-	+	-	-	-
g	+	-	+	-	-	-
m	+	+	-	+	+	-
n	+	+	-	-	+	-
ŋ	+	+	+	-	-	-
f	-	-	-	+	+	+
s	-	-	-	-	+	+
ç	-	-	+	-	-	+
i	+	-	+	-	-	+
u	+	-	+	+	-	+
a	+	-	-	-	-	+

c) Binarity

We have assumed that features are binary (a segment is either nasal or it is not) following Jakobson's original formulation of distinctive feature theory and this premise was adopted in Chomsky and Halle's Sound Pattern of English. There were many reasons why Jakobson advocated a binary approach. Firstly, as we have seen, this is the most efficient way of reducing the phoneme inventory of a language. Secondly, he argued that most phonological oppositions are binary in nature (e.g. sounds either are or are not produced with a lowered soft-palate and nasalisation) and he even proposed that it has a physiological basis i.e. that nerve fibres have an 'all-or-none' response. But the binary principal is certainly not adopted by all linguists, and many phoneticians in particular have argued that some features should be n-ary (where "n" is any relevant number of degrees or levels - see for example, Ladefoged's 1993 treatment of vowel height which is 4-valued to reflect the distinction between close, half-close, half-open, and open vowels).

d) Phonetic interpretation

According to Jakobson, the distinctive features should have definable articulatory and acoustic correlates. For example, [+nasal] implies a lowering of the soft-palate and also an increase in the ratio of energy in the low to the high part of the spectrum. Chomsky and Halle abandoned the acoustic definitions of phonological features (inappropriately, as Ladefoged, 1971 and many others have argued: for example [f] and [x] are related acoustically but not articulatorily and they participated in the sound change by which the pronunciation of 'gh' spellings in English changed from a velar to a labiodental fricative e.g. 'laugh', [lQx]'![lQf]).

Many of the features are defined loosely in phonetic terms. This is perhaps to be expected. Phonology has established highly abstract representations to explain sound alternations (i.e. to factor out what are considered redundant or predictable aspects of a word's pronunciation) and this abstraction is partly opposed to the principle in phonetics of describing in articulatory and acoustic terms the characteristics of speech sound production that are shared by linguistic communities. Nevertheless, if phonology is to be related to how words are actually pronounced, the features are required to have at least some phonetic basis to them.

e) An Overview of Commonly Used Distinctive Features

The features described in Halle and Clements have been commonly used in the phonology literature in their analyses of the sound patterns of various languages. They incorporate many insights of the original features devised by Jakobson but are mostly based on those of the Sound Pattern of English, taking into account some modifications suggested by Halle and Stevens. Most of these are also discussed below.

I. Major Class Features

Four features [syll], [cons], [son], [cont] (syllabic, consonantal, sonorant, continuant) are used to divide up speech sounds into major classes, as follows. Note that [syll] means "syllabic" (syllable nucleus), [cons] means "consonantal", [son] means "sonorant" (periodic low frequency energy), [cont] means "continuant" (continuous airflow through oral cavity), and [delrel] means delayed release (release is not "delayed", but there is a longer aspiration phase than oral stops - nb. voice onset is what's actually delayed).

	syll	cons	son	cont	delrel
vowels	+	-	+	+	0
oral stops	-	+	-	-	-
affricates	-	+	-	-	+
nasal stops	-	+	+	-	0
fricatives	-	+	-	+	0
liquids	-	+	+	+	0
semi-vowels	-	-	+	+	0

Note that the approximants have been divided into liquids (eg. in English/r, l/) and semi-vowels (eg. in English/w, j/). In this, and most other distinctive feature sets derived from Chomsky and Halle.

Semi-vowels (being [-syll, -cons]) form a class of sounds intermediate between vowels ([+syll]) and consonants ([+cons]). The approximants can be defined as a class by the features [-syll, +son, +cont] and can be further sub-divided into liquids and semi-vowels using the [cons] feature. Note that "0" means irrelevant feature for these classes of sounds (there's nothing to release).

We also have a feature [nasal] which, as its name suggests, separates nasal from oral sounds. In the above table, [nasal] would have been redundant as the nasal stops are already defined uniquely as [-syll, +cons, +son, -cont] (ie. as sonorant stops). However. the feature [nasal] is required to define nasal stops, nasalised vowels and nasalised approximants as a single natural class.

II. Source Features

These are related to the source (vocal fold vibration that sustains voiced sounds or a turbulent airstream that sustains many voiceless sounds).

The feature [voice] is self-explanatory (with or without vocal fold vibration). The feature [spread glottis] is used to distinguish aspirated from unaspirated stops (aspirated stops are initially produced with the vocal folds drawn apart).

We can therefore make the following distinctions:

	voiced	**spread glottis**
p	–	–
b	+	–
p	–	+

The [strident] feature is used by Halle and Clements for those fricatives produced with high-intensity fricative noise: supposedly labiodentals, alveolars, palato-alveolars, and uvulars are [+strident]. There seems to be little acoustic phonetic basis to the claim that labiodentals and alveolars pattern acoustically (as opposed to dentals). In this course, we will use Ladefoged's feature [sibilant] which is defined by Ladefoged in acoustic terms as including those fricatives with 'large amounts of acoustic energy at high frequencies' i.e. [s *f* z ']. The English affricates would therefore also be [+sibilant]:

}	**cont**	**sibilant**
oral stops	-	-
affricates	-	+
sibilant fricatives	+	+
non-sibilant fricatives	+	-

This may be an oversimplification, however, as the alveolar oral stops might also be described as sibilant, so sibilant isn't sufficient to separate oral stops and affricates (and we still need spread glottis).

III. Vowel Features

There are four dimensions to consider: vowel height, backness, rounding, and tensity. Vowel height is classified using the [high] and [low] features. Palatal and velar *consonants* are also [+high, -low] and, with the use of the [back] feature, a relationship can be established between high vowels and their corresponding glides:

	high	low	back	syllabic
i	+	-	-	+
j	+	-	-	-
u	+	-	+	+
w	+	-	+	-

(*NB*: [u] is presumed to be a back vowel here as in cardinal vowel 8).

In different languages vowel systems can vary in terms two to four vowel height contrasts.

Vowel systems with only two levels of height simply use [+high] or [-high] to represent high and low vowels respectively.

	high
High vowels	+
Low vowels	-

Vowels systems with three levels of height contrast use the features [high] and [low]. High vowels like [i u y] are [+high, -low]. Mid vowels like [e o] are neither high, nor low, i.e. [-high, -low]. And open vowels like [a] are [-high, +low].

	high	low
High vowels	+	-
Mid vowels	-	-
Low vowels	-	+

Vowel systems with four levels of height contrast require a third feature [mid]. (This feature is additional to the set of features defined in Halle and Clements, but will be used in this course).

	high	mid	low
Close vowels	+	-	-
Half-close vowels	+	+	-
Half-open vowels	-	+	+
Open vowels	-	-	+

The question of vowel *tensity* is more controversial. In English there is a class of vowels which are more central in the vowel space (i.e. further away from the four vowel space corners) and that cannot end monosyllabic words: in Australian English, these include the short vowels

In 'had', 'head', 'hid', 'hood', 'hod', 'hud'. While that is perhaps not so controversial, the issue of whether they can be defined by an articulatory [-ATR] (minus advance tongue root), indicating that the tongue root is not drawn forward to the same degree as [+ATR] vowels (all the 'long' vowels that *can* end words in English) is a good deal more problematic. It definitely doesn't make sense to apply [+ATR] to lax back vowels.

As Halle and Clements note, [ATR] appears to "... never co-occur distinctly in any language..." with another feature pair "tense/lax" [+- tense].

Whilst the tense/lax distinction is also defined by Halle and Clements in articulatory terms similar to those used for [ATR], the use of the term "tense" versus "lax" to describe respectively the "long" and "short" vowels of English is very familiar to phoneticians.

The use of an alternative feature pair "long/short" is avoided because some languages have a distinction between tense and lax vowels which do not appear to be realised acoustically in terms vowel duration (ie. long versus short). In this course the feature [tense] will be used rather than the feature [ATR].

IV. PLACE OF ARTICULATION

The [ant] 'anterior' and [cor] 'coronal' features, in combination with [high] and [back] and [sibilant] do most of the job of consonantal place classification. These features will be defined in the next section.

For example, for fricatives:

	ɸ	f	θ	s	ʂ	ʃ	ç	x	χ	h	ʍ
ant	+	+	+	+	-	-	-	-	-	-	-
cor	-	-	+	+	+	+	+	-	-	-	-
labial	+	+	-	-	-	-	-	-	-	-	+
high	-	-	-	-	-	+	+	+	-	-	+
back	-	-	-	-	-	-	-	+	+	-	+
sibilant	-	-	-	+	-	+	-	-	-	-	-
distr	+	-	+/-	-	-	+	+	+	+	+	+

(*[ʍ] is a labial-velar fricative*: the fricative equivalent of [w]).

Note that, by having abandoned [strident] (or replaced it with [sibilant]), we leave ourselves the problem of how to differentiate [x] from [f]. Halle and Clements also define a feature [distr] (distributed) that they say can be used, amongst other things, to distinguish bilabial [+distr] and labiodental [-distr] sounds (nb. [θ] is [+distr] if it is lamino-dental, or [-distr] if it is apico-dental). [+distr] sounds have a greater area of contact than similar [-distr] sounds. For example, [+distr] bilabials have two lips in contact so there is a greater area of articulator contact than for [-distr] labiodentals (as the lower lip is in contact with the smaller area of the tips of the upper teeth). Also, apicals use the smaller area of the tongue tip whilst laminals use the greater area of the tongue blade.

DISTINCTIVE FEATURES USED IN THIS TOPIC

The following set of distinctive features follows the set defined by Halle and Clements, but with the following exceptions:

- The feature [ATR] (advanced tongue root) has been omitted, in favour of [tense].
- The feature [strident] has been replaced by Ladefoged's feature [sibilant].

- The feature [rounded] has been omitted as it seems to be mostly redundant given the presence of the feature [labial].
- The feature [mid] has been added to deal with vowel systems with four contrastive levels of height.
- The feature [-cont] does not automatically include all laterals. In this course laterals are [+cont] if approximants or fricatives and [-cont] if lateral clicks or laterally released stops.
- The feature [front] has been added. It is used here exclusively as a vowel feature and is used for languages or dialects, such as Australian English, which exhibit three levels of vowel fronting. The original set only had [back] as American English vowels could be described as [+back] or [-back] (for front) and the central vowel in the word "heard" was disambiguated by a [+rhotic] feature.

When quoted text occurs in the following descriptions, it is taken from Halle and Clements and this is indicated by **(HC)** following the quote.

1. *Syllabic/non-syllabic [syll]*: Syllabic sounds constitute a syllable peak (sonority peak). [+syll] refers to vowels and to syllabic consonants. [-syll] refers to all non-syllabic consonants (including semi-vowels).
2. *Consonantal/non-consonantal [cons]*: Consonantal sounds are produced with at least approximant stricture. That is consonantal sounds involve vocal tract constriction significantly greater that that which occurs for vowels. [+cons] refers to all consonants except for semi-vowels (which often have resonant stricture). [-cons] refers to vowels and semi-vowels.
3. *Sonorant/obstruent [son]*: Sonorant sounds are produced with vocal tract configuration that permits air pressure on both sides of any constriction to be approximately equal to the air pressure outside the mouth. Obstruents possess constriction (stricture) that is sufficient to result in significantly greater air pressure behind the constriction than occurs in front

of the constriction and outside the mouth. [+son] refers to vowels and approximants (glides and semi-vowels). [-son] refers to stops, fricatives and affricates.

4. *Coronal/non-coronal [cor]*: "Coronal sounds are produced by raising the tongue blade toward the teeth or the hard palate; noncoronal sounds are produced without such a gesture." (HC) This feature is intended for use with consonants only. [+cor] refers to dentals (not including labio-dentals) alveolars, post-alveolars, palato-alveolars, palatals. [-cor] refers to labials, velars, uvulars, pharyngeals.
5. *Anterior/posterior [ant]*: "Anterior sounds are produced with a primary constriction at or in front of the alveolar ridge. Posterior sounds are produced with a primary constriction behind the alveolar ridge." (HC) This feature is intended to be applied to consonants. [+ant] refers to labials, dentals and alveolars. [-ant] refers to post-alveolars, palato-alveolars, retroflex, palatals, velars, uvulars, pharyngeals.
6. *Labial/non-labial [lab]*: Labial sounds involve rounding or constriction at the lips. [+lab] refers to labial and labialised consonants and to rounded vowels. [-lab] refers to all other sounds.
7. *Distributed/non-distributed [distr]*: "Distributed sounds are produced with a constriction that extends for a considerable distance along the midsaggital axis of the oral tract; nondistributed sounds are produced with a constriction that extends for only a short distance in this direction." (HC) [+distr] refers to sounds produced with the blade or front of the tongue, or bilabial sounds. [-distr] refers to sounds produced with the tip of the tongue. This feature can distinguish between palatal and retroflex sounds, between bilabial and labiodental sounds, between lamino-dental and apico-dental sounds.
8. *High/non-high [high]*: "High sounds are produced by

raising the body of the tongue toward the palate; nonhigh sounds are produced without such a gesture." (HC) [+high] refers to palatals, velars, palatalised consonants, velarised consonants, high vowels, semi-vowels. [-high] refers to all other sounds. Note, however, the discussion above on how this feature is used in combination with [mid] to describe the distinction between four contrastive vowel heights.

9. *Mid/non-mid [mid]*: Mid sounds are produced with tongue height approximately half way between the tongue positions appropriate for [+high] and [+low]. This vowel height feature is only required when a language has four levels of height contrast and remains unspecified for languages with fewer vowel height contrasts. [+mid] refers to vowels with intermediate vowel height. [-mid] refers to all other sounds.
10. *Low/non-low [low]*: "Low sounds are produced by drawing the body of the tongue down away from the roof of the mouth; nonlow sounds are produced without such a gesture." [+low] refers to low vowels, pharyngeal consonants, pharyngealised consonants.
11. *Back/non-back [back]*: "Back sounds are produced with the tongue body relatively retracted; nonback or front sounds are produced with the tongue body relatively advanced."(HC) [+back] refers to Velars, uvulars, pharyngeals, velarised consonants; pharyngealised consonants, central vowels, central semi-vowels, back vowels, back semi-vowels. [-back] refers to all other sounds.
12. *Front/non-front [front]*: This is an additional vowel feature added to assist in the description of the vowel systems of languages such as Australian English. To describe the central vowels of Australian English its necessary to define them as [-back, -front].
13. *Continuant/stop [cont]*: "Continuants are formed with a vocal tract configuration allowing the airstream to

flow through the midsaggital region of the oral tract: stops are produced with a sustained occlusion in this region." (HC) For some reason it has been traditional to include lateral consonants as stops in distinctive feature theory. Since laterals can have approximant, fricative or stop (click) stricture there seems to be no justification in including all laterals with the stops, and in this course laterals are not necessarily stops (as is the case for the lateral clicks) but can also be continuants (as is the case for the lateral approximants and fricatives. [+cont] refers to vowels, approximants, fricatives. [-cont] refers to nasal stops, oral stops.

14. *Lateral/central [lat]*: "Lateral sounds, the most familiar of which is [l], are produced with the tongue placed in such a way as to prevent the airstream from flowing outward through the centre of the mouth, while allowing it to pass over one or both sides of the tongue; central sounds do not invoke such a constriction." (HC) [+lat] refers to lateral approximants, lateral fricatives, lateral clicks. [-lat] refers to all other sounds.
15. *Nasal/oral [nas]*: "Nasal sounds are produced by lowering the velum and allowing the air to pass outward through the nose; oral sounds are produced with the velum raised to prevent the passage of air through the nose." (HC) [+nas] refers to nasal stops, nasalised consonants, nasalised vowels. [-nas] refers to all other sounds.
16. *Tense/lax [tense]*: The traditional definition of this feature claims that [+tense] vowels involve a greater degree of constriction then [-tense] (lax) vowels. Tense vowels need not be any different to lax vowels in terms of constriction (e.g. the tense/lax pair /PĐ,P/ in Australian English are produced with the same tongue position but differ in duration). The tense/ lax distinction in vowels seems to be related to some kind of strong/weak distinction. In some languages

this is realised as a distinction between more peripheral vowels (closer to the four corners of the vowel quadrilateral) and less peripheral vowels (vowels that are either more centred, more mid, or both more centred and more mid). In other languages, a long/short durational distinction is what is often the main acoustic distinction between tense and lax vowels. Note, however, that short vowels are more likely to be produced with under-realised targets (more mid-central) during connected speech than are long vowels because the long vowels have more time to reach their targets. [+tense] refers to tense vowels or long vowels. [-tense] refers to lax vowels or short vowels.

17. *Sibilant/non-sibilant [sib]*: Sibilants are those fricatives with large amounts of acoustic energy at high frequencies. [+sib] refers to [s ʃ z ']. [-sib] refers to all other sounds.
18. *Spread glottis/non-spread glottis [spread]*: "Spread or aspirated sounds are produced with the vocal cords drawn apart producing a nonperiodic (noise) component in the acoustic signal; nonspread or unaspirated sounds are produced without this gesture." (HC) [+spread] refers to aspirated consonants, breathy voiced or murmured consonants, voiceless vowels, voiceless approximants. [-spread] refers to all other sounds. It should be stressed that during the occlusion of both voiceless aspirated and voiceless unaspirated (0 VOT) stops the glottis is open. The difference is during the period following release where, for aspirated stops, the glottis stays open much longer than for unaspirated stops.
19. *Constricted glottis/non-constricted glottis [constr]*: "Constricted or glottalized sounds are produced with the vocal cords drawn together, preventing normal vocal cord vibration; nonconstricted (nonglottalized) sounds are produced without such a gesture." (HC)[+constr] refers to ejectives, implosives,

glottalized or laryngealised consonants, glottalized or laryngealised vowels. [-constr] refers to all other sounds.

20. *Voiced/voiceless [voice]*: "Voiced sounds are produced with a laryngeal configuration permitting periodic vibration of the vocal cords; voiceless sounds lack such periodic vibration."(HC) [+voice] refers to all voiced sounds. [-voice] refers to all voiceless sounds.

AUSTRALIAN ENGLISH VOWEL FEATURES

a) Australian English Monophthong Vowels

When Chomsky and Halle were using their system of Distinctive Features to analyse American English vowels, they argued that it was necessary to define three levels of height:

1.	high	[+high] [-low]
2.	mid	[-high] [-low]
3.	low	[-high] [+low]

but only two levels of fronting:

1.	front	[-back]
2.	back	[+back]

Whilst its not impossible to describe Australian English vowels in terms of [high, low, back, round, tense] so that all monophthongs are provided with a unique featural specification the resulting system doesn't match the phonetics of Australian English vowels. In each category, front, central and back there are several vowels.

To call both the central and the back vowels [+back] doesn't capture this pattern satisfactorily. For example, the vowel/‰Ð/has been moving forward over several decades and for most speakers its a high, central, rounded vowel.

For some speakers it has moved even further forward (half way between central and front), but isn't yet a front rounded vowel. It makes a lot of sense to regard this as a high rounded vowel that isn't explicitly front or back (i.e. [-front, -back]).

So now we can define three degree of vowel fronting:

1.	front	[+front, -back]
2.	central	[-front, -back]
3.	back	[-front, +back]

As stated (and justified) in the previous section, we don't use a length feature (e.g. [long]) to indicate the distinction between long and short monophthongs. We can instead refer to long vowels (and diphthongs) as tense and short vowels as lax. Instead we use the [tense] feature to distinguish between tense [+tense] and lax [-tense].

Whilst we can sometimes determine that schwa is in some sense a reduced form of some other vowel (e.g. when vowel quality changes when we add or subtract affixes, such as the first syllable of "phonetics" versus "phonetician") for many words its now impossible to determine what the original vowel might have been (or even if there ever had been an original unreduced vowel). Because of this it seems sensible to treat schwa as a phoneme in English.

We treat schwa as a vowel phoneme that has the feature [+syllabic], but is unspecified ("0") for [tense]. All other features are context dependent (ie. optional) so its probably best to also treat these features as unspecified ("0") as well. Whilst schwa could be said to be the least tense (most lax) of all vowels it shares an important property with the [+tense] vowels. It can, in English, occur in open syllables (syllables that end with a vowel).

The only other vowels that can occur in open syllables in English are the [+tense] vowels (long monophthong vowels and diphthongs). Traditionally this has been explained as being due to schwa, in these contexts, being the reduced form of a tense vowel (and therefore "underlyingly" tense) but as we have described schwa as an independent phoneme this explanation no longer works. None of the other short vowels can occur in open syllables in normal words (except perhaps in interjections). If we make [tense] unspecified for schwa then we can devise a single rule that determines which vowels can occur in open syllables, i.e. "[-tense] vowels cannot occur in open syllables but all other vowels can". There are other precedents for "0" specifications for a feature. For example the delayed release [delrel] feature can only be applied to phonemes that have a release (i.e. oral stops and affricates). All other phonemes have a "0" specification for this feature. Some specifically vowel features have a "0" specification for consonants and vice versa.

Feature Table for Australian English Monophthongs (All Are Also [+Syll, -Cons +Son +Cont])

	high	low	front	back	round	tense
iː	+	-	+	-	-	+
ɪ	+	-	+	-	-	-
eː	-	-	+	-	-	+
e	-	-	+	-	-	-
æ	-	+	+	-	-	-
ɐː	-	+	-	-	-	+
ɐ	-	+	-	-	-	-
ɔ	-	-	-	+	+	-
oː	-	-	-	+	+	+
ʊ	+	-	-	+	+	-
ʉː	+	-	-	-	+	+
ɜː	-	-	-	-	-	+
ə	0	0	0	0	0	0

b) Centring Diphthongs

Mitchell lists three centring diphthongs for Australian English: /jY/,/[Y/ and /ŠY/.

There was also a possible 4th centring diphthong /oə/ which appears to have been described for Australian English by McBurney, although we have no way of knowing whether words like "poor" [poə] were pronounced as one or two syllables and therefore as a diphthong or as two monophthongs.

This fourth centring diphthong is occasionally described for some varieties of British English. Further, Bernard found that 22 out of 112 //vowels produced by Australian speakers in an/h_d/context had an "inglide" (ie. [oə]). Bernard considered this inglide to be no more than an idiosyncratic or allophonic variant of the phoneme/oÐ/ and no phonetician argues for the existence of /oə/ as a phoneme in modern Australian English.

The continuing existence of /Šə/ as a phoneme in Australian English is doubtful. It was confidently described by Mitchell and most phoneticians up until the 1960's to be a phoneme of Australian English realised as a centring diphthong [Šə]. Its status as a phoneme in Australian English has become quite unclear in recent years. If it still exists, it is a very low frequency phoneme.

There is a lot of idiosyncratic variation in the survival of diphthongal realisations of this phoneme (those that still possess an audible or measurable in-glide). Even words such as "tour", which have often been cited as late survivors of words containing /Šə/are nearly always now found to contain either [oĐ] (a monophthong) or [‰Đə] (two monophthongs, ie. two syllables).

Of the remaining two centring diphthongs, only /jə/ (a) is common and (b) is produced as an in-gliding diphthong by a majority of Australian English speakers (but a fairly large minority are now pronouncing).

The phoneme previously labeled /[ə/ or /eə/ is now produced as a long mid-high monophthong [eĐ] by the majority of Australian English speakers in CVC contexts (e.g. "paired") and has been transcribed phonemically by most Australian English phoneticians as /eĐ/ since the early 1990's. It should be noted, however, that there is evidence that the same people who pronounce it as [eĐ] in a CVC context pronounce it as [eə] in CV contexts (e.g. "hair").

Why is this discussion of centring diphthongs of relevance to the current topic? The answer lies in the extent to which the centring diphthongs can be accounted for by the features used in tables 1 and 2 if they undergo the process of monophthongisation.

The inclusion of /eĐ/ in the list of Aus.E. monophthongs causes no problem for this system of distinctive features. /eĐ/ is simply the tense equivalent of the lax vowel /e/ and the tenseness of /eĐ/ is realised phonetically as either a long vowel or as an offglided diphthong (varying with speaker and phonetic context).

If this system of distinctive features has any cognitive validity, it might help explain the reason why /eĐ/ has evolved from the earlier /eə/ vowel described by Mitchell in the 1940's whilst /jə/ has been resistant to such a change. It might also explain why/Šə/ and a possible earlier diphthong /oə/ have disappeared (either by merging with an existing tense monophthong, or by splitting into a sequence of a tense monophthong plus schwa).

In table 2 there was a vacant slot for /eĐ/ and, if this distinctive feature model is correct, there was therefore nothing to prevent the diphthong from surviving the process of monophthongisation by becoming a distinct tense vowel. All other centring diphthongs lack such an empty slot to fit into.

So what is happening to /jə/ and how should we view its distinctive features?

The phoneme /jə/ is realised in one of three major forms:

1. [jə] This is the most common form used by the majority of Australian English speakers, especially when preceding a pause (eg. "ear" uttered by itself or at the end of a sentence). Many of these speakers produce [jĐ] when there is an intrusive /r/ (that is, an [y]inserted between a certain vowels, such as /jə/ , and a following vowel) or a following alveolar consonant. This pattern of pronunciation appears to be a feature of General and Cultivated Australian English.
2. [jĐ] A growing minority of Australian speakers produce this form even when preceding a pause. As mentioned above, many speakers of Australian English (who normally produce[jə] before a pause) also produce this form when there is a following intrusive/r/or a following alveolar consonant.
3. [iĐə] This seems to be a feature of the speech of some speakers of Broad Australian English but this is probably best analysed as two vowel phonemes.

It should be noted that the vowel quality for the [jÐ] allophone is usually that of the lax vowel /j/ rather than that of the tense vowel /iÐ/ but it should also be noted that the targets of /iÐ/and /j/ are becoming more alike (Cox, 1996 - see the page on Australian English Monophthongs).

The vowel /iÐ/ maintains its distinctiveness due to its onglide and length. Acoustically, and auditorily, the targets of /iÐ/ and the [jÐ] allophone of /jə/ are likely to be distinct for older Australians, but not distinct for younger Australians, but from the point of view of the above system of distinctive features they would be identical. That is they would both be [+high, -low, -back, -round, +tense].

Is this therefore evidence against the cognitive validity of this particular distinctive feature model? Well, possibly! If it can be determined empirically that /jə/ is more resistant to this kind of change than /eÐ/ was, then this might be because there is no available slot for it as was the case for /eÐ/. But, why should it not simply disappear as is almost the case for / Šə/? The answer to this question may be lexical rather than phonological or phonetic.

There are far more words with this phoneme than there ever was with the phoneme /Šə/. Phoneme merger would cause numerous word pairs to become phonetically identical. This argument is weakened, however, when we realise that / jə/ and /eə/ merged into one phoneme in New Zealand over the past 30 years.

This merger caused many pairs of words to become homophones (e.g. "cheer" and "chair"). The loss of distinctiveness of these word pairs did not prevent the change from occurring.

There may be another explanation for the pattern of changes occurring for /jə/. The [jÐ]pronunciation may be more common for those speakers of Australian English who produce the most salient on-glide when pronouncing /iÐ/. These are particularly speakers of Broad Australian English who produce a strong on-glide (ie. /iÐ/ = [^{Y}iÐ]).

In these speakers, it could be said that/jə/ is becoming a

high front unrounded tense monophthong as /iÐ/ is becoming more like a diphthong. This, however, overlooks the well-established fact that the vast majority of Australian English speakers produce/i:/with an onglide (regardless of whether they are broad, general or cultivated speakers). This onglide varies from a long onglide ([ʸiÐ]) of broad speakers, through the shorter, but acoustically similar, onglide of general speakers to the short onglide (something like [ʲiÐ]) of cultivated speakers.

For those Australian English speakers who move between [jə] and [jÐə] sequences in different phonetic contexts, the phoneme /jə/ may (according to transformational theory) be described to be "underlyingly" a sequence of the phonemes /j/ + /r/ (or perhaps /iÐ/ + /r/).

If this is so, then the process of monophthongisation of the centring diphthongs may be the result of a more fundamental process whereby the underlying/r/component of the sequence is deleted.

Even in American English, which is a rhotic dialect of English, the surface representations of the underlying post-vocalic/r/phonemes varies greatly. In American English /Y⊖/ the following /r/is most often entirely represented by the surface rhoticisation of the vowel.

In the Eastern New England variety of American English the post-vocalic/r/in many words is not as rhoticised as is the case of most American English varieties, but the/r/still exists as an alveolar, but not retroflexed, approximant.

The next table represents a possible feature representation for the three high front vowels of Australian English speakers. The feature "onglide" is proposed here as a feature that accounts for the virtually universal existence of an on-glide for/i:/in Australian English.

Table. Feature Table for Australian English/I?/,/?/and/??/

	high	low	front	back	round	tense	onglide
/iː/ = [ᵊiː] [ᶦiː]	+	-	+	-	-	+	+
/ɪ/ = [ɪ]	+	-	+	-	-	-	-
/ɪə/ = [ɪə] [ɪː]	+	-	+	-	-	+	-

c) Feature Analysis of Diphthong Vowels

Diphthongs are single vowels with two targets. In other words the tongue must attempt to move from one position to another in order for the diphthong to be fully pronounced.

In the following discussion /eÐ/ is excluded because it as regarded as a tense monophthong (with an optional offglide) and /ʊə/ is excluded because it is either extinct or is almost extinct.

One way of performing a distinctive feature analysis of diphthongs is to analyse each target separately. This type of analysis appears to assume that diphthongs are "underlyingly" a sequence of two monophthongs. In this approach, each target would be allocated a full set of features. This approach has the advantage of not requiring the invention of new features. Its weakness is that implicitly it treats diphthongs as two vowels.

In Australian English all diphthongs are pronounced with distinct first targets and very brief or sometimes absent second targets. They are realised as having a clear first target followed by a long offglide in the direction of some intended second target, which may have a very short or even a zero length. In unaccented contexts (i.e. not affected by sentence stress) diphthongs may be reduced to a monophthong (often similar to the first target) or even to schwa.

Australian English diphthongs can be divided into three classes of diphthongs on the basis of the direction of their offglides. These directions are centring /Iə /, high-fronting /æj, Qe, Tj/, and a third class of diphthongs /æI, Y‰/ whose offglide moves toward a high-central, high-back or a back position. We have already dealt with /Iə / above and so we will omit it from this analysis.

These classes could be differentiated by inventing three new features:

1. *[Offglide]*: true for all diphthongs
2. *[Centring]*: true for centring diphthongs (where the vowel glides to a more central position following the first target)

3. *[Fronting]*: true for the high-fronting diphthongs (where the glides move toward the position of [i]).

The feature [centring] seems redundant, however, as the centring diphthong can be treated as a [-fronting] diphthong. Further, all of these diphthongs can be distinguished by the features for the first target so the fronting feature, whilst descriptive, is redundant.

In the following table, offglide indicates the presence of a second target whilst the other features describe the quality of the stronger first target.

Table. Feature Table for Australian English off Gliding Diphthongs

Phoneme	high	low	front	back	round	tense	offglide
æɪ	-	+	+	-	-	+	+
ɑe	-	+	-	+	-	+	+
ɔɪ	-	-	-	+	+	+	+
əʉ	-	-	-	-	- (+?)	+	+
æɔ	-	+	+	-	- (+?)	+	+

The main problem with this analysis is its failure to capture the rounding gesture into the second targets of/ə ‰/ and/æT/. This also results in/æj/and/æT/having identical feature specifications.

This failure is a possible argument for providing a featural specification of both diphthong targets. However, if we apply [+round] to any diphthong that contains a round lip gesture in either target. We continue to apply height and fronting features based on the first target.

We will now bring all of this together into a single table of all Australian English vowel phonemes. Vowels are defined as being syllabic, con-consonantal, sonorant, continuant speech sounds and therefore they all share the following features [+syll, -cons, +son, +cont].

The following table includes only those vowel features necessary for distinguishing between vowel phonemes. In the following table "0" means "inapplicable feature" whilst "+/-" means optional (either are possible as are intermediate values).

Phoneme	high	low	front	back	round	tense	offglide	onglide
iː	+	-	+	-	-	+	-	+
ɪ	+	-	+	-	-	-	-	-
ɪə	+	-	+	-	-	+	+/-	-
eː	-	-	+	-	-	+	+/-	-
e	-	-	+	-	-	-	-	-
æ	-	+	+	-	-	-	-	-
ɐː	-	+	-	-	-	+	-	-
ɐ	-	+	-	-	-	-	-	-
ɔ	-	-	-	+	+	-	-	-
oː	-	-	-	+	+	+	-	-
ʊ	+	-	-	+	+	-	-	-
ʉː	+	-	-	-	+	+	-	-
ɜː	-	-	-	-	-	+	-	-
æɪ	-	+	+	-	-	+	+	-
ɑe	-	+	-	+	-	+	+	-
ɔɪ	-	-	-	+	+	+	+	-
əʉ	-	-	-	-	+	+	+	-
æɔ	-	+	+	-	+	+	+	-
ə	0	0	0	0	0	0	-	-

Note that schwa explicitly has no onglide or offglide. Its too short to have multiple targets or complex target onsets or offsets. In fact, its generally too short to even have a clear target. We can also see from this table that we are assuming that Australian English has 19 vowel phonemes.

This is based on the following assumptions:

- /ə/is really a phoneme and is not merely a reduced allophone of many vowel phonemes.
- The occasionally attested examples (only 2 or 3 minimal pairs) of a distinction between/æ/and/æĐ/are not strong enough evidence to support two phonemes.

These examples are controversial and there is no agreement on whether they are true minimal pairs or whether they also vary in some other way (grammatical, morphological). For example, the "bad" [bæĐd] versus "bade" [bæd] example is weak because the latter word is absent from most people's vocabulary, and the durational distinction claimed to exist between them is less than the normal intrapersonal (same-person) variation in the length of this vowel. It is the most variable Australian English vowel in terms of its duration and can be produced relatively long or short. Further, it has been suggested that the distinction between "bad" and "bade" may merely be evidence of some underlying morphophonetic effect ("bade" being an inflected past tense form of "to bid").

- The old phoneme /ʊə/ is now extinct and can no longer be considered a phoneme in Australian English.

ENGLISH CONSONANT FEATURES

The following table brings together (especially in sections 4 and 5) all of the consonants of English into a single table. It is simplified somewhat. For example, dark (velarised or vocalised)/l/is ignored in this analysis (being an allophonic variation it doesn't really require a phonological feature). The most common features of the most common allophones of each consonant as they exist in Australian English are used as the basis of this table. This table, whilst based on Australian English, is applicable to most dialects of English with only minor changes.

	syll	cons	son	cont	delrel	sib	voice	nas	high	back	ant	lab	cor	distr	lat
p	-	+	-	-	-	-	-	-	-	-	+	+	-	+	-
b	-	+	-	-	-	-	+	-	-	-	+	+	-	+	-
t	-	+	-	-	-	-	-	-	-	-	+	-	+	-	-
d	-	+	-	-	-	-	+	-	-	-	+	-	+	-	-
k	-	+	-	-	-	-	-	-	+	+	-	-	-	-	-
g	-	+	-	-	-	-	+	-	+	+	-	-	-	-	-
tʃ	-	+	-	-	+	+	-	-	+	-	-	-	+	+	-
dʒ	-	+	-	-	+	+	+	-	+	-	-	-	+	+	-
f	-	+	-	+	0	-	-	-	-	-	+	+	-	-	-
v	-	+	-	+	0	-	+	-	-	-	+	+	-	-	-
θ	-	+	-	+	0	-	-	-	-	-	+	-	+	-	-
ð	-	+	-	+	0	-	+	-	-	-	+	-	+	-	-
s	-	+	-	+	0	+	-	-	-	-	+	-	+	-	-
z	-	+	-	+	0	+	+	-	-	-	+	-	+	-	-
ʃ	-	+	-	+	0	+	-	-	+	-	-	-	+	+	-
ʒ	-	+	-	+	0	+	+z	-	+	-	-	-	+	+	-
h	-	+	-	+	0	-	-	-	-	-	-	-	-	-	-
m	-	+	+	-	0	-	+	+	-	-	+	+	-	+	-
n	-	+	+	-	0	-	+	+	-	-	+	-	+	-	-
ŋ	-	+	+	-	0	-	+	+	+	+	-	-	-	-	-
l	-	+	+	+	0	-	+	-	-	-	-	-	+	-	+
r	-	+	+	+	0	-	+	-	-	-	-	-	+	-	-
w	-	-	+	+	0	-	+	-	+	+	-	+	-	+	-
j	-	-	+	+	0	-	+	-	+	-	-	-	+	+	-

If you carefully examine this feature matrix you will note that no two consonants have the same pattern of features. It is clear that this feature set is sufficient to distinguish between all of the consonants of Australian English.

If you were to consider the distinction between the two main allophones of/l/(clear/l/and dark/l/) it would be a simple matter of changing the [-back] to [+back] to indicate the velarising of the dark/l/. That is, its possible to also use distinctive feature to distinguish between allophones of a phoneme. Its not clear how valid it would be to do this as the distinctive features were developed as phonological rather than phonetic features and were in tended to distinguish between phonemes, but distinctive features can be used in rules that explain the selection of competing allophones.

POSSIBLE OBJECTIONS TO DISTINCTIVE FEATURES

Distinctive features are based on binary features. This was a choice made early in their development and is based on Trubetzkoy's privative (binary) distinctions. The choice was made because it simplified the writing of phonological rules. You should note, however, that Trubetzkoy also allowed for gradual distinctions. This type of feature has been taken up by phoneticians (e.g. Ladefoged, 1971, used a single feature for height with up to four levels for the same feature). It also seems desirable to represent consonant place of articulation as an "equipollent" continuum of independent features only one of which may be selected for a simple articulation (e.g. alveolar for/d/). For complex articulations, two or more such features might be selected (e.g. labial plus velar for/w/).

The nature of some of the features (e.g. distributed) seem quite arbitrary and motivated by the need to disambiguate unseparated vowel or consonant pairs. Sometimes these feature choices are not supported by phonetic research and their sole strength is their usefulness in the writing of rules.

The motivation to develop a system that optimises the expression of rules begs the question - what justifies the belief that humans use rules of this kind? If we can't prove that humans use phonological rules (particularly rules of the kind used in this kind of phonology) then we can't use the need to write simpler rules as a justification for binary features.

Another problem is the way in which distinctive features are related to the articulatory or acoustic properties of a sound. Initially it seemed that a feature should be described in terms of acoustic and/or articulatory correlates. The idea was that such properties were only physical correlates of an internal cognitive entity (i.e. distinctive features exist only in the brain). Further, acoustic correlates were dropped from many descriptions of distinctive features (e.g. Chomsky and Halle, 1968). The notion of distinctive feature became increasingly abstract as their description moved away from Jakobson's idea that the features should be clearly defined in terms of their physiological and acoustic correlates.

Moving away from such externally measurable correlates might be argued to be justified on the grounds that physical and mental reality are not identical, but doing so also moves away from the possibility of hypothesis falsifiability, the basis of modern science. "Falsifiability (or refutability or testability) is the logical possibility that an assertion can be shown false by an observation or a physical experiment".

The above issues bring us to the question of psychological reality. Do human brains use distinctive features, or more generally features of any kind, in the specification (and production and perception) of phonemes? If we do, then do we use the features that have been described above (or similar sets of features)? Sometimes phonological proof has resembled the strategies formal logic whereby proof may consist of providing a logically internally consistent system of rules and features. Do human brains use rules in normal speech cognition?

ARTICULATORY FEATURES

In more recent years there have been a number of developments in phonological theory. Generative phonology, the theoretical context of distinctive feature theory, has evolved into Optimality Theory (Prince and Smolensky, 1993) which holds that cognitive rules and features are related to measurable surface phenomena (e.g. speech production and perception) by various constraints. For example, phonological change motivated by the desire for ease of articulation is constrained by the need to maintain perceptual distinctiveness (Boersma, 1998). Such constraint based approaches illustrate the need for phonological theory to keep in mind both speech perception and speech production.

In speech perception research and theory, the motor theory of speech perception (Liberman, Mattingly and Turvey, 1967, Liberman and Mattingly, 1985) has long asserted a model that relates speech perception to speech production. More recently, the direct-realist theory of speech perception (e.g. Fowler, 1986, Best, 1995) posits the idea that when we perceive speech we directly perceive speech gestures without the intervening step of analysing into abstract phonological features.

Also, speech physiological research has led to the realisation that the syllable, rather than the phoneme, is the basic unit of articulatory planning. Gestures are known to interact to a greater extent within syllables than across syllable boundaries.

Increasingly gestures, particularly at the level of the syllable, are being seen as important in speech production, speech perception and phonology. At the very least, any modern development of distinctive feature theory needs to be more explicitly based on gestures. If basic phonological features do exist (in contradiction to the claims of the direct realist theory) then they are likely to be based on gestures. This is the basis of articulatory phonology, which is basically a theory of articulatory features, some privative (binary), some gradual and some equipollent.

In this theory gestures, and therefore features, may operate across the syllable, but which features occur and where they occur depend upon which phonemes are found in the syllable. Gestures are not synchronised with each other or with boundaries (such as the mostly imaginary phoneme boundary). Timing of gestures is context specific. The features specify articulator (i.e. lips, jaw, tongue tip, tongue body, velum and larynx), degree of constriction.

GENERATIVE PHONOLOGY

PHONOLOGY AND UNDERLYING REPRESENTATIONS

We have considered so far two different levels of abstraction in representing the sound structure of a language: a phonetic level of representation which includes aspects of pronunciation which are at least shared by a community/ dialect group, and which above all includes the variability due to context effects; and a phonemic level of representation which is formed from a finite number of phonemic units and which factors out the contextual influences.

It has been a particular hallmark of a branch of phonology known as Generative Phonology, that came to prominence with Chomsky and Halle's *Sound Pattern of English,* to consider a more abstract representation which will call an *underlying representation* that allows phonological rules and principles to be more transparently and economically stated.

Their emphasis in the *Sound Pattern of English* is to eliminate *redundancy* from phonological analyses. We already do this to a certain extent, of course, in representing words using the phonemic rather than a phonetic representation: that is, there are some aspects of pronunciation that are redundant (e.g. aspiration of oral stops in English) and so we factor out this redundancy and subsequently fill it in by rule. We therefore of course also necessarily end up with a considerably more abstract sound representation of the word (e.g. /pIn/ rather than[p^hIn]) i.e. one which is one stage further removed than a phonetic transcription from the actual details of the production of speech and how the vocal organs are coordinated.

In the *Sound Pattern of English,* one of the main aims is to factor out many more redundancies from the words' phonological representations and to fill in these redundancies by rule. This in turn results in a representation which is a good deal more abstract than the phonemic forms we have been considering. Furthermore, these highly abstract representations are presumed to form part of the talker's knowledge of the language. — they might be how the words are encoded in the mental lexicon.

As an example, consider some data reported by Mohanan and discussed in Kenstowicz. In Singapore English, as in many dialects of English, talkers simplify word-final consonant clusters by deleting the final stop.

For example, words like 'task', 'lift', 'list' are produced as/tQs/,/lIf/,/lIs/, i.e. without the final /t/. Now consider the pluralisation rule (in all standard accents of English) in which a /ə z/ suffix is added to words that end in /s/. For example, the plural of 'class' and 'dress' are /klQs ə z/ and /drɛ ə z/ in standard forms of English.

The question is: how do these kinds of Singapore talkers who regularly reduce consonantal clusters form plurals in words like 'tasks' and 'lists'? Since their singular productions end in/s/(/tQs/,/ljs/) and since the pluralisation rule requires an /Yz/, they should produce /tQsYz/ and /ljsYz/ (analogous to 'classes' and 'dresses') if it is the phonemic/s/ which is responsible for plurals in /ə z/.

But these Singapore English talkers do no such thing: their plural forms of 'tasks' and 'lists' are the same as their singular forms i.e. /tQs//ljs/ even though they do produce the plural forms/klQsYz/ and /dr[sYz/ for 'classes' and 'dresses'. How can we explain this?

The Generative Phonology solution would be to propose that the underlying forms of 'task' and 'list' in this dialect of Singapore English are /tQsk/ and /ljst/ i.e. with a full consonantal cluster that is not pronounced. Or from another point of view, these talkers' mental representations of these words — that is; the way in which these words are stored in their mental lexicons — include phonological forms (final /sk/ , final /st/) *that are never pronounced* (by them). Generative Phonologists would then model the actual pronunciations of the singular and plurals in terms of phonological rules, as follows:

	'task'	'tasks'
underlying representation	task	task+s
cluster simplification	tas	tas+s
output (phonetic form)	tas	tas

Therefore, because Singapore English talkers'know' that'task' really has a final/k/(even though they do not pronounce it), they do not add the plural suffix/ə z/(which is reserved for words like'dance' which have a final/s/), but the plural suffix/s/, analogously to words that end in a final voiceless non-sibilant consonant ('tap','block' etc. which form plurals by adding/s/thus/tæps/,/bl?ks/etc.).

The significance of this example (and there are many others like it) lies not so much in the details but rather in the idea that the way in which the pronunciation of words is stored in the mental lexicon may be a good deal more abstract than the phonemic representation of the actual pronunciations would suggest. If we accept this premise, then we must also accept the idea that there are phonological rules that link these often highly abstract underlying forms to the phonetic forms (or 'surface' forms, to use terminology from Generative Phonology) because otherwise we cannot explain how underlying forms are related to pronunciation (this is exactly parallel to our earlier phonemic/phonetic distinction: once we represent words phonemically, we have to have rules that fill in the redundant or predictable aspects of pronunciation like aspiration; the difference in the Generative Phonology model is that the underlying forms that are being proposed are more abstract than phonemic forms — resulting in many more rules to explain the predictable and redundant aspects of pronunciation — and they lay much greater emphasis on the claim that these underlying forms are in some sense 'psychologically real' i.e. part of the talker's linguistic competence).

Examples of Uuderlying Forms Reconstructed

Generative phonologists often use evidence from

morphological alternations which are a very productive source of sound variation, to reconstruct underlying forms. In English, underlying forms have been reconstructed from alternations such as opaque/opacity, electric/electricity, serene/serenity, digress/digression, confuse/confusion etc. Again, the argument is that these alternations include predictable aspects of pronunciation that can be succinctly expressed by applying phonological rules to abstract underlying forms. We will take a first example from Indonesian to illustrate how underlying forms are reconstructed and the way in which phonological rules apply to derive the 'surface' phonetic forms.

In Indonesian, there is an alternation between a simple and a prefixed form. By studying these alternations, we have to try to come up with a plausible underlying form for the prefix and an appropriate set of rules. Here is the data:

simple form	**prefixed form**	
lempar	məlempar	'throw'
rasa	mərasa	'feel'
wakil	məwakil	'represent'
jakin	məjakin	'convince'
masak	məmasak	'cook'
nikah	mənikah	'marry'
ŋaco	məŋaco	'chat'
ɲaɲi	məɲaɲi	'sing'
hituŋ	məŋhituŋ	'count'
ɡambar	məŋɡambar	'draw a picture'
kirim	məŋirim	'send'
dəŋar	məndəŋar	'hear'
tulis	mənulis	'write'
bantu	məmbantu	'help'
pukul	məmukul	'hit'
d͡ʒahit	məɲd͡ʒahit	'sew'
t͡ʃatat	məɲt͡ʃatat	'note down'
ambil	məŋambil	'take'
isi	məŋisi	'fill up'
undaŋ	məŋundaŋ	'invite'

We can see that there is some variation in the phonetic

shape of the prefix. For example, we have[mə] in the first 7 forms, [mər] for 'sing', 'sew' and 'note down', [mYm] for 'help' and 'hit', [məK] for many other forms and so on. We can also note that the phonetic shape of the simple form is usually copied in the prefixed form (e.g. [lempar] and [məlempar]), but not always (e.g. [pukul] but [məmukul]). Our task is to see if we can explain this variation in terms of phonological rules and come up with a single underlying representation for the prefix to reflect the fact that we are dealing with the same prefix in all cases, even though its phonetic shape does vary.

As with the problems in complementary distribution, we must look for some pattern than might explain the variation in the shape in the prefix. The most striking feature seems to be that it is affected by the place of articulation of the following consonant.

For example: Initial consonant of the stem final consonant of the prefix e.g.,

bilabial	bilabial	məmbantu
alveolar	alveolar	məndəjar
palato-alveolar	palatal	məɲd͡ʒahit
velar	velar	məŋgambar

This is a rule of *anticipatory assimilation* which occurs in many languages: a final consonant changes to the place of articulation of a following consonant. This happens in English as well in some contexts. For example, at a faster speech production, we can get [siÐm meIbl] for 'seen Mable', [siÐK kærən] for 'seen Karen' etc.

We need at least another rule to explain why the first consonant of the simple form is deleted when the prefix is added in 'send', 'write' and 'hit'. Do the first consonants of these words have anything in common? Yes, they are voiceless stops. Perhaps, then, when the prefixed form begins with a voiceless stop, it is deleted in the prefixed form. To verify this assumption, we have to look at all words to make sure that none of them begin with a voiceless stop that is not deleted when the prefix is added. An inspection of this data shows that only 'send' 'write' and 'hit' begin with voiceless stops and in all three cases these are deleted in the prefixed form. We can therefore tentatively propose a second *deletion* rule that will delete voiceless stops in the prefixed form.

The other two prefix shapes that are not accounted for are /mə/ and /məK/. We get/mə/ + the simple form in the first eight words (down to 'sing'). The fact that we have already demonstrated an assimilation rule in which the prefix is affected by the following consonant might lead us to look for some pattern in the following consonant to explain the occurrence of [mə].

The initial consonants of these words are [l r w j m n K r]. Do these have anything in common? They are all non-syllabic sonorant sounds i.e. [-syll, +son]. Is it therefore the case that we get [mə] whenever the simple form begins with a non-syllabic sonorant? An inspection of all the other forms shows that this is indeed the case.

Finally, leaving aside 'send' and 'draw a picture', whose prefix can be explained by the anticipatory assimilation rule given earlier, we get[məK] in 'chat', 'count', and the last three, 'take', 'fill up', and 'invite'. These do not seem to have much in common as far as the initial sound of the simple form is concerned. However, the last three all begin with a vowel in the simple form ([ambil], [isi], [uṅdaK]), so we can at least propose that [mYK] occurs when the simple form begins with a vowel (and this is consistent with the rest of the data).

We have suggested various rules in the preceding analysis. We now have to try to reconstruct an underlying form that the rules will apply to. There will always be more than one possible way of reconstructing an underlying form (we have no way by looking at phonetic data to know what underlying form might be in a talker's head); so when there is more than one possibility, we have to argue for one over the other.

The way we might do this for the present data is as follows. (But we do not want to stray from the idea that there will be ONE underlying form for the different shapes of the prefix to express the idea that we are basically dealing with the same prefix, at least in terms of morphology).

One possibility is to pick one of the possible shapes of the prefix as the underlying form. Let's pick,/mə m/. In this case, we would be proposing that the underlying prefixed forms are all/mə m/ and that we derive the surface forms by rule. For example, for the first word we would have UR (underlying representation) /mə mlempar/, and a deletion rule which would discard the /m/ of the prefix to derive [mYlempar]. There would also have to be an assimilation rule to change our proposed UR /mə maambar/ into[mə Kaambar]. However, when we come to 'count', and the last three words 'take', 'fill up', and 'invite' that all begin with a vowel, we have a problem. There is certainly nothing to stop us writing a rule that will change /mə misi/ into [mə Kisi], but this *rule has no phonetic basis to it at all* (and is therefore not well motivated). Specifically, why should a bilabial /m/change into a velar [K] before a high front vowel? And above all, why should it change into a velar [K] before /h/ ('count') and three vowels at different height and backness (the last three words) that seem to share no phonetic features in common? We have no answer and therefore we should look for a different solution.

What about if we propose /mə / as the UR of the prefix? In this case, the UR and surface forms of the first eight words would be the same (no rules needed) and we would have to insert a final nasal in all of the other cases. But we quickly see that we run into the same problem as before. Although we could propose a well motivated rule that would insert a nasal consonant at the same place of articulation as the initial consonant in the simple form (i.e. insert /m/ in the proposed UR /mə bantu/ to derive the phonetic form [mə mbantu] etc), we have no answer to why /K/ should be inserted in the proposed UR /mə isi/ to derive [mə Kisi].

Let's try a different tack. The UR of words should consist of segments that cannot be explained or reduced further by phonological rules. For example, there's probably no reason to suppose that the UR of the English word 'pick' is anything other than /plk/. We can't explain the /I/ vowel by the presence of the neighbouring consonants (whereas we *can* explain the presence of the/m/ in 'impatient' by the presence of the following bilabial /p/) and there's no reason to suppose we can exploit any redundancy in the UR of 'pick' by looking at the morphological relatives ('pick', 'picked', 'picking' etc). So since we can't explain away any of the three units in/plk/ by rule, they must form part of the word's underlying representation in the (mental) lexicon.

Similarly, since we can't account for the existence of /K/ in some words, let's propose that it forms part of the UR of the prefix. In other words, if we choose a UR of /mYK/ as the prefix, we have no explaining to do (no rules to write) for 'count', 'take', 'fill up' or 'invite': their URs and phonetic forms are the same.

Now let's recap on the rules that we need to derive the other surface forms:

- *An assimilation rule*: assimilate the final nasal consonant of the prefix to the place of articulation of the following consonant
- *Deletion rule A*: delete voiceless stops after the final nasal consonant of the prefix
- *Deletion rule B*: delete the final nasal consonant of the prefix before a non-vocalic sonorant.

Let's see if these rules generate the appropriate surface phonetic representations of the prefixed forms. Here are some examples.

UR:	məŋlempar
rule 3	məlempar
UR:	məŋŋaco
rule 3	məŋaco
UR:	məŋgambar
rule 1	no change (the assimilation rules applies vacuously)
UR	məŋtulis
rule 1	məntulis
rule 2	mənulis

We can see from the last example that the derivation of

the surface phonetics form may require the application of more than one rule, and also that the rules have to be *ordered*. Consider what the result would be if we applied rule 2 first..

UR:	məŋtulis
rule 2	məŋulis
rule 1	(cannot apply -- the voiceless stop has been deleted)

i.e. the incorrect phonetic form [m ə Kulis] is derived.

Finding Patterns of Alternation

Setting up an underlying form from phonetic data requires some practice in formulating phonological rules. This section provides an example of developing a set of phonological rules without explicitly setting up any underlying forms.

EXAMPLE

The data below is from Tagalog and shows an alternation between a simple form and a suffixed form that occurs before the suffix [an] (i.e. the suffixed form of 'open' is [buksan]). What phonological rules would you need to convert the simple form into the suffixed form?

Simple form	Suffixed form	
bukas	buks	'open'
kapit	kapt	'embrace'
posod	pusd	'tuft'
bata	bath	'suffer'
polo	pulh	'ask for trifles'
banig	baŋg	'mat'
tanim	tamn	'plant'
talab	tabl	'penetrate'
opos	ups	'stop'
bili	bilh	'buy'
dipa	diph	'open'
damit	damt	'clothe'
ganap	gamp	'fulfil'
atip	apt	'thatching'
laman	lamn	'fill'

From the first three forms, and indeed many others, we can see that the vowel in the second syllable is deleted in the suffixed form.

For example: bukas + an becomes buksan

Secondly, there seems to be an alternation between [o] in the simple form and [u] in the suffixed form. This seems to be entirely 'context-free' i.e. [o] changes obligatorily to [u]regardless of the context (or at least that's all we can say from the information that we have). So from this rule and the deletion rule above, we get from:

opos	
ops	(deletion rule)
ups	(vowel raising rule: i.e. raise the phonetic height
of [o])	

Thirdly, the alternation of [bania] and [baKa] suggests an assimilation rule. Is it generally the case that [n] assimilates to the place of articulation of the following consonant (after vowel deletion has taken place)? This does happen in [aanap] which becomes [aamp] (i.e. [p]is bilabial so [n] assimilates to the same place of articulation and becomes a bilabial as well), but it doesn't happen in [tanim] which alternates with [tamn].

It would seem from this limited data that the assimilation rule must be highly context-sensitive: i.e. [n] only assimilates when the following sound is an oral stop (so such a rule will apply to [bania] and [aanap], because, after vowel deletion, [n] precedes [a] or [p] which are both oral stops, but it won't apply to[tanim] because [m] is a nasal stop).

Fourthly, some of the consonants in some forms undergo *metathesis* in which they swap places after vowel deletion (this is in fact quite common in morphological alternations in many languages).

For example, we have:

atip	simple form
atp	vowel deletion
apt	metathesis of the last two consonants

A closer inspection shows that metathesis occurs whenever an alveolar consonant immediately precedes a bilabial consonant.

For example:

talab	simple form
talb	vowel deletion: [l] is alveolar, [b] is
bilabial	
tabl	metathesis
tanim	simple form
tanm	vowel deletion: [n] is alveolar, [m] is
bilabial	
tamn	metathesis

Finally, we need a rule to deal with alternations such as [bili]/[bilh] in which the suffixed form has an . Those forms that do have an in the suffix all end in a vowel in the simple form ([bata],[polo],[bili],[dipa]). One possibility is that is inserted when the suffix is added (this is a kind of liaison rule, similar in nature to the insertion of [t] in the interrogative French 'a-t-elle?' that is derived from 'elle a' meaning 'she has').

Specifically, we can propose:

bili	simple form
bilih	h-insertion
bilh	vowel deletion

We therefore have five rules that apply when the suffix [an] is added:

1. Delete the vowel in the final syllable of the simple form
2. [o] becomes, [u]
3. [n] assimilates to the place of articulation of a following oral stop
4. when an alveolar precedes a bilabial they metathesise
5. insert a final if the simple form ends in a vowel

Clearly, rule (1) must apply before either rules (3) or (4): if we did not delete the vowel first (rule 1), there would be no context for either rules (3) or (4) to apply. For example, this is the outcome of an ordering of rule (3) before rule (I):

ganap	simple form - rule (3) doesn't apply because [n] and [p] aren't adjacent
ganp	by rule (1) -- this is not the correct form for the suffix

We must also apply the assimilation rule (3) before the methathesis rule (4). Otherwise, we would again derive an incorrect result:

ganap	simple form
ganp	rule 1
gapn	rule 4 metathesis

i.e. we would have [aapnan]. Finally, rule (5) must apply before rule (1) to derive the correct suffixed forms with . If rule (1) applied first, we would have:

bili	simple form
bil	by rule 1

and then no context for the -insertion rule to apply (because is only inserted after a vowel), thus incorrectly deriving the suffixed form [bilan].

So in summary, the order of the rules is 5-1-3-4; rule (2) being a context-insensitive rule is free to apply at any stage in the derivation of the suffixed forms.

Underlying Forms and Phonological Rules

EXAMPLE

The following shows phonetic data of alternations in Zoque (a language in Mexico) between the plural form, 1st person singular plural, and 3rd person singular plural.

- Set up an underlying form for each word and the affixes for 'my' and 'his
- ·Describe the phonological rules that are necessary to link the underlying forms to the phonetic data.

The way to begin such problems is firstly to look across the rows (at the paradigmatic variations of each word) and make a few mental notes of the alternations. For example, in the first row we note that [pama] is prefixed by [m] in 'my' and infixed with [j] for 'his'. When you have looked carefully across the rows, compare the rows (words) with each other to see if you can find evidence of a similar kind of alternation that you can explain by rule.

plural	my	his
pama	mbama	pjama
tatah	ndatah	t͡ʃatah
tuwi	nduwi	t͡ʃuwi
kaju	ŋgaju	kjaju
t͡sin	nd͡zin	t͡ʃin
mok	mok	mjok
ʔatsi	ʔatsi	ʔjatsi

For example: does a similar kind of prefixing and infixing occur for the other forms? This is so for some of the words (e.g. [kaju],[Kaaju],[kjaju]), but the phonetic form of the 'my' prefix changes form word to word (and does not appear in 'corn' or 'brother'). Also, the [j] does not appear in the 'his' forms of 'father', 'dog', 'pine' and the initial consonants of these words have turned into a palato-alveolar affricate.

Let's begin more systematically with the 'my' forms. The fact that there is an alternation between[m],[n],[K] before a following consonant at the same place of articulation suggests an*assimilation* rule. There seems to be no basis from the data for choosing either /m/,/n/, or/K/ as the UR of the 'my' suffix. So let's choose /n/ on the grounds that it is prone to assimilation in many languages (e.g. 'seen Mable' and 'seen Karen' in which/n/assimilates to/m/ and /K/ respectively at faster rates of speech in English).

The assimilation rule applies appropriately to the first five forms (vacuously in fact to 'father', 'dog', 'pine' in which /n/ 'changes to' [n]), but we have to deal with 'corn' and 'brother' in which the prefix seems to have disappeared. We can handle these cases with a *deletion rule.*Firstly, we can say that when two nasals at the same place of articulation follow each other, one of them is deleted (this is appropriate because perceptually there is unlikely to be a lot of difference between [mmok] and [mok]). In other words, by the assimilation rule we get from / nmok/ to /mmok/ and then one of the nasals is deleted to produce the phonetic form [mok]. Secondly, since it's impossible to assimilate the /n/ to a glottal place of articulation ('brother'), we shall say that /n/ is deleted before glottal stops.

The rules we have so far, then are:

- Assimilate /n/ to the place of articulation of a following consonant
- Delete one of two homorganic nasal consonants (homorganic = at the same place of articulation)
- Delete /n/ when it precedes a glottal stop

We still have to deal with the alternations of [p] and [b] ('clothes'), [t] and [d] ('dog'), [k]and [a] ('horse'), and [tas] and [daz] ('pine'). This is clearly an alternation in the voicing of the stop. The question is: which one do the words have as part of their UR? The answer is that it must be the voiceless one and for two reasons. Firstly, the voiceless stop/ affricate also appears in the 'his' forms and secondly it would be an odd rule indeed if voiced sounds became voiceless after the attachment of the *voiced* /n/ prefix in the 'my' forms! So we need another rule.

- Voiceless consonants become voiced after /n/

Focusing now on the 'his' forms, the data suggests that 'his' is /j/ in Zoque and that this prefix metathesises with the first consonant. In other words, we are proposing that / j + pama/becomes /pjama/ (analogously 'horse', 'corn' and 'brother'). We have to account for the 'his' forms with /taƒ/ in 'father', 'dog', 'pine'. This is more than likely another assimilation rule in which /tj/ turns into an affricate (another common occurrence: consider in English the alternation between [djdj‰] and [djda'‰] 'did you' or [tj‰n] and [taƒun] for 'tune' etc). So in summary, the URs for the words are exactly as represented in the plural forms; the UR for 'my' is / n/ and the UR for 'his' is /j/.

We then have 6 rules:

1. Assimilate /n/ to the place of articulation of a following consonant

2. Delete one of two homorganic nasal consonants (homorganic = at the same place of articulation)
3. Delete /n/ when it precedes a glottal stop
4. Voiceless consonants become voiced after /n/
5. Metathesise /j/ and a following consonant
6. Alveolars assimilate to palato-alveolars before /j/ (and delete the /j/)

For example, the derivation of 'his pine' is as follows:

/j t͡sin/	UR
t͡sjin	rule 5
[t͡ʃin]	rule 6

AUTOSEGMENTAL PHONOLOGY

AUTOSEGMENTAL PHONOLOGY

In the Generative Phonology that followed from Chomsky and Halle's publication of the*Sound Pattern of English* (SPE), morphemes are represented as underlying representations (URs) that consist of underlying units each defined by a distinctive feature matrix.

In the SPE model, there are phonological rules that apply to URs (such as to the prefix /mYK/ in Indonesian that we considered earlier) and that then convert these into one or more surface phonetic forms (such as [mYm]) We have also seen that there are often multiple rules, which implies that the UR may have to go through many different kinds of transformation before the appropriate phonetic form is reached.

The most important development since the SPE model of phonology is to recognise that URs may be *multidimensional* in which segments are arranged on separate or *auto*nomous levels or tiers (hence the name *auto*-segment). Phonological rules could apply independently to the segments at these autonomous levels, although the segments always remain linked to each other.

The development of multidimensional phonological representations was largely motivated by the realisation that the SPE framework, in which URs consisted of linear (one-dimensional) segments, was not able to explain adequately certain properties of tone languages, nor in fact various aspects of prosodic phonology such as lexical stress in English. We consider some data from Margi (a tone language) that can be used to argue for URs that have segments and tones arranged on independent tiers.

Consider firstly a fairly simple example from English for the autonomous representation of syllables and phoneme-size segments. As you may know, there are at least two different ways of saying the first few sounds of a word like 'parametre'. The first is the citation form way recorded in most dictionaries in which the word has four syllables and, the first three segments are [p ə y]i.e. with a medial schwa. The second, and more common way in fact, is to not produce the medial schwa and to have a syllabic [y)] segment i.e. [py)æmYtY]. Notice that this initial cluster is quite different phonetically from the initial segments in monosyllabic 'pry' in which the /r/ is realised as a voiceless approximant: in 'parametre', we still have four syllables but the schwa has been deleted.

Let's see why the two variant pronunciations [p ə y] and [py)] are a problem in an SPE type model. Assuming that we have the form with the schwa in the underlying representation, we have to write a rule which is going to delete the schwa and yet somehow keep the [+syllabic] feature (from the schwa) which then gets carried over onto the [y] segment. Specifically, remember that the schwa's distinctive feature matrix must include (amongst other things) the features [-consonantal, +syllabic].

What we would like to be able to do is to delete every feature except the [+syllabic] one, and then attach the [+syllabic] feature to the feature matrix of [y] so that it becomes [+syllabic] (remember that initially [y] will be defined as [+consonantal, -syllabic]). But the problem in SPE is that, when you delete segments, you also have to delete their entire feature matrices (you can't retain bits of a feature matrix). Therefore when the schwa is deleted so is its entire feature matrix, including the feature [+syllabic] that we want to keep.

An intuitively more satisfying explanation is to represent the syllabic feature and the segments on autonomous levels and then to have a rule that deletes the schwa without affecting the syllabic level. That is, in our UR, we would start out with a representation like the one immediately below. This has two separate levels which are linked by association lines (the vertical lines).

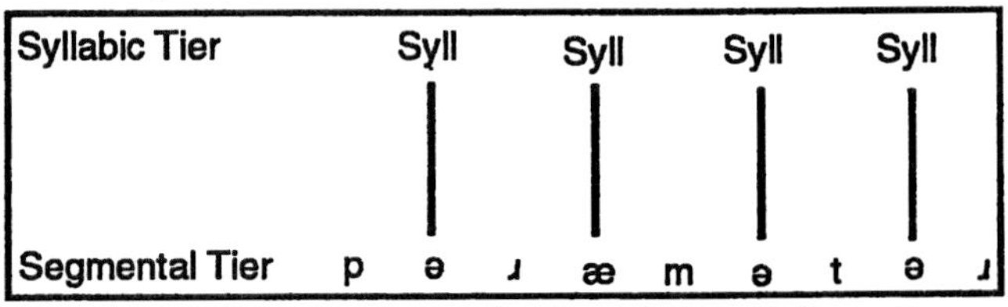

We would then have a rule that deleted the schwa at the segmental level while leaving the units at the syllabic level unaffected (and therefore leaving a dangling, or unattached, association line):

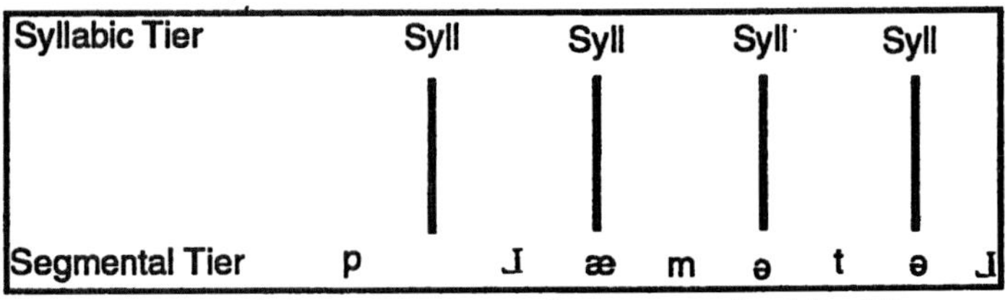

A rule would then associate the unattached [syll] segment rightwards to the nearest sonorant segment, i.e. to [y]:

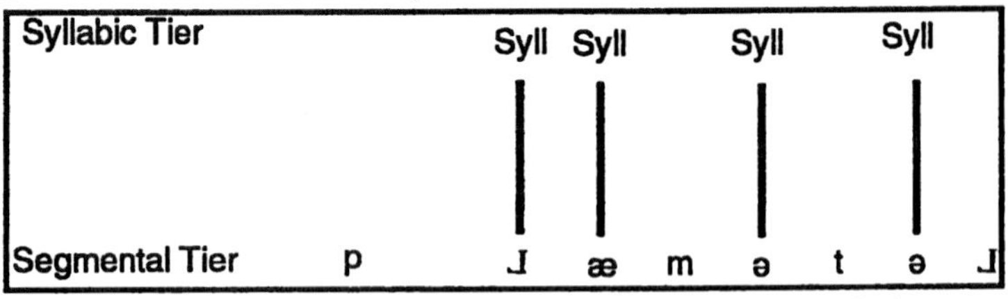

We have thereby deleted the schwa, retained the same number of syllables, and also marked the[y] segment as syllabic (by its association line to [syll]).

An important implication of the autosegmental treatment, which represents a radical departure from the *Sound Pattern of English,* is that not all features are necessarily *properties* of segments. For example, in SPE, lexical-stress in English was a property of a vowel segment: in 'pattern', the/æ/ vowel was marked as [1 stress] (primary stress) - thus [1 stress] was a property of this vowel, in the same way that the feature [+low] formed part of this vowel's feature matrix. By analogy, the same applied to tone languages: a vowel's feature matrix might be marked as [level-high] for syllables produced with a high-level tone (and that's why, if a vowel was deleted, its stress and tonal features were also necessarily deleted, since these were simply considered to be inherent properties of the vowel's feature matrix). What the autosegmental treatment does is to take some of the features out of the segment and to put them onto their own level or *tier* so that rules that apply at the segmental level need not necessarily apply to them as well.

The value of this autosegmental analysis was clear in Goldsmith's analysis of tone in African languages. He argued for an autosegmental representation on the grounds that there are phonological rules that apply independently to the tonal and segmental levels. In one of the well-known examples, he showed that there are rules that delete a segment but which can leave a tone that is associated to a segment unaffected. The data is shown below. First, however, we will need to learn some new notation to interpret the tones, as follows.

High and low level tones are marked with an acute and grave accent respectively, thus:

é	high level
è	low level

These are level tones. A rising tone on the same vowel is equivalent to a low tone immediately followed by a high tone. This is reflected in the notation by combining the low and high tone representations as follows:

e	rising

By analogy, a falling tone (High followed by Low) is marked as:

ê	falling

and in the few occasions when we need to mark a mid-level tone, we will use

ë	mid-level

Goldsmith's data was from Margi (a language spoken in Nigeria), in which he analysed phonologically the change in the tonal shape of an [ari] suffix when segments were deleted. The addition of an [ari] suffix turns an indefinite into a definite. As these examples show, when the indefinite ends in a consonant, there is no change to the definite and the suffix is always [aMrM]:

indefinite	definite	
sál	sálárì	'man'
kátsákár	kátsákárárì	'sword'
àgám	àgámárì	'ram'
kùm	kùmárì	'meat'

When the definite ends in a vowel, there are various changes both to the vowel of the suffix and to its tone. Consider first the case when the final vowel of the indefinite ends in a high tone:

indefinite	definite	
kí	kjárì	'compound'
kú	kwárì	'goat'
tágú	tagwárì	'horse'
ʃèré	ʃèrérì	'court'
tóró	tórórì	'threepence'
ncálá	ncálárì	'calabash'

The above cases can in fact be handled in a linear SPE model. We can have a rule which turns a high vowel into a glide when it precedes a vowel (thus [i] and [u] become [j] and [w]respectively) and in which the vowel of the stem replaces the vowel of the suffix elsewhere: thus [toro+ari] becomes [torori], [ʃere+ari] becomes [ʃereri] etc).

Now consider the following cases in which the indefinite ends in a vowel with a low tone.

We see exactly the same segmental changes as before (change a high vowel to a glide, replace the vowel of the suffix with the last vowel of the indefinite elsewhere), but additionally, the tone of the penultimate vowel changes from *high* to *rising:*

indefinite	definite	
fa`	fǎrì	'farm'
tì	tjǎrì	'mourning'
hu`	hwǎrì	'grave'
cédè	céděrì	'money'

These cases are more difficult to handle in an SPE framework in which the tone would be assumed to be an intrinsic part of the vowel's feature matrix. This is because a closer analysis shows that the vowel of the suffix is deleted although its tone is not.

For example, we can analyse[céderì] as:

cédè + aìrì

Now delete the vowel of the stem, as before, *but do not delete the tone:*

cédè + `rì

We are left with an unattached high tone (the ì tone which is left after the [a] vowel has been deleted). We now need a rule which says that unattached tones must be attached to the nearest vowel.

Consider in the light of this that the final vowel of [cédè] is low (L) and the unattached tone is high (H). The combination of the two gives a low tone followed by a high tone (L then H) which is the same as a rising tone (or equivalently: cédè + ì becomes céde).

Phonologists would deal with these rule changes in an *autosegmental representation* in which tones and segments appear on separate levels.

For example, the UR for the definite form of 'farm', [farì], would be:

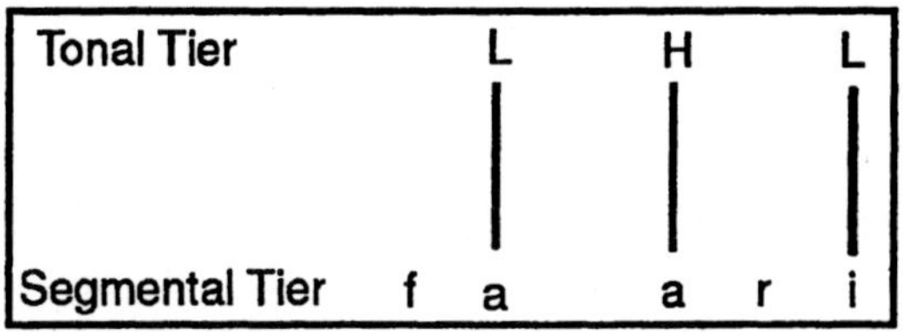

A rule applies to the segmental level to delete the vowel of the suffix when it is preceded by a vowel:

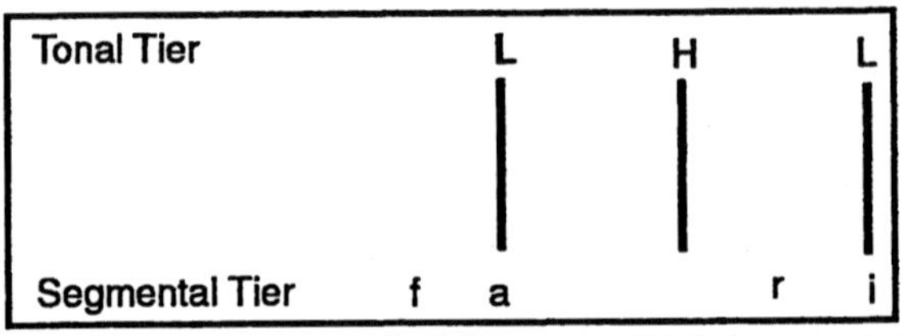

We now have an unattached H tone which is associated to the nearest vowel:

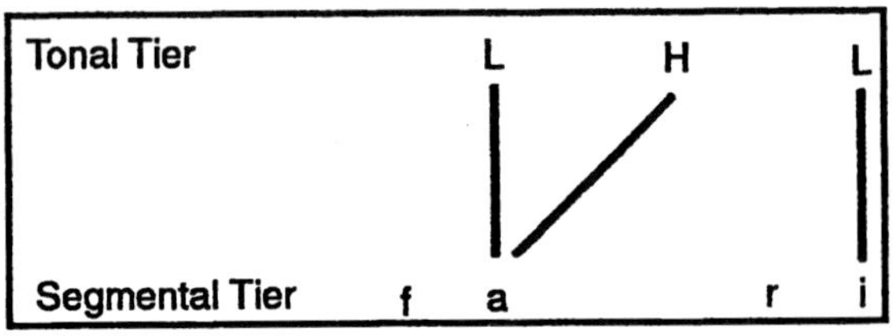

In other words, we have an LH (=rising) tone attached to the first vowel i.e. we correctly derive[farì].

The cases in which the vowel of the indefinite is turned into a glide ('mourning', 'grave') can be dealt with in a similar autosegmental way, but in this case we have to have a rule which says that tones can *only* associate to vowels. Specifically, the UR for the definite 'grave' would be:

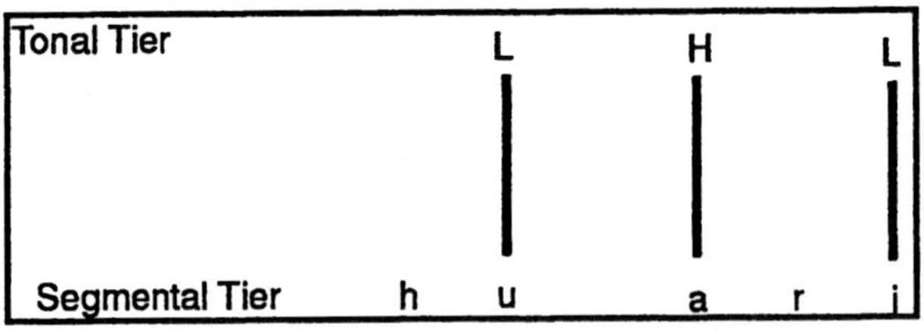

We apply a rule to the segmental level which says that high vowels turn into glides when they precede a vowel:

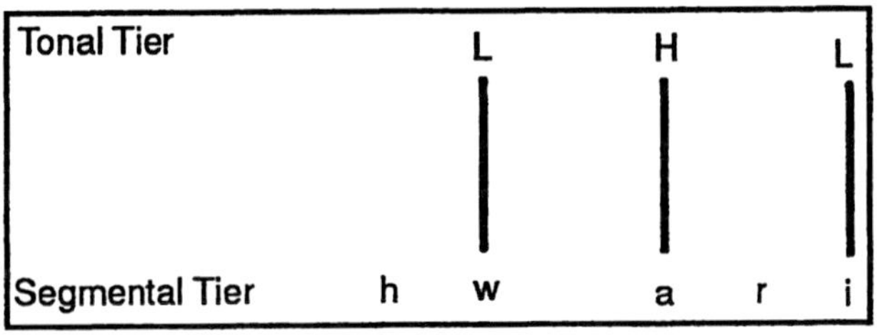

But we now have a tone (L) associated with a consonant

[w], which is disallowed (because tones can only associate to vowels). We therefore need a rule at the tonal level that will link the L tone to the nearest vowel (i.e. to the following [a]):

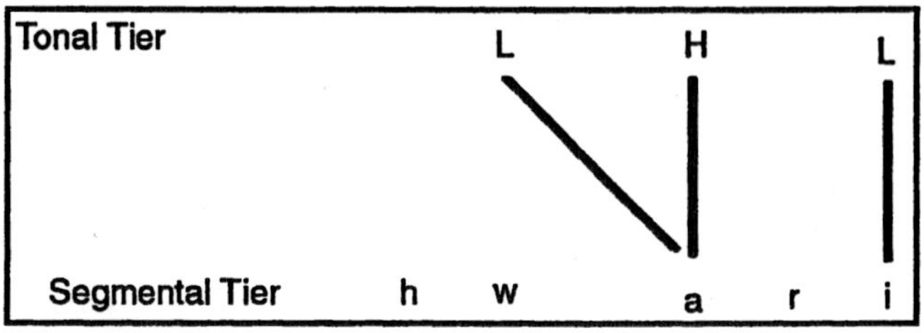

= [hwarì]

THE PHONOLOGY OF INTONATION

INTRODUCTION TO PROSODY

What is Prosody

Prosody is the study of the tune and rhythm of speech and how these features contribute to meaning.

Prosody is the study of those aspects of speech that typically apply to a level above that of the individual phoneme and very often to sequences of words (in prosodic phrases). Features above the level of the phoneme (or "segment") are referred to as suprasegmentals. A phonetic study of prosody is a study of the suprasegmental features of speech.

At the phonetic level, prosody is characterised by:

- Vocal pitch (fundamental frequency)
- Loudness (acoustic intensity)
- Rhythm (phoneme and syllable duration)

Phonetic studies of prosody often concentrate on measuring these characteristics.

Prosody has been studied from numerous perspectives by people belonging to differing linguistic schools. There has been great diversity of approaches to prosody. Different approaches examine prosody from the perspective of grammar, of discourse, of pragmatics and of phonetics and phonology

Prosody can be regarded as part of the grammar of a language. Discourse approaches examine the prosody of normal interactions rather than stylised, constructed, fluent, scripted interactions. Functionalist approaches integrate the study of prosody with the study of grammar and meaning in natural social interactions.

Pragmatics examines the distinction between the literal meaning of a sentence and the meaning intended by the speaker. Prosody can have the effect of changing the meaning of a sentence by indicating a speaker's attitude to what is being said (eg. it can indicate irony, sarcasm, etc) particularly when prosody works in conjunction with the social/situational context of an utterance.

Prosody overlaps with emotion in speech. The same acoustic features that are used to express prosody (intensity, vocal pitch, rhythm, rate of utterance) are also affected by emotion in the voice. For example, I can simultaneously be sad and ironic or fearful and sarcastic.

Speech contains various levels of information that can be described as:

- *Linguistic*: direct expression of meaning
- *Paralinguistic*: may indicate attitude or membership of a speech community
- *Non-linguistic*: may indicate something about a speaker's vocal physiology, state of health or emotional state

Paralinguistic aspects of speech are those aspects that are not strictly linguistic, but which contribute to the meaning of an utterance. Paralinguistic features may help to indicate a speaker's attitude, although this may overlap with emotional aspects of speech.

Another paralinguistic aspect of speech are those features that indicate a speakers membership of a speech community. These are effectively sociolinguistic markers of speaker identity. eg. Australian versus New Zealand pronunciations, styles of speech of farmers versus bankers, etc.

Some speech communities might prefer broader pronunciations. Some speech communities might prefer more nasal voices. Some speech communities might speak louder or faster.

Gender has both paralinguistic and non-linguistic aspects. Some features may be regarded as more masculine or feminine by a particular speech community (eg. degree of pharyngealisation in Arabic)

But, features that are purely a consequence of physiological differences are non-linguistic aspects of speech

A speaker's emotional state is often evident in the speaker's voice. These features are linguistic to the extent that they are relevant to the meaning of the current utterance. On the other hand, our current emotional state might be a non-linguistic undertone to what is being said (ie. if its not very relevant to what's being said).

Our state of health can be evident in our speech. This would be a non-linguistic aspect of our speech. Note, however, that even this distinction can blur when the health issue is cognitive and affects the expression of meaning.

Segmental and suprasegmental features of speech are both affected by linguistic, paralinguistic and non-linguistic forces.

The main acoustic correlates of prosody (rhythm, intensity and fundamental frequency) are also correlates of paralinguistic and non-linguistic phenomena, particularly emotion.

SCHOOLS OF PROSODY

There have been many theoretical approaches to prosody. The earliest such schools dealt with the metrical structure of poetic verse

(eg. the ancient Greeks).

Often the British and American approaches to prosody are contrasted, but this dichotomy is a simplification of the diversity of theoretical and experimental perspectives.

British Schools

Crombie listed the following three British approaches to intonation:

- Syntactic approach
- Affective or attitudinal approach
- Discoursal approach

Crombie states that the British schools have the following elements in common:

- "Dividing the flow of speech into tone groups or tone units (tonality)"
- "Locating the syllables on which major movements of pitch occur (tonicity)"
- "Identifying the direction of pitch movements tone)"

British schools tend to focus on pitch contours or tunes whilst American schools tend to focus on pitch levels. Different tunes are associated with different meanings.

Central to British models of prosody is the idea of the "tone group".

A tone group is a sequence of speech dominated by prominent or accented word. The accented word is the focal point for the tonal characteristics of the tone group. It contains the strongest, most prominent syllable (usually its primary stressed syllable). The accented syllable, or rather the strongest syllable in the accented word, is often referred to as the nuclear syllable or the tonic syllable. A tone group can contain one or more rhythmic feet. Each foot is dominated by a stressed syllable. In English a foot starts with a stressed syllable and ends with the last unstressed syllable before the next stress.

As an example of a British school we will examine the approach of Michael Halliday and Systemic-Functional linguistics.

Halliday

"It is not enough to treat intonation systems as if they merely carried a set of emotional nuances... English intonation contrasts are grammatical"

In contrast, Pike, a founder of the American school said that intonation " is merely a shade of meaning... superimposed upon... intrinsic lexical meaning according to the attitude of the speaker".

A consequence of Halliday's view of intonation was that being a part of grammar it should be analysed in the same way as other grammatical systems. Halliday utilises the British concept of tunes which extend across a section of text. These tunes have a "nucleus" which is the "first (salient) syllable in the tonic foot".

Tonality, according to Halliday, is related to the number of tone groups in an utterance and each such tone group is seen as one "move" in a speech act. Tone is "... a complex pattern built out of a simple opposition between certain and uncertain polarity."

Halliday describes 5 simple and 2 compound primary tones for English. They are:

- Tone 1 - falling
- Tone 2 - high rising
- Tone 3 - low rising
- Tone 4 - falling-rising
- Tone 5 - rising-falling
- Tone 13 - falling plus low rising
- Tone 53 - rising-falling plus low rising

"If polarity is certain, the pitch of the tonic falls; if uncertain, it rises." Polarity refers to the truth of a statement ("true" or "false" in fact or in belief) or to whether something is "known" versus "unknown". From these tones and the idea of polarity, Halliday builds up a complex pattern of relationships between tone and meaning.

- *Tone* 1: falling tone - "polarity known... the unmarked realisation of a statement" (also a question with known polarity)
- *Tone* 2: rising tone - "polarity unknown... the unmarked realisation of a yes-no question"
- *Tone* 3: low rising - "not yet decided whether know or unknown... dependent on something else"
- *Tone* 4: falling-rising - "seems certain, but turns out not to be. It is associated with reservations and conditions"
- *Tone* 5: rising-falling - "seems uncertain, but turns out to be certain. It is used on strong, especially contradicting assertions... It often carries an implication of 'you ought to know that" (the above is from Halliday, 1985, 281-282)

Some examples:

- Tone 1 (falling) "That's a dog." - statement
- Tone 1 (falling) "Is Fido a dog?" - question with known polarity
- Tone 2 (rising) "Are you coming?" - I don't know if you are coming but want to know. cf. Tone 1 (falling) "Are you coming?" - this is a bit more like a command.
- Tone 3 (low-rising) "I think I'll come tomorrow." - but not really sure.
- Tone 4 (falling-rising) "Bill is coming if he's allowed." - conditional statement.
- Tone 5 (rising-falling) "You ought to know that."

TONE IN INTONATION AND LEXICAL TONE

The use of the word "tone" in some theories of intonation and prosody needs to be clarified.

This usage must not be confused with lexical tone in tone languages, where changing the pitch contour of a word changes its meaning.

For example, changing the tone on "ma" in Mandarin Chinese may change the meaning from "horse" to "mother". That is, changing the tone means that you have selected a different word.

Lexical tone in tone languages is usually attached to a single syllable.

Prosodic tone is attached to a higher level entity such as a tone group (a phrase or sentence characterised by a particular prosodic pattern). Occasionally a tone group might only consist of a single word, which might in turn be a single syllable, but very often it consists of more than one word.

AMERICAN SCHOOLS

American schools of prosody are often described as relying on a phonemic or levels approach to intonation. For example, Bloomfield referred to "differences of pitch... as secondary phonemes". (but note that Bloomfield, like the British, used pitch contours rather than pitch levels).

Pike used:

- Pitch heights to characterise intonation contours (contours are sequences of pitch height)
- A systematic approach to speaker attitude
- The interdependence of intonation, stress, quantity, tempo, rhythm and voice quality

(the above summary is after Chun(2002))

Pike utilised four levels of pitch because "four levels are enough to provide for the writing and distinguishing of all the contours which have differences of meaning so far discovered." "These four levels may, for convenience, be labeled extra-high, high, mid and low respectively..." (Pike, 1945). The ToBI framework for transcribing prosody (eg. Pierrehumbert and Beckman, Beckman et al. (2005)) is an intonation transcription system based on two relative levels (low and high). ToBI is particularly suited to phonetic analyses of prosody but increasingly it is used in studies of prosody and meaning.

The remainder of this topic will concentrate on the ToBI framework of Pierrehumbert, Beckman and others.

SENTENCE OR UTTERANCE PROSODY

Sentence-Stress or Accent

Some words sound more prominent — they 'stand out' to a greater extent than others.

The relative prominence of words depends very much on how the *intonation* is associated with the words, or with the text, of the utterance. Above all, the same string of words can be *accented*in different ways.

[marianna made the marmalade]

[marianna made the marmalade]

PROSODIC PHRASING

The same set of words can be broken up into *prosodic phrases* in different ways. At the boundaries between prosodic phrases we often hear a change in the rhythm of the speech or a pause.

[marianna] [made the marmalade]

INTONATION

The same set of words can be associated with any number of different *tunes* that are signaled by the rise and fall in pitch — there is always *one* tune for *each* prosodic phrase

[marianna made the marmalade?]

How do we Hear Accented Words

One of the main reasons why we hear certain accented words as prominent is because of*intonation*. Specifically, a speaker synchronises a unit of intonation known as a *pitch-accent* with the *vowel of the primary stressed syllable* of each word that is accented.

We represent this as follows:

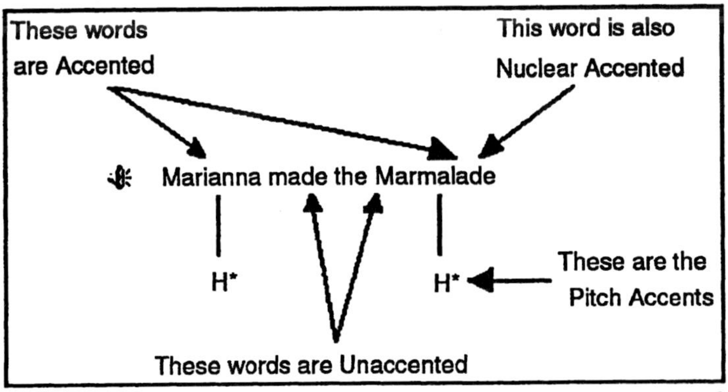

Another unit of sentence stress is known as the *nuclear accent*. The last accented word in any prosodic phrase is *nuclear accented*. (*Prosodic phrase* is still to be defined: assume that there's one prosodic phrase above that extends from the beginning to the end of the sentence).

Prosodic phrases

Every utterance consists of one or more prosodic phrases. In every prosodic phrase, there is one (and only one) nuclear accented word.

You can often hear if an utterance has more than one prosodic phrase because:

- You can sometimes hear a pause between intonational phrases
- A speaker 'slows down' at the end of a prosodic phrase which makes the last syllable a bit longer (known as phrase-final lengthening).
- There can be a marked change in pitch either at, or just before the end, of a prosodic phrase.

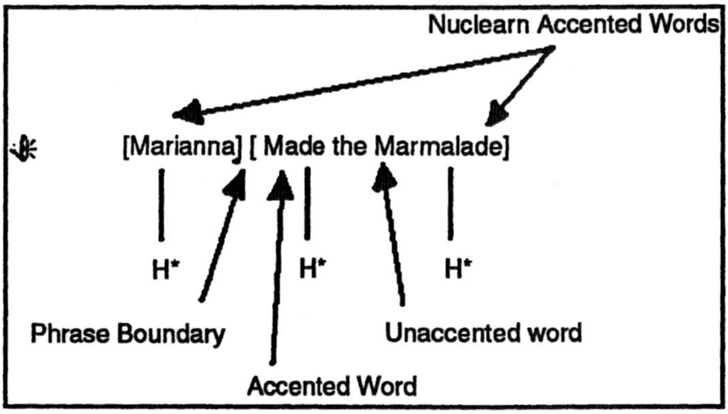

Two Example Prosodic Phrases

Amongst her friends she was considered beautiful
The museum hires musicians every evening

Intonation and Tunes

Speakers can select one of a number of tunes to be associated to each prosodic phrase.

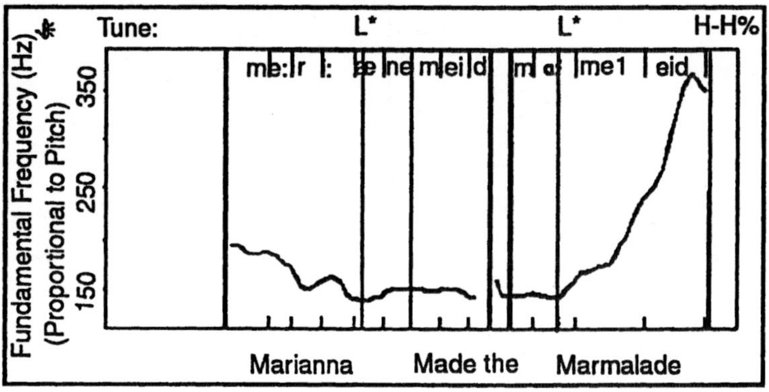

TheHE Anatomy of a Tune

A tune is composed of:

- pitch accents: H* or L*
- boundary tones: L-L%, L-H%, H-H%, H-L%

The association of tune and prosodic phrase:

- one pitch accent is associated to each accented word
- one boundary tone is associated to the end of each prosodic phrase

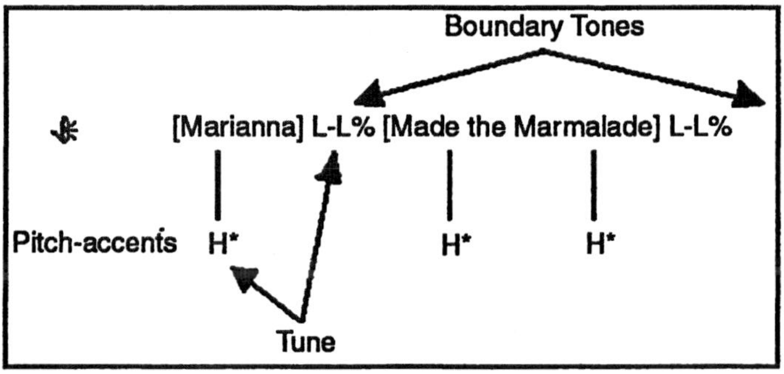

Pitch-Accents

H*	L*
There should be a pitch peak on, or near, the accented word's primary stressed vowel. Preceding consonant is voiced (e.g. 'bit')	There should be a pitch trough, on, or near, the accented word's primary stressed vowel
H* 	L* 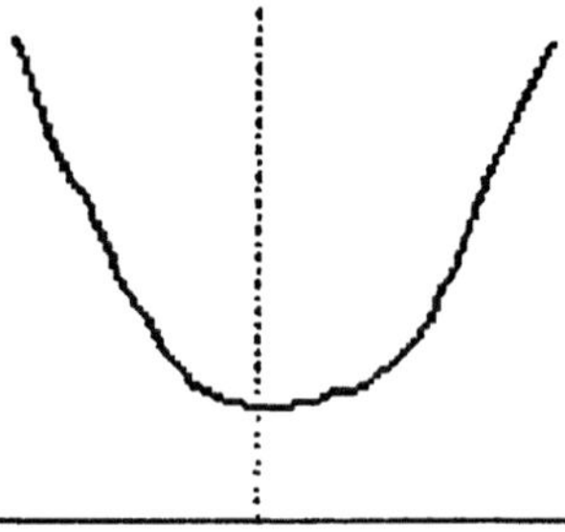
Sometimes this is labeled L+H* if there is a long rise to the peak	

Examples Of H* Tones

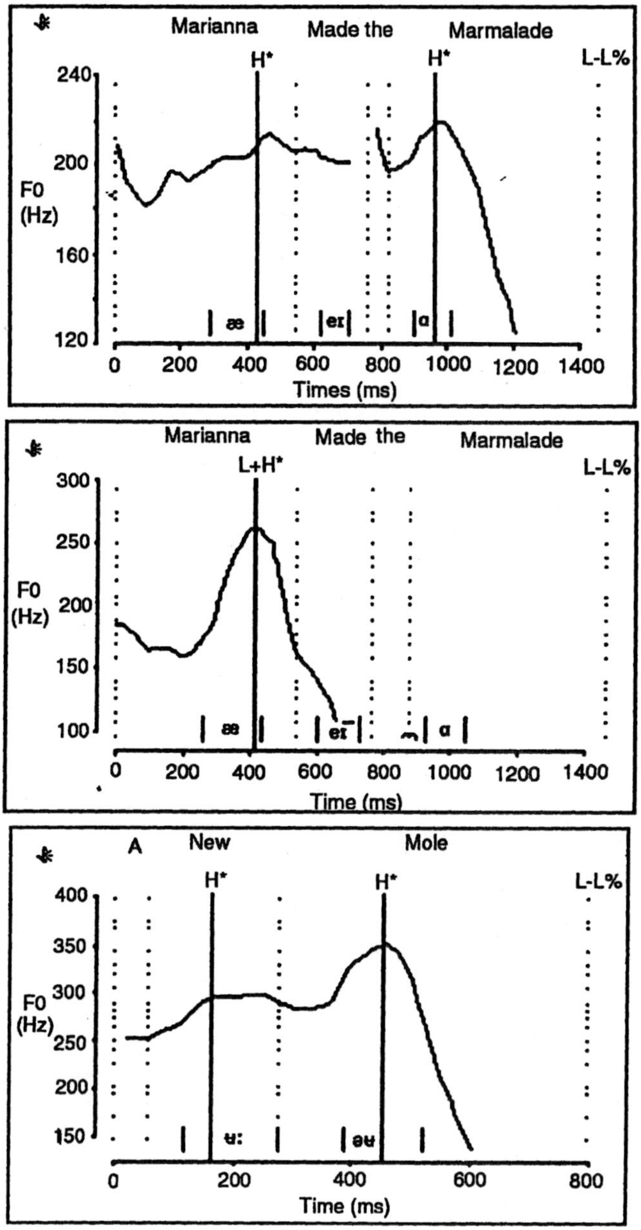

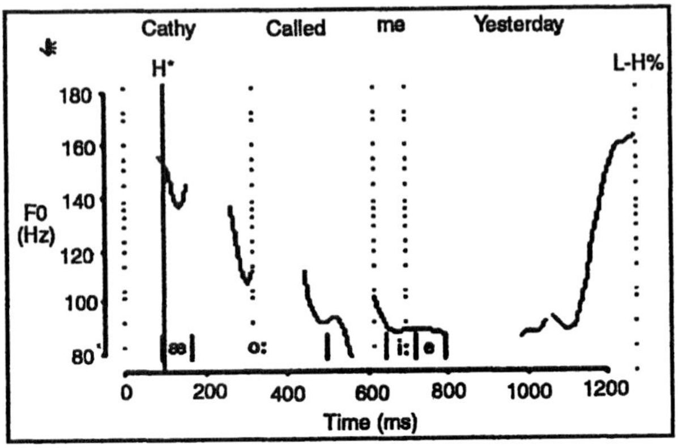

Examples of H* and L* Tones

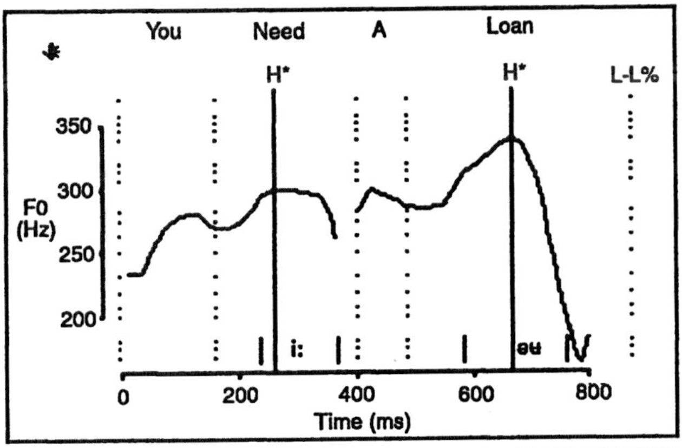

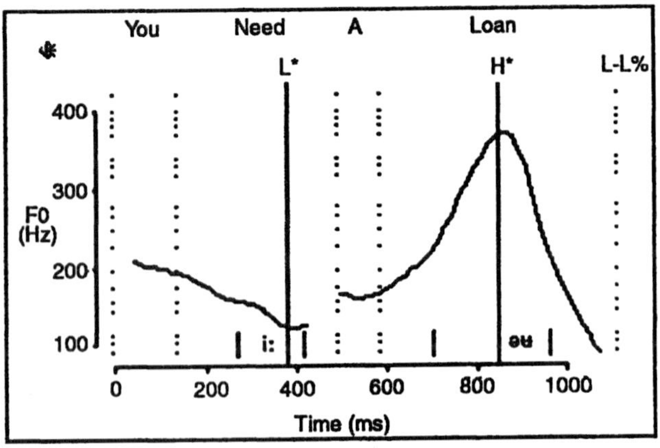

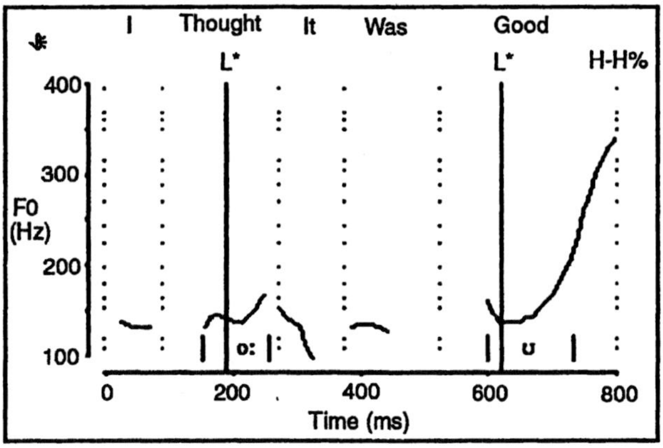

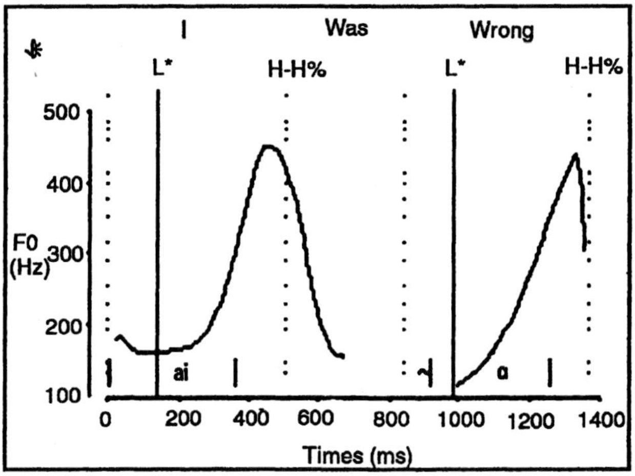

Boundary Tones

A boundary tone influences the pitch contour between the tone target of the nuclear accented word and the right boundary of the prosodic phrase,

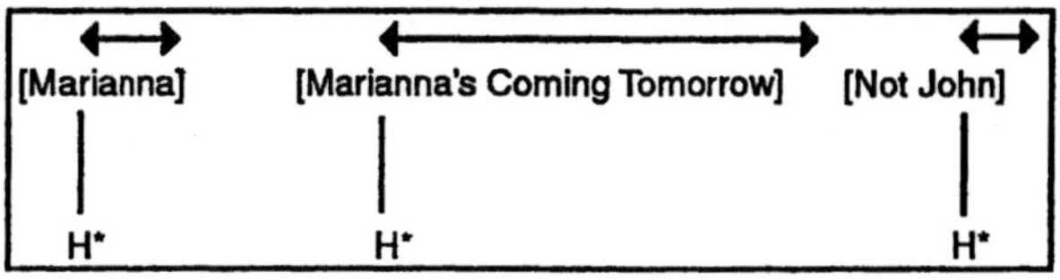

(the part of the pitch contour influenced by the boundary tone is shown by the horizontal line with arrows).

There are four kinds of boundary tones...

1. L-L% Boundary Tone

- L-L% The pitch ends at a low value at the end of the prosodic phrase. This boundary tone is common in 'neutral' statements.

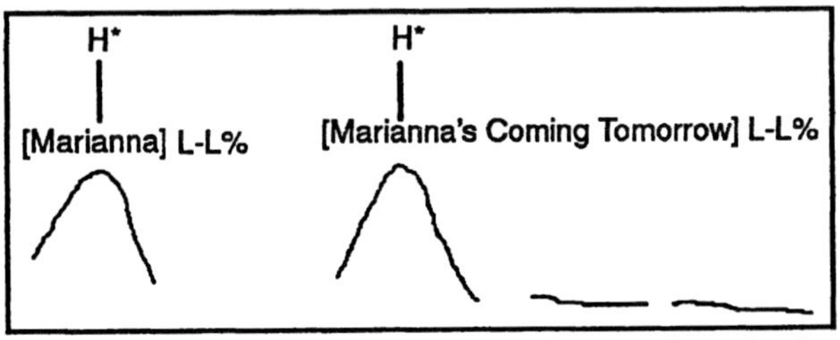

The L-L% boundary tone causes the pitch to be low after the tone target of the nuclear accented word; if there are only one or two syllables after the last H* tone target (left), the result is a fall in pitch; if many syllables follow the H* tone target, then the pitch falls as before, but then stays low to the end of the phrase (right).

2. H-H% Boundary Tone

- H-H% The pitch ends at a high value at the prosodic boundary
  "Yes-no" questions: "did you say Melbourne?"
  In many statements in Australian English (known as high-rising-terminals).

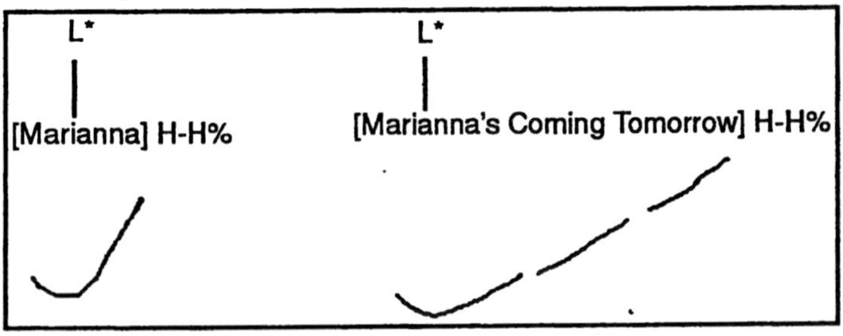

3. L-H% Boundary Tone

L-H% (continuation-rise)The pitch is low and then rises at the end of the prosodic phrase.

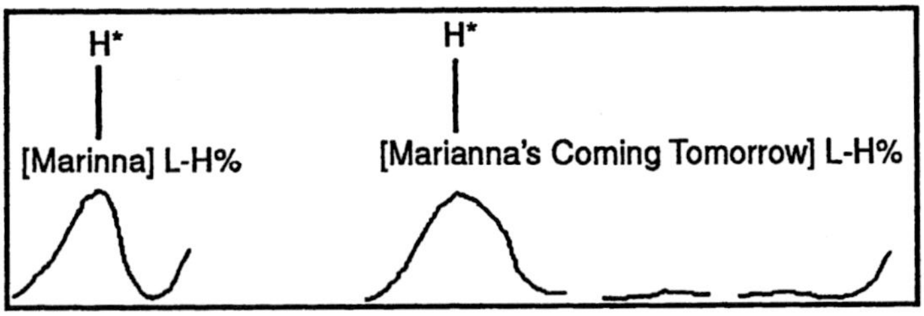

Some common usages of L-H%:

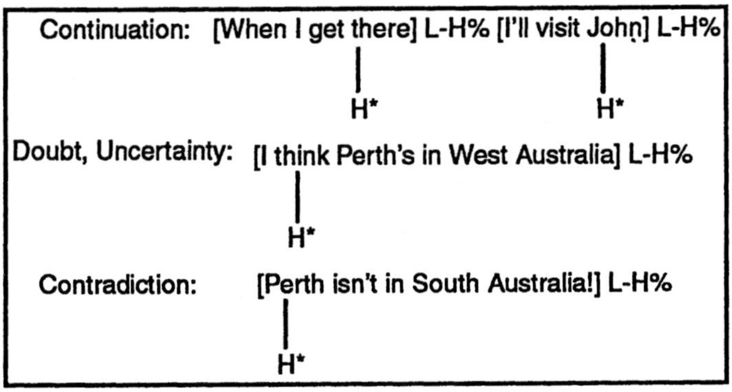

Examples of L-L% (1), H-H% (2), L-H% (3):

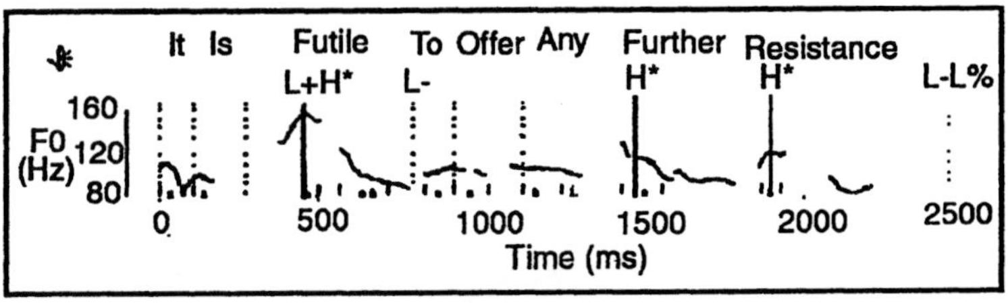

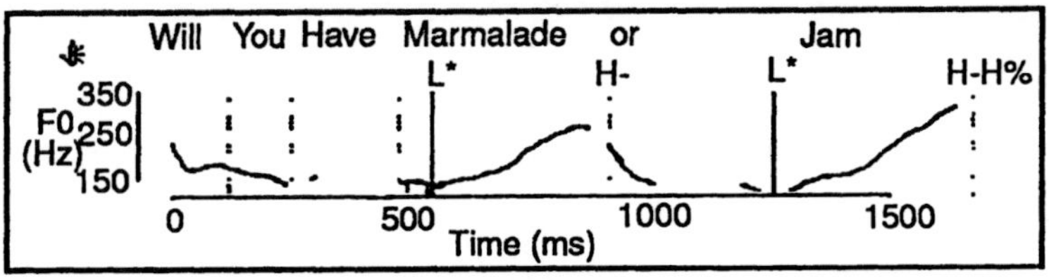

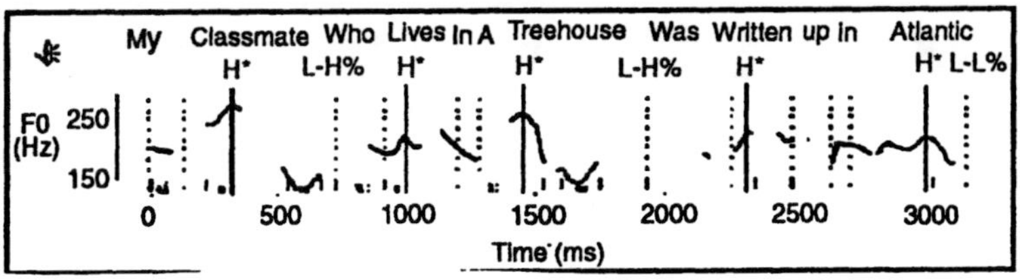

4. H-L% BoundaryTone

H-L% The pitch is high and then falls slightly at the end of the prosodic phrase.

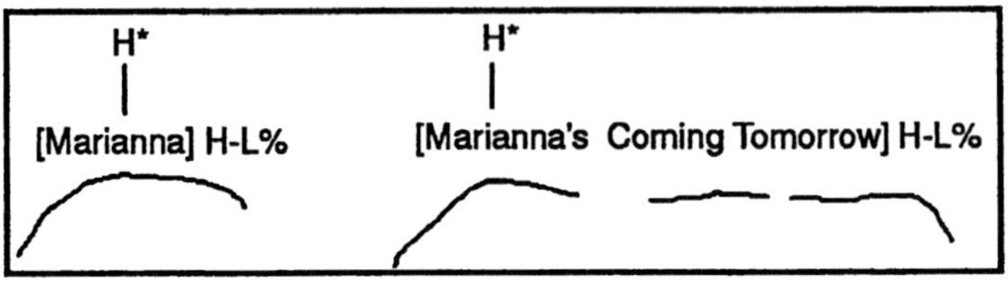

It is sometimes used in list recital to convey a somewhat disinterested tone

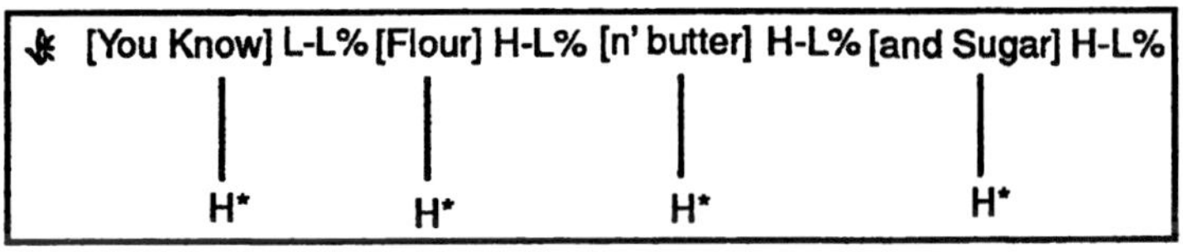

Pitch Contours and Boundary Tones

When the nuclear accented word is early in the prosodic phrase the pitch contour of a large part of the prosodic phrase is controlled by the boundary tone.

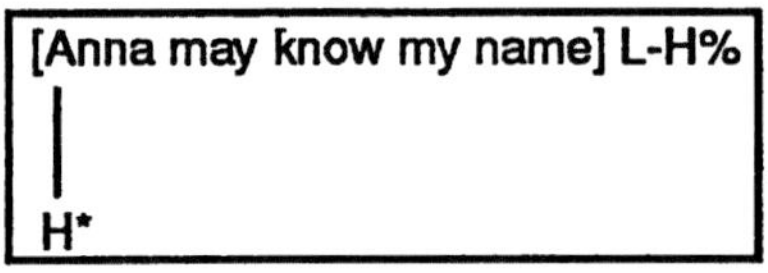

The pitch falls immediately after the /æ/ of 'Anna', then stays lows until the end of the phrase when it rises.

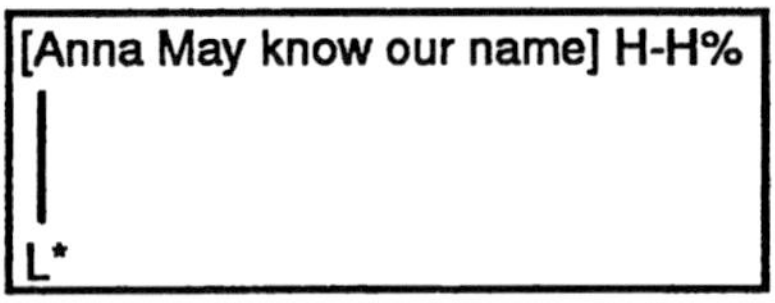

The pitch is low on the /æ/ of 'Anna', then rises continually to a high value at the end of the phrase.

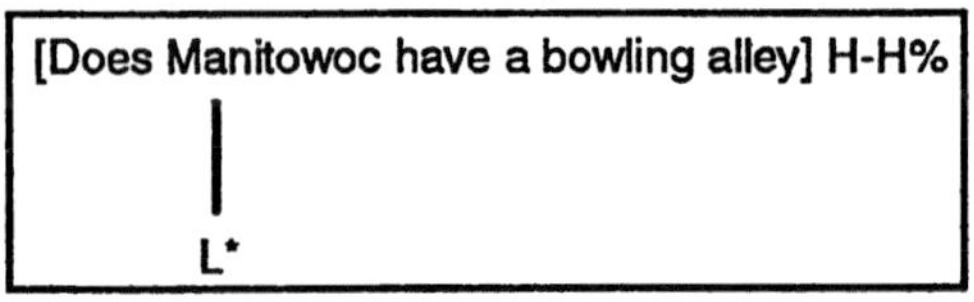

As above,

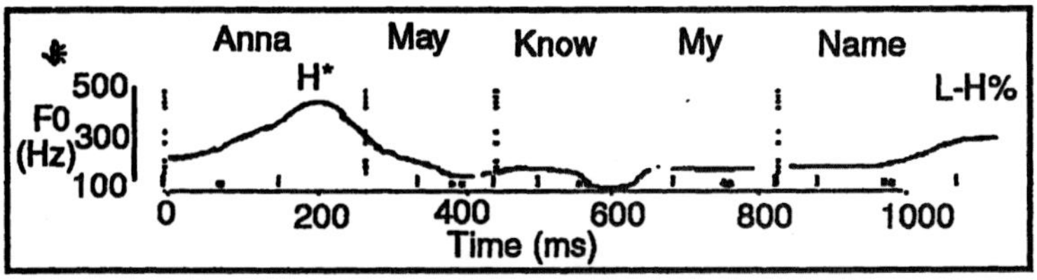

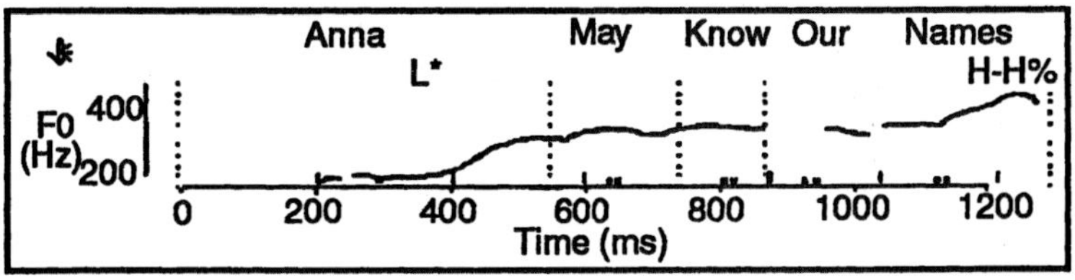

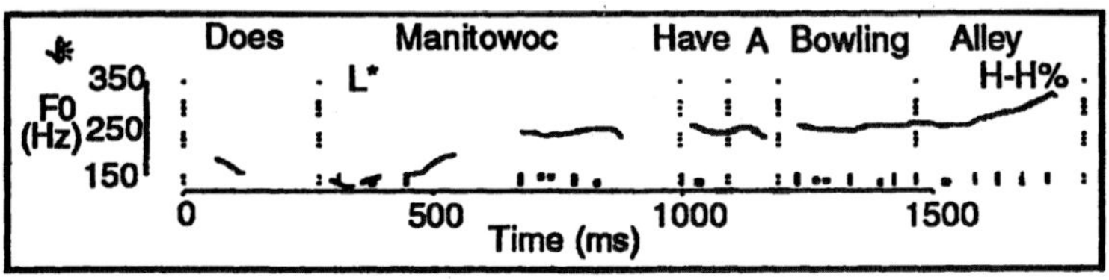

INTONATIONTRANSCRIBING WITH TOBI

Transcribing Intonation

The object of this tutorial is to introduce you to some of the main components of transcribing intonation in English.

There are three main parts to consider when transcribing intonation: dividing an utterance into one or more prosodic phrases; deciding which word is the nuclear accented word and which of the remaining words in the utterance are accented or unaccented; and finally assigning a tune, consists of one or more pitch accents and a boundary tone to each prosodic phrase.

Prosodic Phrases

Every utterance has one or more prosodic phrases (even if you say only a single word, that will still count as a prosodic phrase). Most of the examples with which you will be presented will consist of only a single prosodic phrase.

We can denote the boundaries of prosodic phrases with square brackets, thus:

[Peter saw Mary].

[Did you see Peter?]

[Peter!].

An example of an utterance that would almost certainly have to consist of two prosodic phrases is as follows:

[when I get to Sydney,][I'll go an visit John]

and in this example 'Sydney' would typically have a fall-rising (continuation-rise) intonational contour.

You can hear the boundaries between prosodic phrases because:

- This is where the speaker sometimes slows down
- You might hear an abrupt change in the pitch
- The last syllable of each prosodic phrase is typically quite long

Accented Words

Every prosodic phrase has to have at least one accented word and it may (and usually does) have unaccented words. So the next thing to try to do, after you have decided how many prosodic phrases there are, is to decide which of the words in each prosodic phrase are accented and which are unaccented. There are two main ways of doing this.

By listening to the utterance: accented words sound more prominent and are sometimes louder than unaccented ones. The greater prominence of accented words comes about partly because, all things being equal, they are often longer than unaccented words, and are acoustically higher in intensity. But the main reason is because there is a *pitch-accent* associated to each accented word which can produce quite dramatic pitch changes in the vicinity of the accented word's primary stressed syllable.

There are two main kinds of pitch accent. A H* (high-star) pitch accent which tends to produce a pitch peak. And an L* (low-star) pitch accent which produces a pitch trough.

For example, have a look at the pitch contour of 'marianna made the marmalade'. Both 'marianna' and 'marmalade' are accented whereas 'made' and 'the' are unaccented. Notice the pitch peaks on the primary stressed vowels of these words: on the [æ] of 'marianna' and the[Q] of 'marmalade'.

These pitch peaks are the acoustic consequences of aligning the H* pitch accents to these words (which makes them accented).

We can denote this as follows: Below shows a typical intonational contour for a 'yes-no' question (one that requires an answer of 'yes' or 'no'). In this case, we have two L* pitch accents on the same words and there is a pitch *trough* in their primary stressed vowels. So we would denote this as:

Nuclear Accented Word

The last accented word in any prosodic phrase is known as the *nuclear accented word* and it often sounds more prominent than other accented words in the same prosodic phrase. In both of the above examples, 'marmalade' is the nuclear accented word. One of the reasons why the nuclear accented word is particularly salient is because there is very often such a dramatic change in pitch from the pitch accent with which it is associated to the boundary tones discussed in the next section.

Sometimes the nuclear accented words can occur early in the prosodic phrase, which often has the effect of marking a word as especially prominent. An example is sentence 3 (compare its pitch contour with sentence 1) in which there is an H* pitch accent on the first word, then a fall in pitch due to the boundary tones. But note that there is no other word which is marked by a pitch accent. We would represent the pitch-accent of 3 as: from which we can immediately see that 'Marianna' is the nuclear accented word and all other words are unaccented (there could not be any other accented words since the nuclear accented word is always the last accented word in the prosodic phrase; therefore, if the nuclear accented word comes first, then all following words in the same prosodic phrase must necessarily be unaccented).

Boundary Tones

These are the other part of the tune and they are associated with the right edge of the prosodic phrase (so we write them after the] boundary). In conjunction with the tone target of the nuclear accented word, they are responsible for perhaps the most salient part of the intonational contour. We will consider four kinds. In all cases, they affect a particular interval of intonation: from the pitch accent of the nuclear accented word to the end of the prosodic phrase. Here are the four kinds.

L-L% (Low) Boundary Tone

This is a common in 'neutral' declarative sentences. The L-L% boundary tone causes the intonation to be low at the end of prosodic phrase. Therefore, the intonation will fall sharply from the H* pitch accent of the nuclear accented word to the end of the prosodic phrase. (You very rarely get tunes which have an L* nuclear accented word in an L-L% phrase). A typical example of an L-L% boundary is in the first sentence considered earlier (sentence 1). It is very clear to see how the pitch falls from the [Q] of 'marmalade' through the rest of the word to the end of the phrase.

H-H% (High) Boundary Tone

This is very common in 'yes-no' questions. It is also a common feature of Australian English declaratives and is known as the *high-rising-terminal*. It causes the pitch to end high at the phrase boundary and it very often co-occurs with an L* nuclear accented word. As a result, the pitch rises dramatically from the nuclear accented word's pitch accent to the end of the phrase. A good example of this is the yes-no question in .

L-H% Boundary Tone

This is known as a *continuation rise*. It can occur in a number of contexts, but it often gives the impression that the speaker still has something left to say. For example, the first phrase of [When I get to Sydney], [I'll go and visit John] would very often have an L-H% type of boundary tone. The effect on the pitch contour is as follows: first it will drop to a low value and then it will rise towards the end of the prosodic phrase. Therefore, if the pitch accent of the nuclear accented word is

H* (as it very often is in this context), the pitch contour over this interval firstly falls to a low value, and then typically stays low until the end of the prosodic phrase where it rises (but not as much as in an H-H% phrase). So over this interval, the pitch goes down and then up again. A good example of this boundary tone is [4] Amelia visited Mary yesterday. This prosodic phrase has two accented words, 'Amelia' and 'Mary' and so 'Mary' is the nuclear accented word. Notice how the pitch falls on 'Mary', then stays low over the first part of 'yesterday', and then rises at the end of the prosodic phrase.

We can annotate this as follows: So in summary, the shape of the pitch contour from 'Mary' to the end of the phrase is falling and then rising.

H-L% Boundary Tone

This is perhaps the least common boundary tone. It sometimes occurs in a somewhat bored recital of lists, and can generally lend a 'disinterested tone' to the utterance. The effect on the pitch contour is as follows: after the pitch accent of the nuclear accented word, the pitch stays quite high and then falls at the end of the prosodic phrase (but not as dramatically as in an L-L% phrase).

Early Placement of Nuclear Accented Words

When the nuclear accented word occurs early in the prosodic phrase, the relationship between the boundary tone and the pitch contour is the same: the boundary tone controls the shape of the pitch contour between the pitch accent of the nuclear accented word and the end of the prosodic phrase. Therefore, when the nuclear accented word occurs early in an L-L% phrase, the pitch contour falls immediately after the nuclear accented word and then stays low until the end of the prosodic phrase - as in the earlier example of 3., which was:

An example of an early nuclear accent placement in an H-H% is, Anna may know our names?: So in this case, the H-H% boundary tone controls the shape of the entire pitch contour from the L* low tone to the end of the phrase, causing it to rise continuously from the pitch trough (associated with the L*) to the end of the prosodic phrase. When the nuclear accented word occurs early in an L-H% phrase, the pitch stays low throughout almost the entire remainder of the prosodic phrase after the nuclear accented word and then only rises at the end of the phrase. An example of this is Anna may know my name with an H* pitch accent on 'Anna'. In this case the boundary tone causes the pitch contour stay low after 'Anna' and it only rises again at the end of the prosodic phrase.

DRAWING STYLISED F0 CONTOURS FROM TOBI TRANSCRIPTIONS

In the final exam students might be asked to do one (or both) of the following two tasks:

1. Given an intonation (F0) contour provide a ToBI transcription
2. Draw an intonation (F0) contour given a ToBI transcription

ToBI transcription from an F0 contour

Real intonation (F0) contours vary greatly and often the position of the accented words are not visually clear without simultaneous recourse to an auditory analysis. ToBI transcription is always done with the aid of a fundamental frequency (F0) contour and simultaneous auditory analysis.

Clearly, this won't be possible in the final exam so the provided contours will be as clear as possible (i.e. we will avoid ambiguous F0 patterns). For example, you will be given a real (or more likely a simplified, abstracted) F0 contour of a short phrase aligned with the words of that phrase. The accented word will be aligned with the main peak or dip and the rest of the words will be placed over the remainder of the contour. You will need to determine what the ToBI transcription of the phrase is, by writing the accent's tone and the boundary tone for that phrase.

This task is essentially the inverse of the next task.

Draw an F0 (pitch) Contour From a ToBI Transcription

In this case you will be given a phrase, will be told which

word takes the accent, and will be given its ToBI transcription (e.g. "John bit the dog". "John" is accented. ToBI transcription is L+H* L-H%) You will need to draw the contour (from the attached contours, or additional similar ones that can be deduced from these patterns) and place the accent word over the main peak or dip. This example is not found in the accompanying drawings but its pattern can be inferred from H* L-H% and from L+H* L-L% (i.e. by taking the start of one diagram and the end of the other).

Some Typical F0 Patterns

- Accents: H* rises moderately from the preceding F0 value.
  L* falls moderately from the preceding F0 value
  L+H* rises steeply from a much lower preceding F0 value.
  H+L* falls steeply from a much higher preceding F0 value.
- Boundary Tones: L-L% falls immediately after the accent (if it isn't already low for a L*) and stays there to the end.
  L-H% falls immediately after the accent (if it isn't already low for a L*) but rises at the end.
  H-H% rises immediately after the accent (if it isn't already high for a H*) and stays there to the end.
  H-L% rises immediately after the accent (if it isn't already high for a H*) but falls at the end.
  The above is greatly simplified but its a helpful way to get used to what to expect in intonation transcription. The ability to deal with ambiguous or unclear contours can only come with practice.

INTERLANGUAGE PHONOLOGY

Pronunciation errors have long been thought to be caused by the transfer of phonological aspects from the L1 to the L2. While a significant portion of errors may be attributed to *interlanguage transfer* (2.1) according to Selinker, inter and intra speaker variables exist which may be attributed to the other recognised items listed (2.2 to 2.9) below. Section (2.10) reviews a hierarchy *significant* pronunciation errors proposed by Jenkins.

INTERLANGUAGE TRANSFER

When a language learner attempts to produce an L2 sound their relative success at approaching the target is reliant on their ability to disassociate their L2 utterance from their repertoire of L1 phonemes and allophones. Disassociation is often necessary because two languages may contain sounds which seem to be the same but are produced by differing articulatory motions. They are therefore acoustically different and may be perceived to be divergent from the target by the listener.

While it is possible for adult speakers to learn to produce acoustically acceptable approximations of targets such as the troublesome /l/ and /r/ distinction over time the level of success varies between individual speakers. It is a common remark that the more successful producers of near-native sounding pronunciation are *rare, gifted* or *talented*. Their success could be more reasonably attributed to their ability to disassociate phonological aspects of the L1 and L2 and thus minimise the transfer of phonological features from one language to the other. Assumptions regarding the variable success of learners' L2 also concern the relative difficulty different *nationalities* encounter in their production of acceptable English pronunciation.

As discussed previously, a very useful observation to consider in the contrastive analysis of various language groups and their L2 English production is that nationalities with a vastly different phonetic inventory to that of English, often find it easier to learn to produce an acceptable phonetic target in the L2 than a nationality whose L1 contains contrasting sounds (Flege's Speech learning model 1987, 1995). For example, Japanese students have an advantage over Koreans when it comes to the production of English vowels. As Japanese only contains five simple monophthongal vowels to Korean's ten, Japanese English speakers only have five vowels to interfere with the twelve monophthongs present in (Australian) English.

Therefore, it may be assumed that it is a simpler task to learn totally foreign sounds than sounds which bear a resemblance to sounds found in the L1.

Furthermore, fossilised errors, which are attributable to the negative transfer of L1 to L2, may more easily be *unlearnt* when they are of the foreign rather than the familiar variety. For example, English /v/, which is totally foreign to Korean and often approximated by /b/, is less of a problem to *unlearn* than the negatively transferred Korean high front vowel /i/ which typically replaces the similar but durationally longer English high front vowel /iĐ/.

Each language has its own pattern relating to the length of vowels. Languages vary widely as to*whether* and how *much* vowel duration is affected by the following consonant. English has extremely exaggerated pre-consonantal vowel duration when preceding voiced consonants. (Takahashi, 1987). There are however some *universal* (inter-lingual) consistencies in vowel length. Low vowels are always longer than high vowels, and back vowels tend to be longer than front vowels. For this reason vowel duration is often regarded to be a *universal*. More of this phenomenon of universals and their significance to interlanguage transfer is discussed.

PHONOLOGICAL UNIVERSALS

Phonological Universals are phonological patterns which are common to all known languages. They are also referred to as being *unmarked*, (common and regularly occurring phenomena), or inversely, as being *marked* (distinctive and unique phenomena). In English for example, /s/ is unmarked and /θ/ is marked. Another notion, *implicational universals*, is that the presence of a marked segment /θ/ in a language implies the presence of an unmarked segment /s/, but the reverse is not true.

Many studies have been undertaken to determine the degree of difficulty in acquisition of the various elements of L2 phonology based on markedness theory of universals.

Takahashi concluded from an analysis of their studies: "Those less *marked* phonetic or phonological characteristics of L1 are harder to unlearn. That is, those characteristics which are acquired early in L1 acquisition and are important (yet commonly occurring) characteristics of L1 are easily carried over in the production of the L2 phonological system and remain persistently as the L2 learner's foreign accent." The development of an absolute hierarchy of markedness in and between languages is an almost impossible task given the enormous number and diversity of languages. Markedness theory has however contributed to a general understanding of the tendencies of simplification adopted by L2 learners. Some of these are outlined below. In all languages there appears to be a universal preference for the open CV syllable. A study by Kozhevnikov and Chistovich showed that in a stressful situation, speakers tended to revert to very simple CV patterns of pronunciation in their own native language.

Tarone has argued that: "the simple open syllable may be a universal articulatory and perceptual unit; that is, that the articulators tend to operate in basic CV programmes in all languages, and the various languages simply elaborate upon this programme by adding various combinations of initial and final consonants."

From this it could be hypothesised that in interlanguage transfer, first languages with a greater propensity towards open syllables will have a greater degree of difficulty in assimilating the syllable structure of English. English has a greater tendency to stray from open syllable structure than Korean and a far greater tendency for this than the Japanese language, which is essentially built upon open syllables. Therefore, the syllable structure of English is more problematical for Japanese than for Koreans.

Other phonological universal tendencies include devoicing of word-final obstruents and affrication of the word-final alveolar fricative /s/.

AVOIDANCE

Avoidance is a general tendency for learners to avoid

those aspects of production that they know to be problematic for them. See Schachter. Avoidance strategies may be employed at the grammatical as well as at the phonemic level. At the grammatical level an article (a/an, the) may be left out of the utterance when the student suspects an article is necessary and yet chooses to avoid using one rather than running the risk of selecting the wrong one. The above newspaper clipping is a clear example of a grammatical avoidance strategy. The source of misperception of the Korean speaker's message could easily be misdiagnosed as a deviance from the L2 target phonemes /æ/ and /p/. However, any English language teacher worth their salt would tell you that L2 learners of English often avoid articles because the internalisation of the rules for correct article use are almost an impossibility. In the above story (if the quotation is accurate) the Korean speaker has avoided the indefinite article *an* and has produced the grammatical utterance "Yes, I need adaptor" *not* "Yes I need *a dapter*." The speaker may have mispronounced /æ/ as something resembling /R/ but this is unlikely, the Korean transfer strategy would produce something closer to /ɛ/ or /ʌ/. However, /p/ could easily be misperceived as /k/ over the telephone's narrow bandwidth. Yet, it is unlikely that *redundancy* would fail to intervene. The listener could have searched their mental lexicon for an appropriate word candidate (or asked for clarification) if the speaker had used the article and said *I need a dopter*. So clearly the salient source of this misunderstanding is grammatical avoidance, not phonemic error.

At the phonemic level a typical example of avoidance is the avoidance of using words which contain *difficult to pronounce* phonemes such as /z/ for Koreans. Therefore, the speaker may give a false impression of the extent of their phonemic pronunciation errors by avoiding the use of words such as *zoo*.

OVER-GENERALISATION AND OVER-ELABORATION

Over- generalisation is described by Richards as the

application of a newly learnt target language rule to an inappropriate form or context. For example, pitch, duration and intensity as features of stress being used too often to highlight every content word in an utterance.

Over-elaboration is usually caused by exposure to language acquisition strategies that are heavily reliant on reading and writing, to the detriment of speaking. In an attempt to produce accurate target language utterances, the learner produces un-native like stilted and formal speech which may be syntactically accurate but unnatural.

HYPER CORRECTION OR OVER COMPENSATION

This phenomenon can be found to occur after students have become aware of a negative transfer effect and arises from the strategy they employ to deal with this. See Wardhaugh. For example, Japanese does not posses the CV /siĐ/ but does contain the CV /ʃiĐ/ (she), so the expected negative transfer effect is the production of /ʃiĐ/ (she) for the word *see*. A Japanese English learner may realise that the sounds /s/ and /ʃ/ must be distinguished before the vowel /iĐ/ in the L2 but has not learnt exactly when to do this. The learner therefore acquires the notion of /ʃ/ + /iĐ/ is not allowed in English and applies it even when it is necessary in the production of the word *she*. Thus the learner overcompensates and produces/siĐ/ instead of /ʃiĐ/.

ELISION AND EPENTHESIS

Elision is the non-articulation of a sound and epenthesis is the addition of a sound to a word in the L2. Both are a negative transfer effect of phonotactic constraints in the L1.

STYLISTIC VARIATION

Variations in style of speech occur according to psycholinguistic factors such as the situation, the context, the addressee(s) and the location. In the gathering of speech data, factors which may effect the authenticity of the data are: the self consciousness felt by the subject and the pressure to perform in the situation of a studio recording; unfamiliarity with the context or lexis of the test sentences; the pressure to achieve a 'good result' for the addressee (the tester); and the artificial environment and discomforts associated with remaining still in a recording studio.

LETTER TO SOUND RULE CONFUSION

Learners of English, whose L1 contains a phonemic orthography, often learn to speak English through reading and writing and consequently attempt to interpret English pronunciation from the orthography. The inconsistent letter to sound rules of English lexis may result in mispronunciation, not because of an inability to produce the phonemes, but due to the interference of spelling.

THE DEVELOPMENTAL MODEL

This model of language acquisition suggests that there are significant parallels between the replacement strategies employed by infant L1 learners of English and infant - adult L2 learners of English. Various studies across a variety of nationalities of L2 English learners have revealed replacement strategies for the production of new phones in L2 which are similar to the substitution strategies found in the L1 speech of infants. For example, in German speaking children Wode found that retroflex [{] is first replaced by /w/ which is the same substitution which occurs in the speech of L1 infant speakers of English. In a study of adult L2 acquisition Flege and Davidian found that Chinese, Spanish and Polish speakers showed two developmental processes, word final stop deletion and devoicing, which are typically found in the speech of L1 English speaking infants. This model therefore suggests there is a hierarchy for substitution of new phonemes (consonants) which is sequential and consistent (perhaps universal) across all languages

SIGNIFICANT ERRORS: CURRENT VIEWS

In an issue of *Speak Out!* Jennifer Jenkins outlines the need for a change in pronunciation modification priorities from systems based on a *native model* of pronunciation towards a system that modifies the errors which impede communication across an *international context*. The motivation for this new system of priorities stems from the assumption that non-native speakers will spend more time speaking to other non-native speakers of English, than to native speakers owing to the fact that there are now far more non-native speakers of English in the world than native speakers. This is particularly the case for EFL learners who usually return to their own countries after studying abroad.

Jenkins' list of priorities was built upon the work of Jenner who sought to establish a*common core* of English phonology:

"Jenner recently advocated the need to "establish what all native speakers of all varieties (of English) have in common which enables them to communicate effectively with native speakers of other varieties other than their own."

Jenkins has adapted Jenner's list of priorities from a list designed to "offer the learner a guarantee of intelligibility and acceptability to native speakers anywhere in the world" to a list of priorities which also takes the listener intelligibility of non-native speakers into account. The following is a summary of her list of nine significant aspects of pronunciation to be focused on for pronunciation error elimination:

a) Vowel quantity

Jenkins believes that because the *extra long* vowels of English vary in length from one NS to another, *"there is little common ground between them. Provided the learner is consistent in use, quality is unlikely to affect intelligibility greatly"*. I disagree with this generalisation and maintain that the length contrast of /iÐ/ versus /j/ being phonemic in English and phonetic in Korean causes a negative transfer effect which is compounded rather than assisted by a NNS to NNS interaction.

b) Diphthongs

Diphthong length but not quality is essential to intelligibility as diphthong quality varies between groups of NS without a great loss intelligibility, length however is more critical. Jenkins herself admits that future research into diphthongs may reverse this decision.

c) Consonant Conflations Except for those Involving /θ/ and /ð/

Jenkins' claims that Gimson has demonstrated consonants tend to be more essential to intelligibility than vowels (no citation was given and no source has been found). Jenkins agrees with this view with the exception of /θ/ and /ð/. She believes the conflations (substitutions) of these sounds with /t/ and /d/ or /s/ and /z/ respectively are common to all NNS varieties and for this reason do not significantly impede intelligibility between NNSs and contextual clues may aid intelligibility in NNS/NS interaction. Gimson and Cruttenden assert the opposite by stating that for minimal intelligibility it is not acceptable to replace /θ/ and /ð/ with dental aspirated /t°/ and /d°. However some relaxation of the dental /ð/ is allowable in weak positions such as in the case of the following /s/ or /z/, e.g., in "What's the time?"

d) Phonetic realizations

The majority of phonetic realisations in the L1, which are transferred to the L2, do not interfere with intelligibility and are merely perceived as characteristics of a foreign accent. Other phonetic transfers do interfere however and may lead to unintelligibility. Jenkins mentions however that there are sometimes alternate pronunciations which may be taught that are acceptable even to native speakers. "Adam Brown recommends ignoring and even teaching for productive use vocalic /Š/ for dark [k] post-vocalically and syllabically in words such as *milk, middle* and*full,* since these are apparently easier for NNSs to produce and are fast becoming incorporated into NS varieties such as Estuary English".

e) Consonant Cluster Simplification (and Consonant Sequencing Restrictions)

Many L1 languages have more phonotactic restrictions on consonants than English does. The predominance of open (CV) syllables in languages other than English as well as restrictions on the position consonants may take within the word are negatively transferable to English. The resulting production is either epenthesis (vowel addition) or omission (consonant deletion). Jenkins believes that where learners use the strategy of epenthesis, intelligibility is rarely effected, since listeners are able to recover the original form, e.g. Japanese [pYrYdŒktoÐ] for *product*. However, consonant deletion causes considerable problems for NNS listeners in particular, since the target form is not recoverable from the output, eg. Taiwanese /pRdŒk/ for *product*.

f) Word Stress

Dalton and Seidlhofer have shown that NS listeners identify words on the basis of their stress patterns, first picking out the stressed syllable and then searching their mental lexicons on the basis of this syllable, judging possible candidates according to how well they fit the unstressed syllables on either side of it. Jenkins asserts that this is more of a problem for NS listeners than for NNS listeners, assuming that NNSs listen more for contextual cues when differentiating similar nouns and verbs such as /Θr[kTd/ and /rYΘkTd/, than stress patterns.

g) Prominence and Weak Forms

Jenkins suggests that failure to produce weak forms represents more of a threat to intelligibility for NS listeners than for NNS listeners, mainly because the ears of NSs are not attuned to this. Learners are likely to find unreduced syllables easier to interpret when speaking amongst each other. Therefore, they are reluctant to attempt reduction in their own utterances. Perhaps it is therefore advisable to abandon attempts to teach weak forms productively and focus on recognition alone in the speech of NSs, and on prominence for NNS production.

h) Tone groups

The tone unit is the basic unit of dividing up the stream

of speech in English. In some L1s the utterances are longer between pauses. When this strategy is transferred to English the listener is deprived of much needed time to process information. It also may result in the breaking up of speech in unexpected places.

i) Nuclear/contrastive stress but not tone

In many L1s, if there is anything comparable to the English system of nuclear stress, it tends to fall on the last word of a group of words (or on the first word in Korean). When this is transferred to the L2 the main stress may fall on unimportant grammatical words (prepositions, articles, etc) instead of function words (nouns, adjectives, verbs and adverbs). When the learner's L1 uses syntactic instead of intonational means to indicate contrastive stress, prominence may be neglected by the speaker. Jenkins' studies have revealed that learners *"very quickly acquire receptive competence in contrastive stress, but they take considerably longer to acquire nuclear stress productively"*. This is not an issue for Korean L2 utterances as prominence is also a feature of the L1. Jenkins' understanding of intonation is limited to anecdotal evidence so a more thorough contrastive acoustic analysis should reveal more significant negative transfer effects.

PRONUNCIATION PEDAGOGY

PRONUNCIATION AND THE DEVELOPMENT OF LANGUAGE ACQUISITION

The teaching of pronunciation has been at-odds with the teaching of grammar and vocabulary ever since it was first studied systematically shortly before the beginning of the twentieth century. In the time that has passed since the acceptance of pronunciation as a contributing factor to language acquisition, it has come in and out of fashion as various progressive movements in language acquisition have prevailed.

An *Intuitive-imitative approach.* This approach assumes that a student's ability to listen to and imitate the rhythms and sounds of the target language will lead to the development of an acceptable threshold of pronunciation without the intervention of any explicit information. The invention of the (recently much maligned) language lab and the audio-lingual method contributed to the support of this approach in the 60's, 70's and right up into the 80's. Indeed, many contemporary second language practitioners still hold to this view but research is needed to ascertain if their beliefs have any foundation.

An *analytic-linguistic approach*. This approach recognises the importance of an explicit intervention of pronunciation pedagogy in language acquisition. Developments in the fields of phonetics and phonology from the latter half of the century are drawn upon and often "watered down" for use in the language classroom. Pedagogical aids such as the phonemic chart, articulatory descriptions, explanations of the form and function of prosody and practical exercises such as minimal pair drills and rhythmic chants form the basis of an explicit programme of accent modification.

Korean language learners are usually not exposed to an explicit method of pronunciation instruction until they venture from high school into a TESOL classroom and have exposure to a native speaking teacher who is skilled in pronunciation pedagogy. Even now the majority of these students still learn English without actually speaking it. In their pre-adolescent and adolescent years when exposure to a native model would most benefit their acquisition of pronunciation, Korean students learn by *Grammar Translation* and *reading-based approaches*. These methods of language instruction will not be treated in the following discussion of the historical development of language acquisition models because they are not concerned with oral communication of the target language and are therefore not concerned with pronunciation.

The Direct Method

This method of language instruction, which gained acceptance in the late 1800's, was formed from observations of children attaining their first language. Students would imitate a model of the target language that was spoken by the teacher (and later by recordings) and attempt to approximate the model through constant repetition. Later models that were built on this approach include Asher's *Total Physical Response* and Krashen and Terrell's *Natural Approach.* The methodology of these models consists of intensive listening comprehension, which persist for an extended period before any speaking is allowed.

Proponents of these naturalistic methods maintain that: "the initial focus on listening without pressure to speak gives the learners the opportunity to internalise the target sound system. When learners do speak later on, their pronunciation is supposedly quite good despite never having received explicit pronunciation instruction."

The Reform Movement

In the 1890's the developers of the International Phonetic Alphabet (IPA), Henry Sweet, Wilhelm ViΛtor and Paul Passy, led a movement in language teaching that was generally known as the*Reform Movement*. These phoneticians did much to influence the teaching of pronunciation with their contribution to the development of a system for describing and analysing the sound systems of languages and by advocating the following guidelines:

- The spoken form of a language is primary and should be taught first
- The findings of phonetics should be applied to language teaching
- Teachers must have solid training in phonetics
- Learners should be given phonetic training to establish good speech habits

Audiolinguism and the Oral Approach

The contribution of the latter analytic linguistic approach to pronunciation pedagogy led to the next noticeable movement in the 1940's and 1950's. In the United States *Audiolinguism* and in Britain the *Oral approach* were two methodologies that were built upon the explicit instruction of phonological aspects of language. These two methods emulated the *Direct Method* by relying on a recording or the teacher to model the target language followed by the students' repetition of that language. However, the teacher also drew from their knowledge of phonetics and for the first time used simplified charts of the IPA and of articulatory models in the classroom. Also introduced was the practice of using minimal pairs for listening practice and oral production.

The Cognitive Approach

The 1960's was the decade which was to have a profound destabilising effect on the teaching of pronunciation. An influential new movement, *Transformational-generative grammar*, (Chomsky 1965) asserted that language was essentially rule-governed behaviour and not habitually learnt. This view, which found widespread acceptance in English language teaching circles, de-emphasised the role of pronunciation in language acquisition pedagogy in favour of grammar and vocabulary because: "its advocates argued,

- Native-like pronunciation was an unrealistic objective and could not be achieved
- Time would be better spent on teaching more learnable items, such as grammatical structures and words. "

The Silent Way

In the early 1970's pronunciation returned to favour with the development of the *Silent Way*. In this methodology (which is still in practice in the U.S.A) segmentals as well as suprasegmentals are highlighted from the very beginning of instruction. As the name suggests, teacher talk in this method is kept to a minimum. Instead of complicated articulatory and phonetic explanations the teacher indicates through gestures what the students should do. Teachers hold up fingers to indicate the number of syllables in a word, tap out rhythmic patterns and model the place and manner of articulation with their own lips and throat or with a *hand puppet* of the tongue and oral cavity. Also central to the Silent Way are visual teaching aids that have been found useful in demonstrating some of the more abstract principals of pronunciation to second language learners:

- The *sound-colour chart.* Each phoneme on a phonemic chart is assigned a colour and is referred to by colour for ease of reference.
- *Fidel wall charts.* A colour categorisation system which segments the letter to sound rules into phonetic bundles. For every letter or group of letters, which represent a phoneme in English, a colour is designated.
- *Cuisenaire rods.* Also used to teach children basic numeracy, these coloured pieces of wood of differing lengths have various uses in the pronunciation classroom. Rods can be used to build and visually demonstrate intonation patterns, vowel duration and lexical stress.

The Communicative Approach

The current dominant methodology, which persists today with criticism from some quarters, sprung into prominence in the 1980's. The Communicative approach holds that *oral*communication is the primary use of language and therefore should be central to the mode of instruction. Although pronunciation is not an explicit feature in this mode of instruction, the importance of pronunciation has been highlighted by it. By focusing more on active communication in the classroom, it has been recognised that pronunciation competence below a certain threshold renders even the most grammatically and lexically advanced student unintelligible.

This renewed focus on pronunciation has raised many new problems for the teacher working within the Communicative Approach. One problem is that the artificial and contrived teacher centred nature of previous pronunciation instruction techniques does not allow for a comfortable fit with the discourse-based Communicative Approach. As a result of teacher training methods centred around the Communicative Approach and the rigidly adhered-to Presentation, Practice, Production (PPP) model of instruction, a generation of teachers impartial to, and inadequately trained in the instruction of pronunciation has been produced.

In an attempt to keep pronunciation communicative, materials writers have developed materials that focus on suprasegmental aspects of pronunciation. Generally, integration of pronunciation was only treated with token significance by material developers in the 1980's and was more or less pushed to the outer to be taught in isolation by practitioners still interested enough in its worth and knowledgeable in its form and function.

ATTITUDES OF TEACHERS AND STUDENTS

Top Down or Bottom up? Inseparable

Many English pronunciation instructors have felt frustrated by their inability to assess segmental production and give accurate feedback to students because of the *black box model* of articulatory/acoustic production. Many learners are unable to produce segmentals acceptably or with any permanency after exposure to traditional methods of minimal pair drills, simplified articulatory explanations and aural discrimination exercises. Instead, learners tend to revert to their fossilised production of L2 segmentals once the model, which has been extensively drilled by their teacher, begins to slip from their memory.

Teachers who have experienced this dissatisfaction associated with teaching segmentals tend to embrace negative assumptions regarding this aspect of pronunciation. A popular assumption which teachers may call upon to defend their avoidance of teaching segmentals and which has been given credence by some current pronunciation course books is: deviate suprasegmental aspects are more of a hindrance to clear communication than deviate segmentals. One writer aligns himself with this popular notion by stating "No one, anywhere has ever walked into a restaurant, mispronounced / r/ and gotten a bowl of lice."

Although redundancy in language is a well known factor and intelligibility will be assisted by an immediate linguistic and situational context in actual communicative situations, it is the frequency and type of error which can possibly obscure meaning, no matter what assistance the message is given by context. In a study of natural continuous Japanese L2 speech Baldwin makes the following observation concerning the seriousness of segmental errors:

Deviations such as "I sink zat people are bery kind" can still be easily understood, however a construction (with a high frequency combination of errors) such as "I sink dzo disizbutuza" cannot. No listener understood what he was saying, even with other contextual cues present. Observation of Sydney being a "bad town though" contains at least 7 substitutions, uttered in a continuous stream of rapid speech.

A swing of preference amongst teachers towards instruction in aspects of prosody over phonemic production in the classroom has been greatly influenced by pronunciation course books such as*Speaking Clearly* and *In tempo* which address suprasegmental aspects exclusively. Defeated by the lack of pedagogy that yields any identifiable results in the area of segmentals, teachers may have chosen to adopt the popular assumption and turned their attention to suprasegmentals.

A Survey of Attitudes and Teaching Practices Related to Pronunciation Teaching revealed that the majority of teachers involved in the study believe TESOL training does not adequately cover the area of pronunciation teaching. Teachers feel overwhelmed by the complexities of pronunciation, not knowing what to teach, when or how, and generally lack knowledge about the phonological systems of other languages.

While the majority of teachers stated they feel the most "comfortable" with their knowledge and skills relating to the phonetic (segmental) system of English, they would like more knowledge about, and skills relating to the teaching of suprasegmental features of pronunciation.

These findings beg the question: If they feel they have been poorly trained in the area of phonetics and phonology and its application to second language acquisition, how can they possibly feel "comfortable" with *any* aspect of pronunciation pedagogy?

From this conundrum has arisen a tendency for teachers to polarise and prioritise top down and bottom up approaches to the teaching of pronunciation. This occurrence is in deference to the fact that segmental and suprasegmental aspects overlap and contribute to each other in several important ways. The elements of pronunciation combine to form a dynamic system that cannot be isolated one from the other. For instance, vowel duration and production of the reduced form schwa /Y/, contributes to the stress of syllables in words and to the prominence of semantically loaded words in sentences. As Taylor has written:

"there is a close connection between word stress and the pronunciation of vowels and the ability to predict and recognise word stress patterns can help learners to pronounce vowels correctly. Conversely, a knowledge of the correct pronunciation of the vowels in a word will give the learners a clear indication of its stress pattern."

The use of traditional approaches and pronunciation resources which segmentalise and polarise aspects of pronunciation, contribute to the complexity which teachers claim to see in pronunciation teaching. So how should teachers structure their lessons? A current belief is that pronunciation should be integrated into the general language lesson instead of being taught as a separate subject. While this view has value it also raises many questions for the phonologically naive teacher: what should be integrated, how and when?

Which English

Regarding his maiden visit to Australia at the close of 1996, American President Bill Clinton was reported to have said that he had difficulty understanding Prime Minister John Howard because of his accent.

One possible cause of this lack of comprehension between two native speakers of the same language is that the cultural exchange between Australia and America has not reached a level whereby Australian English is identifiable to

Americans *en masse*. In Britain the cultural exchange has been more complete, our Australian actors and entertainers mix freely within their society and Australian exports containing our language enjoy enormous success. In America on the other hand, Australian actors have been required to undergo accent training to adopt an American accent when they appear in American films and Australian blockbusters have often been dubbed with American speakers prior to release. The cause of this confusion could also be attributed to the similarities in pronunciation shared by General Australian English and the English found in the vicinity of London, recently named Estuary English, which are not shared by General American English.

In terms of population of native English speakers the United States of America dominates over the other nations. The other major populations of native speakers follow in the order of Canada, Britain and then Australasia. Group Canada together with the U.S.A and call it Northern America and the dominance of American-accented English is overwhelming.

So often the question arises in pronunciation pedagogy circles: which English do we teach? If the dominant model were to qualify the pronunciation of choice should clearly be North American. If an historical angle were to be taken some variety of British English should be chosen. For the last century Received Pronunciation (RP) which is only spoken by approximately 3% of the British well-to-do population (according to Crystal 1988) was preferred. These notions which are based on the idea that there is, or should be a *Standard* English do not match the reality of language acquisition. English is taught on every continent on the globe by every conceivable variety of native and non-native speakers possible. Yet as long as the question of dialect superiority is still raised the debate will continue to influence the attitudes of English language teachers and students alike.

In Australia, though the mode of English instruction seeks to be Australian in form and content, the teachers themselves are often from diverse linguistic backgrounds. Many of them are travellers or temporary residents and to model any other accent other than their own would be absurd. So the notion that foreign language students arriving in Australia will acquire aspects of native Australian-accented English is not a reality. This is also the case for the other national centres for English language instruction around the globe. English is no longer *owned* by the English or by any one particular dominant group and therefore to search for a *standard* model built upon one dialect for pronunciation instruction is not realistic.

Instead, intelligibility of speech should be the *modus operandi* when considering what should be taught. Any native speaker of English may teach suprasegmental aspects of pronunciation, irrespective of their nationality or the country in which they are teaching. The choice of a model for segmentals however is not so straightforward. The best solution to this dilemma would seem to be to reserve instruction of segmentals to a native speaker of the variety of English in the country of instruction. That is, a native Australian should teach segmental aspects of pronunciation in Australia, a native northern American speaker should model segmentals in their homeland and so on. This may appear to be a solution except that the previous section outlining the inseparable nature of segmental and suprasegmental aspects of pronunciation negates this option, as does the Communicative Approach to language teaching which seeks to teach through discourse and not through explicit analysis.

The dialect superiority misperception also contributes to the reticence of some language teachers to tackle pronunciation teaching for fear of being accused of being an *inferior model*. If the bulk responsibility for pronunciation instruction were to be taken away from teachers and given to an audio-visual tool such as a computer which could consistently model and far more accurately analyse speech and also give diagnostic feedback to the student, many teachers would have no cause to object.

TRADITIONAL PEDAGOGY

In traditional pedagogy, pronunciation has been viewed as the sum of three components. The components are *sounds, stress and rhythm,* and *intonation.* Perhaps it is due to the complexity of these components, that traditionally in the classroom these components have been explicated separately. As has already been mentioned, many teachers tend to regard these components with varying degrees of importance and may choose to focus on one of them in preference to the others. The teacher's degree of phonological knowledge may also inform the selection.

Critical observations on the limitations of teachers and their methods have their place but for the purpose of this discussion a more positive pragmatic view will be taken in an attempt to unearth those aspects of traditional practice which have merit. This section will summarise some of the novel ideas that have been used in the classroom.

The most common method of modification at the phonemic or *sounds* level is based on minimal pair drills. This method assumes that the speaker cannot perceptively or productively distinguish minimally distinctive sounds such as the vowels in *ship* and *sheep* because these distinctions do not occur in their L1. Traditionally, minimal pairs, or minimally distinctive sets of more than two sounds in the target language are randomly modeled by the teacher from a list and the students guess which sound in the pair or group has been produced. This is an effective exercise for elicitation of the student's perceptual problem areas and for awareness building of the sound contrasts in English.

However, problems are encountered in giving feedback to the students on their production errors, particularly with problem vowel sounds. The traditional practice of production uses articulatory diagrams to explain the position of the articulators, followed by a drill of the contrast. In a classroom situation teachers don't have sufficient time to focus on students individually, nor to analyse the phonetic/phonemic transfer effect occurring between the L1 and the L2 or any of the intra-personal sources of error which could possibly occur. This difficulty can be partly overcome by focusing on students individually outside the classroom in a one-on-one clinic. This however is not an option for most language schools.

The author has observed the operation of one such clinic run by speech pathologists for Japanese learners of English at Cumberland College, Sydney University, Lidcombe. An effective technique they have developed is as follows. The speech pathologist models a target sound within a carrier word. Then the student is asked to produce it two or three times, depending on how many attempts it takes to produce an improved production of the sound.

Then the student is asked which sound they think was better, the first, the second or the third? Surprisingly, using this method, the student can often perceive or *feel* which utterance was closer to the model. By asking the student to reflect on what they feel is a fair production of the model, the closer attempt is thereby reinforced in a way which can not be attained if the teacher was just to comment *good* or *better* or *try again*. It would seem from this example that gaining an intuitive awareness of the accuracy of one's production skills of the sounds in a second language is a significant step towards improved production.

The minimal distinctions between monophthongal vowels in AE may be; mainly durational as in the contrasts /i/ versus /I/ and /aÐ/ versus /Λ/, or it may be due to other acoustic cues expressed by varying articulatory motions and realised as formant frequency differences. In diphthongs the salient cues are the production of the first element, the length of the glide and the direction of the glide. This however also varies considerably between native speakers. For consonants the salient acoustic cues are related to the manner of articulation and place of constriction. These qualities which separate these L2 sounds are interesting in their own right, but what is the significance of these distinctions to the second language learner? Perhaps it is pertinent to ask, what is the point of drilling contrasting L2 sounds? Contrasting L2 sounds with durational difference may be valid for listening practice. However, why compare the student's production of two L2 vowel targets such as /uÐ/ and /Ʊ/ when the student probably can't come close to producing either accurately. In this case neither can be relied upon as a point of reference for the other.

An alternative to the minimal pair drill practice is offered below. Firstly, the fundamental inadequacies of minimal pair drills will be outlined.

The practice of minimal pair drills presupposes the following:

- The L2 speaker can already approximate acceptable acoustic cues for both target phonemes but confuses them;
- Drilling one minimal pair in relation to another will modify the acoustic cues towards more native-like speech;
- The L2 listener has the ability to perceive production of English sounds in the same way the L1 listener does.

These presuppositions are flawed for the following reasons:

- In many instances the learner will not yet be able to produce acceptable acoustic cues for the target phonemes in question, so any drilling to reinforce the contrast between the minimal pairs is putting the cart before the horse;
- If the L2 speaker can not as yet produce acceptable acoustic cues for the sounds in question they have a spurious point of reference on which to contrast the production of the two sounds;
- The L2 listener does not have the ability to perceive speech in the same way the native English speaker does. The L2 listener is constantly influenced by the inventory of acoustic cues from their L1. For this reason the L2 speaker should not be expected to gauge the accuracy of their own production, especially before their production of L2 sounds has reached an acceptable proximity to the target.

A better strategy than contrastive drilling of L2 minimal pairs would be to use the closest corresponding target from the L1 as a point of reference for an L2 target. In classroom pronunciation teaching this has never been an option because a teacher cannot possess native productive and perceptive competence in L1 and L2 phonology. Nor can they visually demonstrate the contrast by any physical model at their disposal. This L1-L2 contrast could however be assessed and visually demonstrated with the computer-based model that is outlined elsewhere.

The more innovative classroom approaches to pronunciation modification have evolved from the pedagogical goal of the *learner-centred* classroom, which has replaced former didactic approaches to teaching. In the learner-centred classroom activities related to the correction of pronunciation errors are designed to meet the student's differing learning styles, namely auditory, visual, tactile and kinaesthetic learning. Conformity to the learner-centred model does not necessarily make the method an effective tool for modification of pronunciation, but it is likely to make the lesson more palatable for the student. The following are examples of what are now being referred to as *low tech* practices, in light of the evolving *high-tech* computer-based approaches.

Traditional practices

SOUNDS

Rubber bands have been employed to both demonstrate and raise individual student awareness of length contrasts between vowels. For example, using a rubber band to model / iÐ/, the students place the rubber band around both thumbs and stretch it to its limit. To model /I/ students pull the rubber band slightly apart. The teacher can also point out the co-articulatory effect on vowels between voiced and voiceless consonants. The students can then identify long and short variance by listening to an utterance and modeling the length contrasts with their rubber bands.

The phonemic chart can be used effectively in class to learn new vocabulary by pointing at the sounds in the chart to elicit a word. This can only be done after the students have had lengthy exposure to the symbols. One way, which I have developed myself, for students to learn the symbols quickly is as follows. Cut up at least two copies of the chart with extra schwa symbols and give the pieces to pairs of students to arrange into words. The chart should have commonly occurring example words under each symbol. Monitor the students, explain any errors they make and point out patterns such as consonant clusters and the use of schwa. Elicit from the students the prominent syllable in each word.

A common drill used to practice minimal pairs which this author takes issue with is tongue twisters. Tongue twisters are pedagogically unsound because they drill sequences of discourse with frequencies of phonemes that do not occur in natural speech. Besides this the difficulty of the exercise is demotivating. It is even too difficult for a native speaker to say *red lorry, yellow lorry*ad infinitum at a rapid pace.

Rhymes or jazz chants may be used to practice difficult sounds in a more enjoyable way than by using isolated words or contrived dialogues with an unnatural repetition of phonemes. Jazz chants are usually used to practice rhythm and stress in functions and common expressions such as the one below for *giving directions*. They can also be used with an integrated focus on problem sounds such as /\Đ/.

Walk three blocks and turn right,
Turn right,
Turn right,
Walk three blocks and turn left,
Turn left,
Turn left,
Walk straight on and turn right, (etc)

The heavy rhyming pattern in Billy Field's song *Bad Habits* is also appropriate:

When you get the urge,
And you have to splurge, (etc)

Songs may also be used to drill sequences of phonemes that conflict with the phonotactic constraints of the L1.

Cuisenaire rods. (Mentioned in 1.5)

Stress and rhythm

A rubber band can be used again to model the prominent syllable(s) in a word or utterance. It can be stretched out during the stressed syllable and left short during other syllables. The point of the exercise is to help certain students avoid transferring their syllable timed language to their production of English.

Clapping, tapping or playing simple rhythm instruments can be an enjoyable way to demonstrate and practise the prominence of content words in discourse or in rhymes. Using natural discourse focuses attention on the often slightly irregular stress patterns that occur in real discourse. Rhymes can be used as an initial demonstration of prominence but should be followed up by real discourse, as their regular metre is in fact a contrivance.

Intonation

When intonation has been dealt with at all in traditional pronunciation practice it has usually been represented by an attitudinal approach. Therefore the traditional techniques used to teach intonation have been informed by an approach which has since been debunked. A summary of the methods used is therefore not relevant. A typical tool used however is a kazoo, which the teacher uses to hum an utterance and thereby exemplify the tune. Such a trite demonstration undermines the complexity of intonation and does nothing to improve the student's production.

Chapter 4

Mechanism of Speech

BASIC DEFINITION

If you want to learn to speak English fluently, it will help you to understand how the human mind produces speech. However, before looking at the mechanics of speech, I want to draw an analogy from machine control because the analogy closely parallels neurological responses in spoken language.

MACHINE CONTROL

An open-loop controller, also called a non-feedback controller, is a type of controller which computes its input into a system using only the current state of the system. A characteristic of the open-loop controller is that it does not use feedback to determine if its input has achieved the desired goal. This means that the system does not observe the output of the processes that it is controlling. Consequently, a true open-loop system cannot correct any errors that it could make.

For example, a sprinkler system, programmed to turn on at set times could be an example of an open-loop system if it does not measure soil moisture as a form of feedback. Even if rain is pouring down on the lawn, the sprinkler system would activate on schedule, wasting water. The control may be a simple switch, or it could be a combination of a switch and a timer. Yet, all it can do is turn the machine on. It cannot respond to anything the machine is doing.

CLOSED-LOOP MACHINE CONTROL

To avoid the problems of the open-loop controller, control

theory introduces feedback. A closed-loop controller uses feedback to control states or outputs of a dynamical system. Its name comes from the information path in the system: process inputs (e.g. voltage applied to a motor) have an effect on the process outputs (e.g. velocity...of the motor), which is measured with sensors and processed by the controller; the result is used as input to the process, closing the loop.

Definition of a closed-loop system subsequently becomes too technical to use here. However, as Suggests above, a sprinkler incorporating a soil moisture sensor would be a simple closed-loop system.

The sprinkler system would have both a timer and a control valve. Either could operate independently, and either could shut the water off, but both would need to be open in order for the sprinkler to operate. The arrangement is shown in above figure.

If the soil is already moist, the sprinkler will remain off whether or not the timer is open. When the moisture probe senses dry soil, the valve is opened. However, after the sprinkler is on, if the soil becomes moist enough, the valve will close even if the timer is still open. Thus, the sprinkler uses feedback from its own operation to control itself.

In a machine application, the calibration function could be a counter which is set so that the machine will produce a certain number of finished parts.

HUMAN SPEECH A CLOSED-LOOP

Human speech is a complex learned skill and is dependent on a number of memory and neurological functions. Speech is a closed-loop system because sensors within the system itself give feedback to the control portion of the system. The control then corrects and coordinates ongoing speech. In this case, the mind is in control of the closed-loop system, the mouth produces the desired product (speech), and auditory feedback from the ears and feedback from the nerve sensors in the mouth allow the mind to coordinate the speech process in real time.

When you speak your own language, your mind stores all of the vocabulary you need. Your mind also controls your tongue, mouth, and breathing. Your hearing is also an important part of the control because your ears hear everything your mouth says.

Therefore, what you say next is partially dependent on the vocabulary and other information stored in your mind. But what you say next is also dependent on what your ears are hearing your mouth say, and on the feedback that is coming from the nerves in your tongue and mouth.

Because you have spoken your own language all of your life, all of this control is automatic — you do not need to think about it. But when you learn to speak English, you must retrain all of these processes so that they will all work together at the same time. It is not enough to simply put new vocabulary words or grammar drills into your memory.

You must retrain your mind to use all of the new sounds your ears will hear, as well as the new movements of your tongue, mouth, and breathing. Yet, since all of these things must happen together for you to speak fluent English, all retraining of your memory, hearing, and the nerves in your mouth must be done simultaneously.

Proprioceptive

Human speech would be impossible without the proprioceptive sense. (*Proprioceptive* refers to the sense within the organism itself which detects or controls the movement and location of the muscles, tendons, and joints which are used to create speech) Our mouth, vocal cords, diaphragm, and lungs incorporate thousands of nerve sensors which the brain uses to control the movement and position of these same organs — the mouth, vocal cords, diaphragm, and lungs. Imagine the complexity of pronouncing even a single word with the need to coordinate the tongue, breath control, and jaw muscles. Now multiply this complexity exponentially as sentences are constructed in rapid succession during normal speech.

Real Time

Unlike an open-loop control system, a closed-loop control

system monitors feedback and corrects the process as the machine is running. The reciprocal path between the control, the feedback sensors, and the process itself is instantaneous. That is, information is not stored for later use. Rather, it is used instantaneously as the sensors detect it.

Calibration

In human speech, the mind must constantly monitor the feedback information from both the speaker's own hearing and the proprioceptive senses which enable the mind to control muscles and create the desired sounds. Thus, the speaker is constantly "calibrating" the feedback to control speech. To change a tense, the speaker may change "run" to "ran," or change the person from "he" to "she," and so on. These "word" changes are achieved by precise control of the muscles used to produce speech.

We "calibrate" our speech frequently as we talk. This is why we can misuse a word, verb tense, or some other part of the initial sentence, and still make corrections in the remaining words of the sentence so that the listener does not hear our mistake.

In human speech is represented as the interplay between the mind, the mouth, and its related organs (represented in the figure by the tongue), two feedback systems, and conscious calibration as the speaker constructs each sentence. In addition, calibration is continuously taking place within the control centre — the mind. However, because it is acting on feedback from hearing and the proprioceptive senses, I am showing calibration as acting on the source of the feedback. It makes no apology for the intricacy of this explanation. The neurological feedback and resulting control of the muscles involved in speech is extremely complex. The mind is involved in a far greater task than simply remembering vocabulary and organizing words into meaningful sentences.

If you are learning English as a new language, all of its unique sounds and syntax must be learned. This is much more than a memory function involving just your mind. Each of these new sound and syntax patterns requires retraining your entire mind, the nerve feedback in your tongue, mouth, and breathing (which is proprioceptive feedback), and the auditory feedback

Even English syntax is dependent on your proprioceptive sense. The statement, "This is a book," *feels* different to the nerve receptors in your mouth than the question, "Is this a book?" We can certainly understand that memory is involved in the use of correct grammar. Just as important, however, is the observation that proprioceptive feedback demands that a question evoke a different sequence of feedback than a statement. This is why we have identified partial syntax control in Table as being a shared function of both the mind (memory) and the mouth (as a proprioceptive sense).

If you doubt that the proprioceptive sense is an important part of speech, try this experiment. Read two or three sentences written in your own language. Read it entirely in your mind without moving your lips. You may even speed read it. Now read the same sentences "silently" by moving your lips without making any sound. Your mind will respond to the first way of reading as simple information which is primarily a memory function, but will respond to the second way as speech because of the proprioceptive feedback from your mouth.

The first reading would elicit the mental activity required when you do a written grammar-based English assignment. The second would result in the same kind of mental activity required when you study English using spoken drills. How quickly you learn to speak fluent English will be directly proportional to your mental involvement when you study.

RIGHT WAY TO LEARN ENGLISH

Two skill areas must be emphasized if you want to learn to speak English fluently. The first is memory (which is involved in both vocabulary and syntax) and the second is proprioceptive responses (which are involved in both pronunciation and syntax).

You may be able to learn simple vocabulary-related memory skills with equal effectiveness by using either verbal or visual training methods. That is, you may be able to learn pure memory skills equally well with either spoken drills or written exercises.

However, it is impossible for you to retrain your proprioceptive sense without hearing your own voice at full speaking volume. Thus, in my opinion, it is a waste of your time to do written assignments for the purpose of learning spoken English.

Surprisingly, it will take far less time for you to learn both fluent spoken English and excellent English grammar by studying only spoken English first, than it will for you to study written English grammar lessons before you can speak English. This does not mean, however, that grammar is not a necessary part of spoken English instruction. It is impossible to speak English — or any other language — without correct use of its grammar. My statement simply means that the best way to learn English grammar is through spoken English exercises.

The Spoken English involves multiple areas of skill working cooperatively in real time, it is mandatory that effective spoken English teaching methods simultaneously train all of these areas of speech..

It is the important area of the proprioceptive sense which has been most overlooked in current grammar-based teaching methodology. When any student over the age of about 12 attempts to learn a spoken language, his or her proprioceptive sense must be consciously retrained for all of the new sounds and syntax. of the mouth, the combined feedback from the mouth and hearing must be simultaneously processed in the mind. Simply said, the student must speak out loud for optimum spoken language learning.

Without simultaneous involvement of all skill areas of speech, it is impossible for you to effectively retrain your proprioceptive sense in order for you to speak fluent English. Yet, this is exactly what grammar-based English instruction has traditionally done by introducing grammar, listening, writing, and reading as segregated activities. It is not surprising that you have studied English so long in school without learning to speak fluently.

Grammar-based instruction has hindered English learning by segregating individual areas of study. Grammar-based English training has not only isolated proprioceptive training areas so that it prevents simultaneous skill development, it has replaced it with visual memory training by using written assignments. Grammar-based language instruction teaches English as though spoken English was an open-loop system. The result for the student is that gaining English fluency requires far more study time, pronunciation is often faulty, and grammar becomes more difficult to learn.

Chapter 5

Rules for Learning Spoken English

RULES

There are four simple rules you must follow when you are learning to speak English:

SPEAK ENGLISH CORRECTLY AND LOUDLY

It is important that you speak loudly and clearly when you are studying spoken English. You are retraining your mind to respond to a new pattern of proprioceptive and auditory stimuli. This can only be done when you are speaking aloud at full volume.

One of the reasons that your English study in school required so much time while producing such poor results is that none of the *silent* study did anything to train your tongue to speak English.

SPEAK FLUENTLY

The proprioceptive sense is not all that you are retraining when you learn spoken English. There is cognitive learning (memory) which must also take place. Grammar-based English instruction has emphasized cognitive learning to the exclusion of retraining the proprioceptive sense. Nonetheless, cognitive learning is an important part of learning to speak English fluently. in syntax development. The more actively your mind is involved in spoken English, the more effective the learning process becomes.

However, just as you will hinder proprioceptive training by trying to study *silently,* so you will also limit cognitive learning by reading from a text rather than constructing the syntax in your own mind. If you are studying English with *Spoken English Learned Quickly,* you may use the written text when you first study a new exercise. However, after repeating the exercise two or three times, you must close the text and do the exercise from recall memory as you listen to the audio recording. You must force your mind to *think* in English by using your recall memory when you are studying spoken exercises. You cannot read from a text.

We will come back to this later in next chapters: Selecting a Text, because there will be times when reading from a text such as a newspaper is an effective language learning tool. But when you are doing sentence responses with recorded exercises, you must force your mind to develop the syntax by doing the exercise without reading from a text.

SPEAKING LOUDLY AND FLUENTLY

Proprioceptive retraining is not instantaneous. It will require a great deal of repetition to build the new language patterns in your mind. As these new patterns develop, there will be progression from a laborious, conscious effort, to speech which is reproduced rapidly and unconsciously.

When you speak your first language, you do so with no conscious awareness of tongue or mouth position and the air flow through the vocal cords. In contrast, it requires experimentation and conscious effort when you first attempt to make an unknown discrete sound in English—this single sound, usually represented by one letter, is called a phoneme. Some new sounds will be relatively simple for you to make. Others will be more difficult.

To add to the complexity, each phoneme has other phonemes or stops adjacent to it which change its sound slightly. (A *stop* is a break caused by momentarily restricting the air flow with the tongue or throat) For example, the simple English sentence, "Why didn't that work?" may be difficult for you to pronounce if your language does not use the English "th" sound. But it may give you difficulty for another reason as well. There are actually two stops in the sentence. When properly pronounced, there is a stop between the "n" and "t" in "didn't" and another stop between the final "t" in "didn't" and the first "t" in "that." Even though the sentence may be said very quickly, the two stops would make it, "Why didn/t/ that work?"

Your objective is not to be able to write the sentence, "Why didn't that work?" accurately in English. Your goal is not even to be able to say it just well enough so that someone could figure out what you meant.

That degree of perfection will require thousands—if not tens of thousands—of repetitions. Therefore—to be somewhat facetious—the more quickly you correctly repeat a particularly difficult phoneme ten thousand times, the more quickly you will be able to use it fluently.

STOP MISTAKE

When you are learning spoken English using the *Spoken English Learned Quickly* method, you are strongly reinforcing the learning process each time you speak. However, when you construct a sentence incorrectly, you have not only wasted the learning time used to construct that sentence, but you must now invest even more time in order to retrain your mind, mouth, and hearing in order to construct the sentence correctly. The more you use a sentence structure incorrectly, the longer it will take for your mind, mouth, and hearing to identify the correct syntax.

Traditional English Study

Traditional methods of teaching English attempt to engage the students in free speech as quickly as possible. Though the goal is commendable, in practice it has a serious drawback. A beginning student does not have enough language background to be able to construct sentences properly. More to the point, the instruction programme seldom has enough teachers to correct every student's errors. Consequently, beginning students regularly use incomplete sentences having incorrect syntax and verb construction. The instructor often praises them for their valiant effort, in spite of the reality that they are learning to use English incorrectly. The student will now need to spend even more time relearning the correct syntax.

Controlled Language Study

The better alternative is to derive all initial spoken language study from audio recorded materials which contain perfect syntax, perfect use of the verb, and perfect pronunciation.

Say, for example, that during the first two weeks of English study, you used only the *Spoken English Learned Quickly* recorded exercises. You would repeat the recorded lesson material which was accurate in every detail. For the entire instruction period, you would work by yourself while repeating the exercise sentences hundreds of times.

Needless to say, in two weeks' time, you would have spoken English correctly far more than had you been passively sitting in a traditional English class. But more to the point, everything you would have learned would have been correct. Your syntax would have been correct. Your use of the English verb would have been correct. And, as much as possible, your pronunciation would have been correct.

To continue the example, say that it was now time for you to begin trying *free* speech. Yet, we still would not want you to make mistakes. Consequently, all free speaking would be taken directly from the many sentences you would have already learned. Your teacher would ask questions from the *Spoken English Learned Quickly* exercises so that you could answer in the exact words of the sentences you would have studied. Subsequently, you would be given questions to answer which would use the same structure as the sentences you already knew, but now you would substitute other vocabulary words which would be in the same lessons.

Making an Application

It is assumed that you are a college student or a young

professional and that you are highly motivated to learn to speak English fluently.

You will do much better if you seek ways in which you can speak English correctly from the very beginning. Strike a careful balance between free speech and forcing yourself to follow a pattern of correct English use. Do everything in your power to use English correctly.

In the early weeks of English study, this may require that you spend more time repeating recorded *Spoken English Learned Quickly* exercises than in trying to engage in free speech. Later, however, you will need to spend a great deal of time talking with others.

Nonetheless, every time you encounter new syntax in English, use controlled language drills long enough so that your mind becomes thoroughly familiar with correct sentence structure and pronunciation. If you are using the *Spoken English* lessons, repeat the exercises until you can say them quickly and accurately with perfect pronunciation. As you progress in your English study, begin reading English newspaper articles aloud. Look for examples of new vocabulary and sentence format.

Chapter 6

Basic and Advanced Spoken Lessons

STUDY

Your perceived needs as you begin studying English will significantly influence how you answer this chapter's title question. If you decide that you need *beginning* English when you start your study, you will spend much time looking for lessons with beginning sentences because English does not speak a *beginning* language. On the other hand, if you decide that the English used in the daily newspaper is what you want to learn, you can easily find that kind of English language.

NEED FOR BASIC AND ADVANCED LESSONS

I am really asking if beginning and advanced students can use the same level of lessons to learn spoken English. Before you give an intuitive answer, I need to ask the question properly. The question is, "Does English have multiple, specialized language divisions?"

The answer is, "No, it does not." There is no *high* English language spoken by the gentry versus a *low* language spoken by commoners. Historically, many languages such as Greek and Chinese, have indeed used two levels. Modern English does not even have a specialized construction for folklore. Many languages in which oral tradition has been preserved have a storytelling form of the language which is distinct from the language used in everyday conversation. In fact, English is so simple in this regard that we do not even have two forms of address for people of differing social standing. French, for instance, has strict conventions regarding the use of "tu" or "vous" when addressing someone.

English has many specialized vocabularies. Any student who has taken courses in anatomy, law, physics, automotive technology, psychology, engineering, geology, or anthropology has spent a great deal of time learning specialized terminology. But the essential English syntax which holds these words together in a sentence is still the language of the street—or the language of the daily newspaper.

So, aside from specialized vocabularies, English has no divisions representing varying levels of language complexity. Almost any individual with at least a secondary school education would make essentially the same evaluation of another speaker's ability to use *good* or *bad* English.

The exception to the above paragraph would be found in technical documents such as legal briefs and the like. However, this style of English is far from the language used in normal conversation.

There is only one kind of English which you need to learn. You do not need two or more different course levels. This is not to say that English is a simple language to learn. Far from it. However, the same complexity is in *all* spoken English, not merely in some higher level.

Why have traditional language programmes insisted that there must be beginning, intermediate, and advanced levels of English study? It is not because there are beginning and advanced levels of spoken English. It is because there are beginning, intermediate, and advanced explanations for English grammar. This means that some rules of English grammar are easy to explain. Some rules of grammar are more difficult to explain. And some are complex enough to require a highly technical explanation. But spoken English is one subject of study, whereas the formal rules of English grammar are quite another.

Now we can answer the question, "Do you need beginning and advanced English lessons to learn the language?" Of course not. There is only one level of spoken English. If you are a beginning student, you must start by speaking normal English sentences. If you have studied English for several years and consider yourself an advanced student, you must continue until you are able to fluently pronounce the words in those same normal English sentences.

There will be a great difference in the fluency between beginning and advanced students. But there is no difference in the level of English sentences they must study. They must use the same English sentences both to initiate, and then to master, the process which will develop the necessary cognitive, motor, and auditory skills used to speak fluent English.

COMPLEX SENTENCES

We need to add an explanation so that what we are saying is understandable. English grammar identifies simple sentences (sentences with one main clause), compound sentences (sentences with two or more main clauses), complex sentences (sentences with one main clause and at least one subordinate clause), and compound-complex sentences (sentences made up of two or more main clauses and at least one subordinate clause). An example of a compound-complex sentence would be, "The Saturday afternoon programme was like a two-ring circus; while one part of the TV screen carried the professional football game, the other part showed scores from collegiate games." Of course, this is not a sentence we would expect beginning English students to use. But the complexity of the sentence is not in the language level of the sentence. Its so-called complexity is only in the punctuation of the sentence which makes it a *complex* sentence by grammatical definition. With very little change, the sentence could become three simple sentences: "The Saturday afternoon programme was like a two-ring circus. One part of the TV screen showed the professional football game. The other part of the TV screen showed scores from collegiate games." Aside from vocabulary, any one of these three sentences are *beginning* level sentences. of English sentences a beginning and advanced student must study, we are not talking about a grammatical definition. I am saying that there is not one language that would be used by commoners and another that would be used by the gentry. Even though the example sentence about the TV's split screen is not a sentence we would want to include in the first lesson, it does not represent multiple, specialized language divisions.

DIFFICULTY TO START WITH NORMAL ENGLISH

Not really. Once you understand the "hello"s and "goodby"s in English, you are ready to begin practicing with normal sentences. Aside from sentences which contain specialized vocabulary, most English sentences use common verbs and syntax construction. This is the English you want to speak. Use it from the very start of your language study.

This is not as difficult as it seems. If you are using the *Spoken English* course, you will discover that Lesson 1 uses normal English sentences, even though it uses only the present tense. previous Lesson uses complete sentences in past, present, and future tenses. The sentences become slightly more complex as the lessons progress, but every sentence in the entire course is one that you will need to master as an "advanced" student. Your objective in using *Spoken English Quickly* is not merely to understand the sentence as though it was part of a grammar exercise.

The spoken language you want to learn is everyday English. It will remove a great deal of stress if you realise that in the very first week of English study, you are learning normal English. By and large, your English study will never become any more difficult than it is when you first begin because you will be studying *normal* spoken English from the first lesson to the completion of your formal study.

It was designed for both beginning and advanced students because our students want to learn *spoken* English, not written English grammar.

TEXT SELECTION

In this chapter, we are using the term *text* to identify a written manuscript. A newspaper in English is usually an excellent source for a study a text. Most newspapers use good syntax, relatively simple sentences, and common expressions. In addition to general vocabulary, newspapers will give you many common political, scientific, economic, and technical words. Generally, newspapers are also a good source of colloquial expressions.

As you begin language study, you will need both a manuscript and an audio recording of the text for pronunciation practice. In your initial selection of a study text, you will be faced with a choice between a printed text from a newspaper or spoken language from a radio broadcast.

We will explain the use of a newspaper as an English text in this chapter because it will help you to understand how the text would be used. However, if you are using the *Spoken English Learned Quickly* lessons, the text and the audio recordings are complete and all of the features in this chapter are already built into that course.

If you are using the *Lesson Text* for your reading, you will have the added advantage of familiar vocabulary and audio recordings to guide your pronunciation. excellent vocabulary—if you continue to read English newspapers aloud. However, at that point you would not need to make audio recordings. Reading aloud and keeping a vocabulary notebook would be all you would need to do. By this time in your study, We are assuming that your pronunciation and voice inflection would be acceptable. If not, you would need to return to the *Spoken English* lessons until your pronunciation was correct.

WRITTEN TEXT TO AUDIO

In this we merely describe the text itself. For the moment, we will assume that you would have a teacher who is a first language English speaker. We are also assuming that you would have audio recording equipment.

By now you realise that the purpose of using the newspaper is *spoken* language practice. You would always read the newspaper aloud, and would frequently read a sentence aloud and then look away from the text, repeating the sentence from recall memory. Everything considered, you would probably find it easier to produce an audio recording from a newspaper text than you would to produce a text from a radio broadcast recording. It would be much simpler to have your English teacher record the text than to have the teacher transcribe the audio recording.

For your study purposes, a printed newspaper text would assure a more precise use of the language, better spelling, and a more easily preserved printed copy. Because live radio broadcasts are difficult to record with inexpensive audio equipment, you would likely have difficulty hearing all of the words. Therefore, it would be easier to get a good text and a usable recording by having the teacher read a newspaper text for the audio recording. The text would be recorded so that there would be adequate pauses for your study.

NEWSPAPER AS VOCABULARY

First, read the article out loud, identifying new vocabulary as you read. Whenever you read a word you do not know, stop and find it in your dictionary. Keep a vocabulary notebook. If a word you do not know is used more than twice in an article, put a check () by it for special study. However, do not check names of places or people. After you finish reading the article for the first time, review the meaning of all of the new vocabulary words. Study these words enough so that you know what they mean when you read the article. Always pronounce vocabulary words—do even your vocabulary study out loud.

After you are more familiar with the process, select other newspaper articles and continue reading aloud while you look for new vocabulary words. When you find a word in a second newspaper article which you have already checked () in your notebook, place a second check () by it. Any word in your notebook with two checks should be memorized as an important word to know.

Whenever you are able to do so, write cognate forms of the same word. For example, *to adhere*, an *adhesive*, and *adhesion* are cognates. It will be helpful for you to learn multiple cognate forms of a word at the same time rather than learning each form as a new vocabulary word when you encounter it. Association of a single word in multiple forms with one root meaning will result in more rapid vocabulary retention. It will also teach you how to develop cognate forms of words as you speak English in the future.

Verbs should be listed in your notebook by their infinitive form (for example, "to remember") rather than by a conjugated form (for example, "she remembers"). After mastering the verb's conjugation, it will be far simpler to learn a single verb form than it will be to attempt to learn each form of a verb as an individual vocabulary word.

Spoken English does an excellent job of teaching English verbs. Since you will learn each new verb in all its persons, tenses, and specialized forms, you will learn the English verb so well that you will be able to use every tense and person of any regular English verb. If you heard a new English verb, you would be able to use every person and tense in a spoken sentence even if you did not know that verb's meaning.

NEWSPAPER FOR SYNTAX DEVELOPMENT

Reading a newspaper article aloud is an ideal way to reinforce your use of grammatically correct English syntax. Your goal is to retrain your mind, hearing, and mouth to understand and use English correctly. Reading aloud from a newspaper is one of the best ways to accomplish that.

The great advantage is that you will be reading a large number of different sentences which will all be organized according to the same grammar rules. Thus, you would be learning the acceptable range of the syntax of that language. That is, there may appear to be many variations from sentence to sentence, yet all of the uses would still be correct. For an example, you would learn that you can place the word "however" at the beginning, middle, or end of an English sentence. You would also learn that the position of "however" can make a slight difference in meaning, or it can enhance the style of the sentence. In many respects, using the newspaper for syntax development is similar to using it for fluency enhancement and as an aid in conversation as mentioned below. The same exercises suggested below would be as profitable for syntax as they would be for fluency and conversation.

NEWSPAPER TO LEARN EXPRESSIONS

Expressions add richness to all languages. Identify expressions as you read the newspaper. Use a special mark to identify them in articles. Many expressions may be divided so that component words of the expression are separated by non-component words.

Try substituting other words while using the same expression. Say or write as many sentences using the expression as possible. To use an example, you may read a sentence in a newspaper which says, "The Governor announced Friday that he will not run for another term, putting to rest months of speculation about his future intentions." Most expressions can be used in different tenses with different people or things. For example, the expression "to put to rest" can be used in the present, He will put his argument to rest," or in the past, "They finally put their rivalry to rest." Notice that in the last phrase, the component parts of the expression are separated: *"They* finally *put* their rivalry *to rest."*

To continue with another illustration, English uses word forms as a type of expression. For example, you may read a sentence in a newspaper which says, "We're getting all kinds of calls from people who are panicking and asking what they can do." This form of expression uses two or more words ending in "...ing" to describe two or more actions that the same person is doing at one time. In this chapter we find that, *"We must never make a mistake when you are speaking."* That objective will be the most difficult when you first begin free conversation. However, using a newspaper article will be a great aid in producing conversation which is essentially free of mistakes.

A newspaper article can give you a great deal of structure for conversation practice. This structure would give both you and your English teacher a defined group of vocabulary words, defined sentences with an understood meaning, and a defined context in which the vocabulary and sentences can be communicated. Your English teacher could use the newspaper article to structure free conversation.

To continue with the illustration, your English teacher could lead you in a discussion stemming from a newspaper article. You could easily have the following discussion after only four weeks of full-time language study. Notice that your teacher would ask each question twice, expecting that you will substitute a pronoun in the second response.

- *English teacher*: "What did the Governor announce Friday?"
- *Your response*: "The Governor announced Friday that he will not run for another term."
- *English teacher*: "What did the Governor announce Friday?"
- *Your response*: "He announced Friday that he will not run for another term."
- *English teacher*: "Will the Governor run for another term?"
- *Your response*: "No, the Governor will not run for another term."
- *English teacher*: "Will the Governor run for another term?"
- *Your response*: "No, he will not run for another term."
- *English teacher*: "When did the Governor announce that he will not run for another term?"
- *Your response*: "The Governor announced Friday that he will not run for another term."
- *English teacher*: "When did the Governor announce that he will not run for another term?"
- *Your response*: "He announced Friday that he will not run for another term."

Assuming that you had only been studying English for four weeks, your initial response to each question would be halting. You would also be looking at the printed text when your English teacher initially asked the question. But at least your answer would be word perfect—you would be training your proprioceptive sense by using perfect syntax.

Chapter 7

Studying Verb

ENGLISH VERB

Probably nothing marks someone struggling to learn English quite as much as improper use of the English verb's person and tense. Therefore, as you study English, you will want to emphasize learning to use the verb correctly as you speak. This will require specialized English verb drills.

Spoken English places great emphasis on the English verb. In all but the first lesson, you will have special spoken drills which will help you learn to use the English verb correctly in all its persons and tenses.

VERB DRILLS

During our initial study, we frustrated by learning only the present tense of a verb, then a week or two later learning its past tense or future tense, only to come back to the same verb later to learn its subjunctive form. It would have been much more effective if you had learned each verb as a complete unit. The verb "etre" (to be) evolved into at least four verbs; first I learned the present tense, later the past tense, still later the future tense, and finally, an entirely new verb called the subjunctive. It would have been much more effective for me to have learned one verb as a unit having four tenses than to have learned four separate tenses as though each was a new verb. Yet, if you learn every tense and person of each new verb simultaneously, it becomes a far simpler memory task. In addition, achieving full use of each verb as it is learned gives greater initial command of a language.

There is, however, another equally forceful argument for learning all forms of the verb at one time. As I have taught the *Spoken English Learned Quickly* course, I have discovered that, in a relative few weeks of learning all new verbs in their entirety, an adult student with no previous English study is able to conjugate verbs which they have never before encountered.

Spoken English was designed to be used as a self-study course. Most students study on their own. However, I have often conducted a weekly two-hour group session as a means of encouraging the students. It is during the group sessions that I have used these spoken conjugation drills.

It strongly encouraged you to learn all forms of each verb the first time you encounter it in your English study. The verb will become much more useful to you in a shorter period of time. The *Spoken English* course contains very useful English verb drills.

In traditional English language instruction, once a particular verb tense is supposedly learned, then it is assumed that the students know that form and no longer need to review it. Yes, the students may be able to write the present tense forms for many regular verbs. But that is not the objective. Can they use all of those forms in spontaneous spoken English? In *Spoken English* we do not stop the instruction merely because our students are able to write the endings of certain verbs. Our goal is to help the students reach a level of fluency in which they can use verbs in all of their tenses and persons correctly in normal speech.

That will also be your objective as you learn to speak English. Do not be satisfied by simply learning verb tenses and persons in written form. You do not *know* a verb until you can use it fluently in spontaneous conversation.

TYPES OF VERBS

In the *Spoken English* we use four verb table formats. All verb tables are used as spoken English drills with recorded audio. In the early lessons, we use only the following format which I will call an "A" format verb drill:

An "A" format English Verb

TO CALL (to call) / He promised to call. (He promised to call):

- Call. (Call)/Please call. (Please call)
- Calling (calling)/It is calling. (It is calling)
- Called (called)/it is called (it is called)/it was called (it was called)/it will be called (it will be called)
- I call (I call)/he calls (he calls)/she calls (she calls) /it calls (it calls)/you call (you call)/we call (we call)/they call (they call)
- I called (I called)/he called (he called)/she called (she called)/it called (it called)/you called (you called)/we called (we called)/they called (they called)
- I will call (I will call)/he will call (he will call)/she will call (she will call)/it will call (it will call)/ you will call (you will call)/we will call (we will call)/they will call (they will call)

Since all of our exercises are recorded audio lessons, you would respond by repeating the words inside parentheses. The parenthetical phrases are included in the written text. Thus, the narrator says, "to call" and you would respond, "to call." The narrator says, "He promised to call." and you would respond, "He promised to call." Everything is spoken, and as soon as you would understand a new exercise, you would put the written text aside and complete the exercise by using only the audio recording without the text.

Repeated use of this format is what allows our students to conjugate an unknown verb correctly. Can you see the fluency they have acquired when they can correctly use English verbs so early in their language learning experience? That is the same fluency you will want to develop as you study English.

A Sentence Completion English Verb

Complete the following sentences with "... them here every evening."

I always meet... (I always meet them here every evening)/ He always meets... (He always meets them here every evening)/You always meet... (You always meet them here every evening)/We always meet... (We always meet them here every evening)/They always meet... (They always meet them here every evening) Complete the following sentences with "... them here after work."

I always met... (I always met them here after work)/She always met... (She always met them here after work)/You always met... (You always met them here after work)/We always met... (We always met them here after work)/They always met... (They always met them here after work)

Complete the following sentences with "... them all before evening."

"B" Format Verb Drill

TO TEST (to test)/He promised to test it. (He promised to test it):

- Test. (Test)/Please test it. (Please test it)
- Testing (testing)/He is testing some. (He is testing some)
- Tested (tested)/It is tested (It is tested)/It was tested (It was tested)/It will be tested (It will be tested)

In this format, we force the students to move from tense to tense using the same person, rather than from person to person using the same tense as we did in the A format drills. Language requires both skills, so we teach the students to do both at normal conversation speed.

However, by this time in the lessons we want the students to be able to do both. Consequently, we alternate between table formats in the same exercise. That is, the first verb is given using the A format, the second verb using the B format, the third verb using the A format, the fourth using the B format, and so on to the end of the exercise. This increases the students' ability to use the verb with all tenses and persons while, at the same time, forcing them to develop spontaneity while using the verb.

Again, this will be your objective in learning English. You want to be able to manipulate spoken verbs quickly and accurately between all persons and tenses. You should also be able to see the great advantage in learning the entire verb with all its tenses and persons at one time. If you learn all the forms of the entire verb each time you encounter a new verb, you have learned one meaning with multiple forms rather than a mix of verb forms and meanings. Learning all the forms of a single verb this way will take you less time than learning the same material using a traditional method.

Most importantly, if you use spoken exercises as a means of learning verb tables, you will find that the conjugation you are learning for one verb will be quickly transferred to other verbs.

In *Spoken English,* you will always study the verb using a spoken exercise without reading from the text after you are familiar with that exercise.

Chapter 8

Success in Spoken English

SPOKEN ENGLISH

It is the world's most widely used spoken English language and it is helps thousands of students around the world to learn English very quickly. If you living in India, for each hour of study, *Spoken English Learned Quickly* would help you learn to speak English twice as fast as you could learn spoken English in a college English class. However, it is much more difficult to learn to speak English fluently in a country where English is seldom used. If you live in a country where you do not regularly hear properly pronounced, grammatically correct English, *Spoken English Learned Quickly* could help you learn to speak English in even less than half of the time it normally takes in your country.

However, even though the course is free on the internet, it will still cost you a great deal to learn to speak fluent English. It will cost you time and a great deal of personal discipline. There will also be the cost of changing your method of studying English. You must stop wasting your time on English grammar and writing lessons and practice *spoken* English instead — even when others tell you that in order to learn to speak English well, you must study English grammar and writing.

ENGLISH LEARNING

Many wonder why *Spoken English Learned Quickly* is free on the internet if it is really as good as claimed. Many probably think that I am trying to sell them something later. The simplest reason that *Spoken English Learned Quickly* is free is that I want to help people. Specially if you want to help those who do not have much money. There is also a practical reason — it is too expensive for me to pay others to market a new product worldwide. But there is still another reason why *Spoken English Learned Quickly* is free. That is true even though it is impossible for me to change the way our universities and colleges teach English in India. There is only one way I can show them that this method is more effective. When hundreds of thousands of students around the world learn to speak English faster and better with *Spoken English Learned Quickly* than they can with any other course, then I will have proved the point. That is why I want you to be successful in learning fluent spoken English with *Spoken English Learned Quickly*.

BASIC RULES

In order to succeed at learning to speak English fluently, you must remember the rules previously given in Chapter:

- To learn to speak English correctly, you must speak it aloud.
- To learn to speak English fluently, you must think in English.
- The more you speak English aloud, the more quickly you will learn to speak fluently.
- You must never make a mistake when you are practicing spoken English.

Now, let's add another new rule:

- Your success will depend upon the amount of time you devote to spoken English study.

There is no alternative to spending a great amount of time in spoken English language study. If you are devoting full time to it, then try to spend a full eight hours a day, five days a week on language study. Ideally, that will be eight hours devoted to actual speaking while using either the *Spoken English Learned Quickly*

BE PERSISTENT

Lack of persistence is the largest reason why you would

fail to learn fluent spoken English. Though grammar-based study is ineffective, it is usually easier for a student to do written English grammar assignments than spoken drills. Written grammar assignments are also used because English classes are often too large for spoken language study, students do not have recorded audio lessons or audio equipment, written assignments make it look like more was accomplished, and because English teachers themselves often do not speak English fluently.

Many *Spoken English Learned Quickly* students fail because they assume that when they understand the meaning of all the sentences, and know the meaning of all of the vocabulary words for a lesson, they have finished that lesson. You will not succeed, however, until you have repeated the spoken English exercises frequently enough so that you can pronounce each sentence exactly like an American. That will take far more time than merely learning what each sentence means.

Another reason *Spoken English Learned Quickly* students fail is because they feel they are too advanced for these lessons. "After all," they think, "I have already studied English for two years, and I already know the meaning of these sentences." They are making the same mistake. They are confusing their understanding of grammar with their ability to speak. I have had these "advanced" students come to one class and then quit. Yet, they could not speak fluent English. They needed to do the exercises from *Spoken English Learned Quickly* just as much as the beginning students, though they probably would have progressed much more rapidly than others in the class. This is why *Spoken English Learned Quickly* is so valuable as a self-study course — each student can progress at his or her own speed.

DON'T TRY TOO HARD

You need to be persistent. But trying too hard to learn spoken English can also hinder your progress. When you studied for important English exams in school, you worked hard to memorize grammar rules, you lost sleep in order to study, you worried about your grade, and you were anxious during the exam. As a result, stress was often associated with English study. On the other hand, when you and a friend were talking in your own language about a soccer game, you were excited about your favourite team's victory. But you were not anxious about the language itself when you were speaking.

To use this new Feedback Training Method to its full advantage, you must hear yourself speaking English correctly. If stress accompanies the language learning process, your spoken English will not be normal.

Be persistent in spending the time necessary to learn spoken English. But avoid becoming stressed. Whether you are reading a newspaper aloud or repeating drills from the Spoken English Learned Quickly lessons, forget that you are studying English and speak naturally just as if you were talking to a friend about a soccer game.

CONTINUE READING NEWSPAPERS

You will have more time to study spoken English with newspapers after you finish the *Spoken English Learned Quickly* course. However, even while you are studying these lessons, you may add variety by reading an English newspaper. Always read aloud using full voice volume. If you are not certain that the English newspapers published in your country use good English (many do not), then go to the internet to find newspapers published in English-speaking countries. If you are studying American English, be certain to use newspapers which are actually published in America in order to get the vocabulary and expressions you want to study.

You may want to use the following internet sources. You can usually print newspaper articles from the internet for your study. If the normal print function on your computer does not work — or if it prints more than just the article you want — you can drag your cursor over just what you want to save to highlight it, click copy, and then paste it into a new document on your computer.

EXPECT SUCCESS

Learning to speak any new language is a difficult task.

But it is not impossible. The *Spoken English* lessons will make it much easier for you.

However, language learning always seems to move in steps. You will study for a period of time and then reach a plateau where it seems as though you are not making further progress. Then, suddenly, you will realise that you have once more made excellent progress. Then, for a time, it will again seem as though nothing is happening.

This is a normal process. These stair steps in spoken English fluency will be much more apparent to you than they will be to someone who speaks English well. If you are studying diligently, a first language English speaker will undoubtedly hear regular progress in your ability to speak English, even when you think nothing is happening.

You are reading this book because you want to learn to speak fluent English. I trust it will help you. Most of all, I think our freely downloadable.

It is the world's most widely used spoken English language course, and it is helping thousands of students around the world learn English very quickly. If you lived in the United States, for each hour of study, *Spoken English Learned Quickly* would help you learn to speak English twice as fast as you could learn spoken English in a college English class. However, it is much more difficult to learn to speak English fluently in a country where English is seldom used. If you live in a country where you do not regularly hear properly pronounced, grammatically correct English, *Spoken English Learned Quickly* could help you learn to speak English in even less than half of the time it normally takes in your country.

However, even though the course is free on the internet, it will still cost you a great deal to learn to speak fluent English. It will cost you time and a great deal of personal discipline. There will also be the cost of changing your method of studying English. You must stop wasting your time on English grammar and writing lessons and practice *spoken* English instead—even when others tell you that in order to learn to speak English well, you must study English grammar and writing. (Has studying English grammar really helped you speak English fluently? This study documented a number of important findings about teaching English reading to language-minority children.

These include:

- English-speaking children making initial attempts at reading understand, if they are successful, the products of their efforts; they read words they know and sentences they understand, and...can self-correct efficiently. Non-English speakers have much less basis for knowing whether their reading is correct because the crucial meaning-making process is short circuited by lack of language knowledge.
- Giving a child initial reading instruction in a language that he or she does not yet speak can undermine the child's chance to see literacy as a powerful form of communication by knocking the support of meaning out from underneath the process of learning. no harm, and it seems likely both from research findings and from theories about literacy development that initial reading instruction in the second language can have negative consequences for immediate and long-term achievement.

The committee therefore urged "initial literacy instruction in a child's native language whenever possible" and suggested that "literacy instruction should not be introduced in any language before some reasonable level of oral proficiency in that language has been attained."

On the question of which language to use when teaching English language learners to read, the committee recommended the following guidelines:

- If language minority children arrive at school with no proficiency in English but speaking a language for which there are instructional guides, learning materials, and locally available proficient teachers, then these children should be taught how to read in their native language while acquiring proficiency in spoken English, and then subsequently taught to extend their skills to reading in English.

- If language minority children arrive at school with no proficiency in English but speak a language for which the above conditions cannot be met and for which there are insufficient numbers of children to justify the development of the local community to meet such conditions, the instructional priority should be to develop the children's proficiency in spoken English. Although print materials may be used to develop understanding of English speech sounds, vocabulary, and syntax, the postponement of formal reading instruction is appropriate until an adequate level of proficiency in spoken English has been achieved.

Chapter 9

English Language

PRESCRIPTIVE AND DESCRIPTIVE ENGLISH

PRESCRIPTIVE ENGLISH

We cannot read books written in languages we do not know. What language do all readers of this page necessarily know? "English" is obviously the answer being prompted. But to say that this page is written in English, and that we all read English, hides a huge assumption: that "English" is one thing, one language. Is that assumption correct? It might seem that if we omit speech, so accents are immaterial, we reach a standard form, but that is not so owing to regional and national dialects; well, if we omit those, surely *then* we have a standard form? Maybe: and the reasons for that "maybe" are the reasons I wrote this page.

A "language" is any set of conventional symbols, and rules for their arrangement, that one user of the language employs to place thoughts in the mind of another user of that language. Keep firmly in mind that definition: *a set of conventional symbols and rules for their arrangement*. Whatever my intent, if I buttonhole you and say "G'por onfer ybr om iwert weyqtx," I have placed no thoughts whatever in your mind save possibly that I am either insane or a refugee from a country you have never heard of. That, obviously, is because I have tried to communicate using symbols with no conventional meaning and used them in accord with no recognizable conventional pattern.

Suppose instead: "Millennium hand and shrimp." Now I have used symbols with conventional meanings, but the pattern of their use does not seem to comport with any recognized convention. The speech is still meaningless.

Then suppose I said: "You like Fred better than me." Aha, one thinks, communication at last. But is it? Did I mean *You like Fred better than I like Fred,* or did I mean *You like Fred better than you like me*? Is there a way to decide which I meant? Yes, there is. The conventional rules for using English words to convey meaning provide that the word "me" in that sentence unequivocally requires the interpretation that your liking for Fred exceeds your liking for me. To convey the other meaning, those rules provide that I would have to say "You like Fred better than I."

While we are in good supposing form, let us next suppose that someone comes along and says that the rules of English should allow a person to use either "I" or "me" indifferently to convey the meaning we thought only "I" could carry in that sentence, but that the other sense still can only be represented by "me." Under*that* rule, if someone says "You like Fred better than I," we have still a definite meaning; but if that someone says "You like Fred better than me," we have ambiguity that cannot be resolved without resort to evidence outside the sentence, which outside evidence may or may not be readily available to us.

Why would anyone propose changing a rule that gives certainty to one that gives ambiguity? Especially when there is no compensating benefit of any kind? That—as the cat who voided into the sugar bowl remarked—remains to be seen. (I suppose that it is not strictly true to say that there is *no* benefit, for we would no longer have to understand and remember quite as much of rule to be able to say that we were using English "correctly.") If we consider it proven, or self-evident, that *some* rules are necessary, the next general question is how simple or complex need or ought they to be? One too frequently hears or reads that, oh, for example, the major and continuing loss of case inflection, or the slow disappearance of the subjunctive mood, is A Good Thing because it "simplifies" English. A useful tool in evaluating trends is to imagine them taken at once to their ultimate end; that is not an absolutely certain thought tool, but it is a sturdy one. So let us simplify English as much as possible: let us imagine an English in which every single sentence is nothing but the syllable "om." The only simplification possible beyond that is no sound (or printed characters) at all. Well, that's pretty simple all right—but, with comic obviousness, it is useless for placing thoughts in the mind of another.

We don't suggest that there is a straight-line relationship between a language's complexity and its power of communication, but a little reflection suggests that, broadly speaking, the two track. The more a language allows us to differentiate, the more subtle its powers of communication: that much seems beyond any but the most outrageous doubt. In practical terms, that conclusion suggests to us that increased differentiation in a language is generally positive and decreased differentiation generally negative.

We say "positive" and "negative"; but I propose a simple and more general test.

A change in the rules of a language that augments the ability of a careful user of that language to place thoughts in the mind of another careful user with precision and elegance is a good change; a change which diminishes that ability is a bad change. ("Elegance" there is meant in the scientist's or mathematician's sense: "pleasing by ingenious simplicity and effectiveness"; but it applies as well in the esthetic sense, "characterized by dignified richness and grace")

We speak of "change" because we are not constructing a brand-new artificial language: we are dealing with an established language, English. To understand what "established" means in this context, a little background is wanted.

English is a relatively new language: If you have any doubts, consider *Beowulf*, circa 1000; Chaucer, the late 1300s; and Shakespeare, the late 1500s. *Beowulf* is for all practical purposes in a completely alien tongue; Chaucer, less than three centuries after, is not simple for a modern to follow without notes or training, but is recognizably writing some form of English; Shakespeare, less than two centuries beyond Chaucer, is readily readable though obviously far from modern; and we today are but four centuries after Shakespeare.

So rapid an evolution meant linguistic turmoil; and in that turmoil, few attempts were made at systematization. For a very long time, English grammar, syntax, diction, and orthography were wildly nonstandard. After the printing press had had time to promote written English to a commonplace, some attempts at assigning formal structure to the language began to appear. Regrettably, most or all of those early efforts were by men with more arrogance than wit or learning—for in their day English usages, while slowly stabilizing, were yet diverse even among careful users, so that these men were not, *could not be,* recording general agreements on right usage, but were arrogating to themselves authority to select from the welter those patterns that peculiarly satisfied their personal esthetics or whatever. Though such follies were enshrined by the half-learned, they had little effect on the continuing evolution and stabilization of actual educated usage patterns in English. The spate of books, magazines, and newspapers that began flowing to the newly emergent and fast-growing class of literate readers substantially accelerated that stabilization, and by about the dawn of the twentieth century, the process was far along.

(Lest some nitpicker suggest that "literate readers" is tautological, remark that even a decent desk dictionary includes under *literate* the meaning "well-educated; having or showing extensive knowledge, learning, or culture.")

Such stability finally made codification of the rules of English a plausible undertaking, and that century thus birthed numerous manuals and texts by authors of sufficient intelligence and scholarship to make those manuals and texts authoritative. The Fowler brothers' *The King's English* was among the first; it was followed by surviving brother Henry's magnum opus, *Modern English Usage*. To name but a few other of the more significant of the century's stream of like works, there was Strunk's (later Strunk and White's) *Elements of Style,* Wilson Follett's *Modern American Usage,* Eric Partridge's *Usage and Abusage,* Theodore Bernstein's *The Careful Writer,* Sir Ernest Gowers' *The Complete Words,* Bryan Garner's *A Dictionary of Modern American Usage,* and that is only some of the usage manuals—there were also grammar texts, such as George O. Curme's classic *English Grammar*. The list makes clear that throughout the twentieth century qualified experts continued to set forth rules and guidelines for correct English at a pace and in a way that demonstrates a substantial interest in and readership for such books.

That is not to suggest that all the authorities were always in perfect accord on every smallest point, that the rules of English were ever at any time held to be embalmed in a single manual figuratively carved in stone. But close examination of those works and most of their kin *will* show a thick cable of continuity, with the occasional points of disagreement few, not often hotly contested, and largely irrelevant to everyday speech and writing. There was not a literal consensus, but there was general agreement on by far the greater part of English usage.

Moreover, as generally stable as English was coming into the century, that stability only became more definite yet as time went on, owing to a feedback process: the manual writers were taking note of how careful, well-schooled writers and speakers used English and codifying those patterns, while those same writers were taking heed of what the authoritative manuals were saying (which is to say, of what their peers were doing with the tongue). The few points of controversy became fewer yet as the century wore on.

That agreement was not confined to the "literati" or academics. Also to be found in the early and middle part of the twentieth century was a manifest, one might almost say ravening, hunger on the part of the great mass of the public to learn and be able to rightly use the acknowledged rules of "correct English"—the proof is the number of books and correspondence courses, widely advertised to and widely purchased by all classes, promising to improve the buyer's English. There was certainly not, in those days, any visible countercurrent or opposition in the public mind to the idea that there is a "correct" English and that it is a good thing to know what it is.

DESCRIPTIVE ENGLISH

As you may recall from somewhere up above here, what remained to be seen, besides the cat's symbolic speech in the sugar bowl, was "Why would anyone propose changing a rule that gives certainty to one that gives ambiguity? Especially when there is no compensating benefit of any kind?"

Be aware that people who want to make changes like that are real, numerous, and clamorous. The movement goes by the name "descriptionism" (or "descriptivism"), and its premise is well conveyed by the epigraph atop this page: that is, they believe that there is literally *no such thing* as "incorrect English." A lot of the fellow travellers of descriptionism—who rarely recognize themselves as such—will say that "literally no such thing" is an exaggeration; but they will have a hard time explaining away the endless academic papers, like the one cited, from the less-reticent ideologues who populate the movement.

There we were, mid-century, with a pretty stable set of rules for English and near-universal acceptance of those rules as defining "correct" English. Then "descriptionism" congeals into a movement; the assertion is made that "rules" are artificial, unnatural constraints on expressiveness, imposed not for clarity and sanity but as symbols of an oppressive patriarchy, or some such blether. In practical terms, the public is led to believe. Such blether will always appeal to a certain large segment of the population. It is part and parcel of a larger anarchic blethering to the effect that most or all rules are false and artificial. The segment such stuff appeals to is the segment that is traditionally unable or unwilling to learn or follow rules; it comports with the belief of such folk that their poor standing in the world is not, after all, owing to their deficiencies, but is purely and simply the result of an evil conspiracy. (Ask yourself what other movements in this age have preached that doctrine) To be sure, a horrible but undeniable half-truth is buried there: when there are no rules, no one can ever be "wrong" in anything—language use, civility, whatever. And there are a lot of "whatevers."

The lazy, the incompetent, and the naturally anarchic are an obvious market for that particular intellectual narcotic. Less obvious is how and why persons with working brains get caught up in it. Again, causes are not my business here: effects are. But one must suspect that the sorts of attractions include a spurious sympathy with the "downtrodden," those poor souls denied advancement in the world owing merely to inability; a sense of superiority and power for being in the vanguard of an iconoclastic movement and even among generally intelligent persons, a sense of relief that they can finally cease worrying about selecting between *who* and *whom.*

It is interesting, and possibly amusing, that the many articles and papers that so vigourously champion linguistic anarchy are almost invariably written in strict accordance with the established "prescriptive" rules of English

Descriptivists set forth many arguments for their position. One cannot deal with all of them, but a few of the more familiar deserve comment.

HISTORICAL FALLACY

One frequently adduced argument is that some given rule is no rule at all because, for hundreds of years, uses both this way and that way were encountered in English—an argument normally buttressed with quotations from some undeniably great writers. We have already discussed the meaninglessness of such a proposition in the light of the anarchic state of even relatively late English, and likened it to proposing that we execute by burning at the stake because that was once commonplace.

We will also note that authors of undoubted excellence, from antiquity to today, make mistakes, sometimes gross mistakes, in language use; it is standard practice in usage manuals to take samples of the error being discussed from the writings of just such fine sources, precisely for the point of demonstrating that no one is immune to error—as the saying goes, "even Homer nodded." Few or none of those authors would, were the error pointed out to them, refuse to accept it as error. Jane Austen notoriously exhibited poor grammar, and accordingly is a common citation by descriptivists; but we fail to see any basis for the implied assumption that had Austen had better knowledge of grammar she either would not have deployed that knowledge or, by deploying it, would have been a lesser writer.

MAJORITARIAN FALLACY

Another common argument is the majoritarian: "practically everybody says it that way." As Wilson Follett once put it,

"Let three thousand say *one of those who believes* while only three say *those who believe*; and as long as the three thousand do not also say *we believes, you believes, they believes,* the three thousand will be wrong from the only point of view that is relevant here, the point of view of form. Mere prevalence can sanctify many sorts of popular error—it can, for example, make words eventually mean the opposite of what they originally meant—but it cannot make a singular verb consort with a plural subject for the convenience of a writer who has not taken the trouble to find out what the subject is."

MENTAL-TELEPATHY FALLACY

This one is the evergreen "ah nuts, you know what I mean." Do I? Too many people seem to make the assumption that because *they* know what they mean (we will grant them that grace), it must follow as the night the day that *any* token effort at expressing that meaning will, in a quasi-magical manner, necessarily convey it to all hearers or readers, as if the ideas in one's mind have the force to communicate themselves to others' minds almost independent of the words used in writing or speaking them. Had I a mere nickel for every time someone who might reasonably be supposed to have a working brain has said something that was at the least equivocal owing purely to a failure to follow the established rules of English usage, I'd be, if not rich, at least comfortably well off.

But even in the many instances in which it is true, that we *do* know what was meant, there are still sufficient reasons to demand that expressing that "what" in incorrect English be held wrong, an *error*.

One, too often overlooked in discussions like these, is esthetics: to a reader or listener accustomed to correct English, an incorrect usage, even when comprehensible, is jarring, distasteful, and distracting. Writers and speakers who are indifferent to whether or not their language jars and distracts their audience so long as it is understood are like folk serving a supposedly fine meal on chipped, cracked, mismatched plates. But there is also a practical point: if our "getting it" engenders any hesitation at all, whether owing to momentary confusion or a mere mental shudder, the flow of the writer's or speaker's ideas is interrupted—and the effectiveness of the communication thus reduced—in proportion to the degree of that hesitation. (One would also think that there would be a certain pride and satisfaction to be had from knowing that one has said one's say as precisely and elegantly—in both senses—as possible, but perhaps such considerations do not appeal to descriptivists)

Another important reason that "you know what I meant" is a deadly argument is that incorrect usages have a steady corrosive effect on correct usages. If we—here, the English-speaking public at large—hear "this is him" for "this is he" often enough, our "ear" for natural case use becomes dulled, to the point that "he's taller than me" starts to sound natural, after which using "you like Fred better than me" to mean that you don't like Fred as much as I do no longer seems wrong or unusual, and Bingo!, there we are, slid some steps back on the slippery road away from Babel that we have been so patiently negotiating through the centuries.

The reference to Babel is not pure ornament. Presumably you know what a dialect is. Whatever else we may feel and think about dialects, we cannot rationally maintain that they augment communication between speakers of a given dialect and speakers of any other form of the language in question, whether another dialect or the "standard" form. ("Standard" is the word that has become the P.C. replacement for "correct," an immediate byproduct of descriptionist harangues about the phrase "incorrect English" being somethingist somethingism) But the descriptionist is not content to encourage mere *dialects*: the descriptionist introduces and lauds the concept of "idiolect." Of the prefix "idio," the OED says "own, personal, private, peculiar, separate, distinct"; from that, we deduce, correctly if shockingly, that the descriptionist is saying that each and every native speaker of English is speaking a unique, private variant version of English—which, up to that point, is a defensible position—and that each of those hundreds of millions of "own, personal, private, peculiar, separate, distinct" Englishes is "correct"—which is not defensible.

SOCIOLOGICAL FALLACY

Yet another argument of the descriptionists is that rules in general (not just in English) are naught but a tool of the ruling class (or classes—they can't seem to decide how many there are), forged to maintain those classes in an artificial and unnatural superiority over the downtrodden, underprivileged, &c. &c. (anyone not living in a cave can fill in the rest), and that language-usage rules are an especially important tool of oppression because no one can long avoid using language. In this argument, we get perhaps a little closer to what descriptionism is all about, which is assuredly not any augmentation of the power of English as a tool with which to place thoughts in the mind of another with precision and elegance.

Now there can be little doubt that language use has been and is used as a badge to identify social class, especially (it seems) in the British Isles—Bernard Shaw's*Pygmalion* (the basis of the musical "My Fair Lady") was a savagely sarcastic comment on that point. Now the badge is not the discrimination, so there are two basic ways of handling the matter: we can remove all the badges, or we can make sure that no two people have one of the same colour. If a given set of people can be identified for purposes of discrimination or of simple snobbery by incorrect use of their mother tongue, which makes more sense: to emphasize and teach correct use, thereby also improving communication? Or to praise, emphasize, and exaggerate differences—hindering communication—on the theory that when every single person speaks differently enough from every other person, group differences will be indistinguishable? Descriptivists have given their answer clearly enough.

ARTISTIC FALLACY

Ancillary to the purported social "benefits" of eroding the definitions of "correct" English are the purported artistic benefits. Rules, descriptivists hold, are shackles chaining the artistic imagination.

Well, as we said earlier, to spot-check an idea, take it to its extreme. Given no rules at all, how does the writer—the artist of words—function at all? His or her random gibberish would then be indistinguishable from anyone else's, or, for that matter, from a chimpanzee's. So: we need *some* rules. Are we next to believe in some linguistic version of the notorious Laffer Curve in economics?

That rules improve communication up to some particular point and then begin to degrade it from there on? In constructing an answer, we need to keep in mind: one, that there are languages with many more and more complex rules than English whose native speakers manage to communicate with grace and fluency without any obvious difficulty; and two, that we are talking about English, real, contemporary English, not some hypothetical unknown or artificial language, or languages in the abstract.

Manifestly, considering the intersection in logic of those two facts, even if there is a Laffer reversal point on the complexity/power curve, it's a *very* long way uphill from the current complexity level of English. (Actual poetry is an exception to the discussion here because the methods and tools of the poet have always been different from those of the speaker or writer of prose—though I think it can be argued that even the poet benefits from clear, accepted language rules because then he or she has a definite baseline from which to vary, and the breaking of rules to a particular purpose may itself be done with precision)

INSIGNIFICANCE FALLACY

The final descriptionist excuse I will consider is that "bad grammar is not The End Of Civilization As We Know It," *aka* "no nation ever fell from bad language use." (Aside: since no one can show a scrap of plausible harm from rigorously following the rules of correct English, all this fallacious flatus from the descriptionists reduces to *excuses,* not *reasons,* for tolerating or even encouraging nonstandard—incorrect—English usage)

The insignificance platitude, usually offered in a sarcastically dispositive tone, seems at first reasonable, even undeniable; it is no such thing. A perusal of works such as Arnold Toynbee's classic *Study of History* shows that civilizations follow fairly regular patterns in their rises and falls.

A society always comprises a dominant class and a socio-economic underclass. What glues a society together during its rise and heyday is a consensus, first that the social and economic divisions between the dominant class and the underclass are neither extreme nor grossly unfair, and second that the dominant class has a sensed moral authority to lead the society. The underclass in such times is valued, and its members have opportunities to achieve both wealth and prestige.

The characteristic pattern of the falling stage is a rapid expansion of the underclass, with an increasing alienation of that swelling underclass from the correspondingly dwindling dominant class. That alienation invariably derives from several simultaneous and inter-related things happening to the underclass in such times: decreasing economic and social status, ever more sharply differentiated values and customs, decreasing schooling and understanding—all things that contribute mightily to a growing sense of "us against them"; and, as another famous man said, a house divided against itself cannot stand.

When alienation erodes and eventually destroys the prevailing consensus, and thus that perception of a moral authority fairly vested in the dominant class, the end is near for that civilization, regardless of its material and cultural accomplishments—which often then reach a feverish apex—during its end days.

Till relatively recently—within living memory, as one says—the western English-speaking nations appeared to be on an ascending arc of civilization, in that class differences owing to wealth, education, opportunity, and their concomitants were slowly, more slowly than might ideally have been wanted but nevertheless surely, eroding. Then, around mid-century, that trend reversed. Leaving aside here the large social context to focus on education and language use, we see the phenomenon encapsulated by the marvelously apt phrase "dumbing down" striking with the suddenness and violence, in cultural terms, of an earthquake.

It does not require deep powers of mind to see that a continued dwindling of the ability of a large segment of the population to use good English is a prime specimen of the major factors that generate and increase the isolation, and thus the alienation, of that segment from the dominant educated class. The jobs available to those with poor language skills become fewer, and invariably substantially lower-paying, than those available to individuals with good language skills. (From the large to the small: it is also often recited by descriptivists that "no one ever died of bad grammar." This is only a note here, not real exposition, because hard data are lacking—but consider:

Jerry Coleman, one-time broadcaster of San Diego Padres' baseball games, was well-known for play calls like this classic: "It's deep, Winfield is going back on the ball, way back, oh my gosh, he's hit his head on the wall, and now it's rolling around on the ground in front of him." Exercise for the student: convert that from comic to serious by varying the circumstances while keeping the form of the error; for bonus points, make the result fatal. For extra credit, answer this question: would you want a paramedic or fireman or policeman who used English like that to be the one to deal with your emergency?

CHOOSING A PLACE

In general, *the* great barrier to any serious consideration of the descriptivist ideology is this: the descriptivist cannot set forth one single harm that would befall from anyone, or everyone, punctiliously speaking and writing 100% textbook-correct English. I know: I have asked descriptionists, in public forums, again and again to set forth one harm, one, that would befall a person writing and speaking ideal "correct" English; the closest thing to an answer that I have ever seen is that some less-capable workmates might occasionally make fun of him or her. Well: that settles that. How could anyone pursue a sound knowledge of English with that awful fate beckoning? Might as well board up all the schools right now. (At the pace the descriptionist ideology and its kissin' cousins are spreading, pretty soon we'll have to anyhow, as no one is very much learning anything anymore anyway)

Understand, please, that in defending the prescribed rules of "correct" English as most of the authorities over the last century have presented them, neither I nor anyone I know of is saying that those rules are perfectly logical and consistent, or that they could not be improved on in many ways. What I, at least, am saying is that they were and in the main still are (at least for careful, considerate users of the language) the baseline; no one without a time machine can change what that baseline is. We thus need to forget about "perfection"—whatever that might be—and deal with the real world. That in turn means considering every divergence from the baseline conventions with but a single criterion: does this divergence on balance augment or diminish the ability of a careful user of English to place thoughts in the mind of another such careful user with precision and elegance? If Yes, we welcome and support it; in No, we reject and argue against it. It's that simple.

Well we lied: it isn't *quite* that simple. Allow me the liberty of a colourful simile: at any given moment, the state of the English language (or any language) can be likened to a battlefield. On this side is the ground held by the fully acceptable usages; across the field is the ground occupied by fully unacceptable usages. But despite the barrages fired back and forth by those two armies, there remains a thin strip of no-man's land between them. Troops from one side or the other are forever worming their way across that dangerous strip, where they are liable to fire from both sides.

Some eventually make it across the barbed wire to the other side and join the opposing army; a few creep back to their own lines; most die there. It is an interesting and—I think—revealing quirk of descriptionism that it is more concerned with sheer defiance of established custom than with any consistent position. As an example, the use of case inflections is continually being attacked: *it's me, this is him, who should I ask for?*, and a parade of like constructions are eagerly touted as perfectly fine English, apparently because they do not require the writer or speaker to take any least trouble to either know what pronoun represents what case or to have any least idea of in what case a given word is (or, for that matter, to have the slightest idea in Hell of what a case is). But when someone pops up with the delightful idea (no, I'm not being sarky) that it would be nice if English reacquired a distinct second-person plural, perhaps in the form*youse,* the descriptionists are all for that too, even though it increases, not decreases, the complexity of the language—primarily if not solely because "youse" is a usage often associated with ignorance or the dialect of scorned classes.

More complex, less complex—who cares as long as it flouts current rules? In your face, man.

Here's another instance: the singular use of *they*. It is a deeply regrettable fact that English lacks a neuter third-person pronoun set: we have to say *he or she, him or her, his or her,* which, admittedly, is tedious and perhaps ugly. So long as women were invisibles who didn't count, *he/him/his* served; but, with enlightenment, that rickety crutch was finally kicked away. The lack is sorely felt: many a valiant soul has contrived and advocated possibilities, some of which seemed rather reasonable—but none has ever caught the public's fancy.

Instead, what has evolved, in lazy minds, is the habit of using *they/them/their*. Lazy minds being the dominant kind, one hears and sees the error so often now that it requires scrupulous care not to fall into it—a fine example of what I mean by the "corrosive effect" I discussed earlier. But, says the descriptionist, so many people routinely employ that usage now that resistance is futile: the battle is over.

Descriptionists do seem to love phrasing triumphs of folly as battles won. Well, what *is* the problem? Doesn't the use answer a real need? Yes, but at a disproportionate price, the loss of clarity when what was uniquely a plural now becomes indeterminate. If I wrote "The team members retired to their cabins, each contemplating their problems," once upon a time—one *not* far, far away—that would have uniquely meant that each was considering the problems confronting the team; now, it might mean that or it might equally mean that each was considering his or her particular individual problems—we don't know and cannot know without information extrinsic to the sentence, nor is the "context will tell" argument available because it is no strain whatever to construct plausible and credibly written text in which the context does *not* tell, yet in which it is important to know which situation the author intended to portray.

And all that quite passes over such wildly inept unintended comedies as "no sooner did the pollen-laden breeze begin to stir than every one of them was blowing their nose," a tribute to the wonders of modern plastic surgery. A marked loss of precision is not a price worth paying to save two short syllables, six printed characters including a space, especially when in the vast majority of cases the problem can simply be avoided altogether by adroit rephrasings (the easiest and commonest being to make the usage plural—*authors* rather than *the author*—but there are several other techniques, Garner, for example, listing five in all).

CAUSES AND CURES

That any who would find fault with the conclusions reached below may see whence those arise, we have here set forth a train of simple propositions in what I trust is a reasonably logical order.

We have kept each simple, and the jumps between them small, not out of disrespect for the reading abilities of visitors, but so that any disagreeing with conditions at the destination may take note of at just which station they felt the need to detrain.

- A language is a tool with which users of that language place thoughts in the minds of other such users. The intended thoughts may be true or false or some of each; they may be meant to inform, to entertain, to please, to stimulate a train of further thoughts, or any of a large number of other things; but placing those thoughts is the end and purpose of language. That is not a discovery or pronouncement or deduction: it is a tautology.
- Languages are purely conventional: they consist of arbitrary symbols with conventional meanings assigned, and of arbitrary rules for arranging those symbols so as to enhance or alter or compound their composite meaning. (There is a belief that some of the most elementary rules of human language may be in part inbred, but there is no conclusive evidence for—and much disagreement over—that idea, conditions that make the conjecture valueless for practical purposes)
- The greater the precision and elegance, in any sense of that word, with which skilled users of a language can place thoughts in the minds of other users—that being the base purpose of language—the more useful (or "better" or "more powerful") the language.

(*Elegant* can mean, as mathematicians and scientists often use the word, "pleasing by ingenious simplicity and effectiveness", or it can mean "characterized by dignified richness and grace"; both are desireable traits for language use)

- Anything that increases the precision or elegance (or both) with which skilled users of a language can place thoughts in the minds of other such users is thus necessarily an improvement to the language; anything that decreases those abilities is correspondingly a detriment.

- The more nearly complete the agreement by the users of a language on the conventions, both of symbol significance and of arrangement rules, the greater the precision and elegance available to those users.

Let me pause to elaborate the obvious: if A uses the symbol—the word—"glorm" to signify the look of the afternoon sky after a thunderstorm has passed, while B, hearing A, thinks of a kind of small, white worm seen only at night, their language has failed A and B badly in its purpose; if A uses that word to signify the general class we call "worm," their language has failed A and B, but not terribly; if they both understand the word-symbol to signify that very type of small white worm, it has served them well.

What is so of the actual symbols is more so of any rules for varying or enhancing the meaning of those symbols by the manner of their arrangement, the potential complexities and subtleties being proportionately greater. It would be supererogation to adduce yet more elementary examples.

- Combining the import of the two propositions above, increasing agreement by the users of a language on its conventions is improvement to the language, while decreasing agreement is detriment.
- Converting a symbol or a rule that had a unique significance to one that has more than one possible significance is a decrease in user agreement on the conventions of the language. It is thus necessarily to at least some extent a detriment.

(Unless you think the sentence "The attorney cited several authorities that sanctioned his actions, but the judge sanctioned him anyway," is admirable communication)

- Supplying a new symbol or rule that makes expressing a given idea with materially greater precision or elegance than before is an improvement.
- Whether a particular change in conventions—which is a change in the language—that has elements of

both improvement and detriment will be on balance an improvement or a detriment depends on whether the harm from the detriment outweighs the gain from the improvement or vice-versa.

- All changes (as opposed to novelties) carry an overhead detriment beyond their actual effect on the power of the language, and that overhead detriment must be included in any reckoning attempting a balance of gain and loss from a particular change.

Change is not Free

Putting aside the comic folly of it, assume that tomorrow every speaker of English in the world freely and enthusiastically agrees that thenceforth the word-symbol "rain" will denote the path of a point moving on a plane so that it remains equidistant from another fixed point on that plane, while the word-symbol "circle" will henceforth mean water that falls from the skies as a consequence of meteorological processes.

Are we no better or worse off than we were? No: we are worse off—because now we have a planetful of libraries chock full of books that describe circles as rain and vice versa (under the new rules, that is). Even those who enthusiastically agreed to the change will soon find making the mental conversions tedious or worse, while succeeding generations will find those books difficult going.

Let us assume that English exists, or existed at some moment of relatively recent time, as a set of symbols and rules to which there was universal agreement by all native speakers. Whether it did or not we put aside for the moment: just grant the assumption.

The assumption does *not* include the premise that that agreed-on English is perfect in its abilities, or even close to perfect: only agreed-on. Implicit in that possibility of error is that, while all users may agree that there is a set of definite conventions that constitute English, not all users know all of those conventions, and some of the ones a particular user may know may be known imperfectly.

The ability of a writer to make mistakes in uses of the language does not conflict with the idea of there being a universal set of conventions. In democratic republics, the citizenry delegates the making of needed laws—many of them complex and concerned with abstruse matters—with equanimity, and does not feel that its collective or individual inability to recite from memory the entire Federal Code in itself vitiates any part of that Code, nor signals disagreement with or disapproval of it.

Indeed, no one can make mistakes unless there is a right form which has not been adhered to: the exception proves the rule. The meaning of that oft-misunderstood legal principle is that if an act is explicitly or implicitly shown to be an exception of some sort, that necessarily implies a rule to which it is an exception. The issuing of written permission for a person to do a certain act implies a rule stating that normally that act—let us say, a "rebroadcast, retransmission, or dissemination in any form"—is forbidden.

Let us next see what some of the consequences are of the state I have asked you to assume.

We have accepted that the conventions are imperfect. They may lack parallelism, and so appear inconsistent one with another, they may be inadequate for succinctly conveying certain not uncommon ideas, or for providing a sufficiency of shades of meaning in common forms, they may require cumbersome constructions in some instances: the list of possible defects is long enough.

None of the prior assertions requires that we suffer such a condition in perpetuity. I say "suffer", but manifestly implicit in the assumption was the corollary assumption that the extant system is working at least tolerably well as it is: that is implicit because otherwise the base assumption, consensus, is an intolerable strain on willing suspension of disbelief.

There is hence no need for massive immediate changes in the conventions. We can, in this assumption, afford to proceed like a subsistence farmer offered new crops: slowly and carefully, a little at a time, until we are confident that the changes are for the better. We have, that is, the leisure to make sure that proposed changes are going to be beneficial—without unintended or unanticipated detrimental consequences. Indeed, we *have* to proceed slowly, lest we lose contact with our linguistic heritage.

That aside raises a point: changes in symbols are less grave than changes in the rules for manipulating those symbols. The world changes: many new things, tangible and intangible, come into existence every day, indeed, every hour, and those things require names. Coining new names—nouns, as we conventionally say—is not only harmless but vital. The only detriments commonly associated with coining are two: occasional infelicity, which can scarcely be helped, and redundancy, which can.

Redundancy is the gravelling practice of coining a term for which a perfectly serviceable word already exists; A pair of examples may amuse.

To "transpire" means—*meant,* I should say—to slowly, invisibly, imperceptibly pass through a barrier by osmosis, and was a fine description, in its common metaphorical use, of the curious way supposedly secret or confidential information often passes into common knowledge. Now, the word simply means "happen"—and what, pray tell, was wrong with "happen"?—while we must fall back for the original idea on terms like "leak," which do not convey that slow, mysterious osmosis but instead imply a distinct, well, *leak.* Water never *transpired* from a badly soldered pipe.

Then there is, or was, "connive at," a term meaning to deliberately turn a blind eye to, to passively allow, by supposedly innocent but actually knowing inaction, an illicit activity to proceed. Now it means something like—the turning has left the term in a bit of a muddle—"conspire with."

There is an immensely complicated jobs it has to do, a definite quality of artifice about grammar. That said, in its fundamentals, it is only sanity: a sane recognition of the real world. Things exist, things have qualities, things do things to other things. We convert our perceptions of those things, and their qualities and actions, into language guided by grammar that, at bottom, reflects those perceptions.

Verbs, in English as in many languages, have forms that correspond to the singularity or plurality of the thing or things performing the action. Pronouns, a marvelous invention, also have forms that reflect data including the number of the noun they are standing in for. On the not-terribly-controversial idea that a thing is equal to itself, pronouns have forms that agree with the nouns they stand in for, as the number forms of verbs correspond to the singularity or plurality of the doer of the action.

English is full of such required correlations between its word symbols, correlations that are a part of what we call the grammar of the language. Those correlations reflect the basic activity of the natural human mind: we don't expect a verb to denote plurality when the active force is singular, nor a pronoun standing in for a singular thing to indicate plurality. That is hardly artifice: it is its polar opposite.

Still operating under that assumption of consensus, what would we make of a sentence in which a plural pronoun was made to stand in for a singular noun? An error—nothing more, nothing less. We would expect that, as before, did we point out the error, presumably made in inadvertence, the maker would be pleased to correct it. But Lo! we find that the maker insists that No, the form is as was intended. On being referred to the conventions of the language, the writer forcefully expresses disdain: the world needs, and is now ready for, a plural pronoun for a singular noun. We no longer conclude that the writer was in error: we conclude that the writer is literally and exactly insane.

It is well to humour the mad: we inquire further. The writer has recognized what myriads of others have recognized: that for a particular generalized noun construction there is no unique correspondingly generalized pronoun, so that—in that generalized circumstance—the disjunction of *two* pronouns needs to be supplied to satisfy the consensus conventions of the language, a less than ideal form of expression. Those inclined to things like checking the water depth at the end of the pool they are contemplating a dive off will be given pause by that curious circumstance; those who—like the fellow in the apocryphal western novel who erupted from his chair at the table, dashed out the saloon door, leapt onto his horse, and rode away in all directions—are less given to reflection on circumstances will be undaunted by the possibility, which will not even cross their minds, that the world may not be here crying out for succor and deliverance just quite so loudly as they fancy—certainly not loudly enough to justify the institutionalized insanity of a plural proxy for a singular thing.

The disjunct pronoun pair at issue is two syllables, printable as nine characters (including spaces). The proposed replacement, the word once uniquely plural, is one syllable of four spaces.

The world-shaking saving effected is one curt syllable or five printed spaces. For that stunning benefit, we are asked to throw away the ages-old innate idea that a thing is equal to itself, and to accept that a long-unique term is now to be ambivalent (ambi-valent, of two values), with the determination of the operative valence a new requirement on the writer to exhibit and the reader to detect.

And all of that wrangling ignores the further consideration that in reality the special circumstances that might require that disjunct pronoun pair are, in the great majority of cases, readily avoidable. Anyone can tell me anything they choose to, and I—not being a telepath—will be unable to contradict that anything; but can you honestly report back to me that at some point in the nine long paragraphs (including this one) discussing a hypothetical writer and sanity in pronouns you said to yourself, "Ah yes, self, a clumsy circumlocution to avoid a gendered pronoun"? Yet that hypothetical writer has been discussed at length, assigned many qualities, made to do and say many things, and we still don't know—and haven't had to deal with—of what sex he or she is.

The dissenters will by now doubtless have packed up and left for a long weekend, but, should any vacillating souls remain, the next issue is the assumption under which we have dealt with that crypto-sexed writer: that there is, or at some moment in relatively recent time was, consensus on the conventions of English. To what extent is that assumption plausible, and to what extent does it affect the conclusions we have tentatively drawn?

Notably more significant, we can turn to the reference manuals. The first thing we need is a consensus, or close to it, as to what the leading reference manuals from in and near that era were. There, I think, we have little difficulty. Far ahead of the rest of the pack is Henry, notably with edition of *A Dictionary of Modern English Usage*; many writers to this hour (Ursula K. Le Guin pops to mind, owing to an explicit remark) feel that a copy of Fowler and a good dictionary are all any sound writer needs.

Well in the running are Theodore Bernstein, with several entries, notably *The Careful Writer*, and (my personal favourite) Wilson Follett with his *Dictionary of Modern American Usage*. That is not a list selected to buttress a viewpoint. It is a list of pretty well all the usage manuals anyone paid any attention to. Omitted are I know not how many equivalents of today's "For Dummies" books about writing, but I think the omissions fair, for while in the main they sold enough copies to sustain the belief I cited earlier that many, many people believed in a standard "correct" English and wanted to acquire it, none by itself was especially influential.

Anyone with an interest in what Lincoln Barnett, in the title of a book, called *The Treasure of Our Tongue* is invited to obtain copies of all of those many reference books and peruse each on this or that matter or topic and see if they don't represent a consensus on the major and most of the minor matters. I elsewhere extracted from most some succinct notes on the use of "they" and variants for a generalized singular; those, being especially relevant here, may stand as an example.

- *Fowler, Modern English Usage (alpha listing at "they")*: *Their* should be *his* (from a wrong example); he continues—about its occasional use in the past—"few modern writers would flout the grammarians so conspicuously."
- *Partridge, Book of Usage and Abusage (alpha at "their")*: "An error commonly found in both speech and writing."

- *Strunk, The Elements of Style (at "Words and Expressions Commonly Misused")*: "They. Not to be used when the antecedent is a distributive expression such as *each* [&c.]. Use the singular pronoun."
- *Strunk and White, The Elements of Style (at "Misused Words and Expressions")*: White not only repeats Strunk's original words, he adds a lengthy emphasis.
- *Nicholson, A Dictionary of American-English Usage (based on Fowler)*: Nicholson, who freely made changes to Folwer where she thought it appropriate, left his words on this matter untouched.
- *Bernstein, The Careful Writer (at "Pronouns")*: "The use of *their* in such contexts is common enough in spontaneous, casual speech, and even occurs occasionally in the work of reputable writers. Yet the writer of craftsmanship and taste will reject the grammatical inconsistency of the combination of a singular noun and a plural pronoun."
- *Gowers, The Complete Plain Words (at "Trouble With Pronouns")*: "You will be wise for the present not to be tempted by the greater convenience of [that usage]." Gowers also quotes Jesperson, whom we do not count separately: "In the third person it would have been very convenient to have a common-sex pronoun, but as a matter of fact English has none and must use.. makeshift expedients.."
- *Barzun, Clear and Simple*: in illustration of his Principle 9, ("Agreement is as pleasant in prose as it is in personal relations, and no more difficult to work for") are a couple of sample sentences using *they* as singular to illustrate pronomial defects.
- *Follett, Modern American Usage (at "antecedents," #7)*: "Liberal grammarians defend and even recommend the plural pronoun after... distributive words.... To the scrupulous the sequence seems unbuttoned, even in speech, and it is rejected despite all innuendos about purism and pedantry."

The one is some imagined prohibition against "splitting

infinitives"; the other is some equally fictitious prohibition against ending a sentence with a preposition. Some quotations from literary lights may help here:

- Bernard Shaw famously observed in a letter to a newspaper editor: "Every good literary craftsman splits his infinitives when the sense demands it. I call for the immediate dismissal of the pedant on your staff [who chases split infinitives]. It is of no consequence whether he decides to go quickly or to quickly go." (Quoted by Wilson Follett)
- Sir Winston Churchill, a writer of no mean abilities, also in a letter to an editor, about prepositions not ending sentences: "This is the sort of arrant nonsense up with which I will not put."

The other authorities I have mentioned all agree on these matters, as do all folk of any sense whatever. But, and count on it, the anarchists will have those zombies lurch out of the closet faithfully at every opportunity, to frighten the unknowing (and will make opportunities when none reasonably exist).

ENGLISH LANGUAGE

Most people who bother with the matter at all would admit that the English language is in a bad way, but it is generally assumed that we cannot by conscious action do anything about it. Our civilization is decadent, and our language — so the arguments runs — must inevitably share in the general collapse. It follows that any struggle against the abuse of language is a sentimental archaism, like preferring candles to electric light or hansom cabs to aeroplanes. Underneath this lies the half-conscious belief that language is a natural growth and not an instrument which we shape for our own purposes.

Now, it is clear that the decline of a language must ultimately have political and economic causes: it is not due simply to the bad influences of this or that individual writer. But an effect can become a cause, reinforcing the original cause and producing the same effect in an intensified form, and so on indefinitely. A man may take to drink because he feels himself to be a failure, and then fail all the more completely because he drinks. It is rather the same thing that is happening to the English language. It becomes ugly and inaccurate because our thoughts are foolish, but the slovenliness of our language makes it easier for us to have foolish thoughts. The point is that the process is reversible. Modern English, especially written English, is full of bad habits which spread by imitation and which can be avoided if one is willing to take the necessary trouble.

If one gets rid of these habits one can think more clearly, and to think clearly is a necessary first step towards political regeneration: so that the fight against bad English is not frivolous and is not the exclusive concern of professional writers. I will come back to this presently, and I hope that by that time the meaning of what I have said here will have become clearer. Meanwhile, here are five specimens of the English language as it is now habitually written.

These five passages have not been picked out because they are especially bad — I could have quoted far worse if:

- It is indeed, sure whether it is not true to say that the Milton who once seemed not unlike a seventeenth-century Shelley. had not become, out of an experience ever more bitter in each year, more alien (sic) to the founder of that Jesuit sect which nothing could induce him to tolerate.—*Professor Hamid Hussain (Essay in Freedom of Expression).*
- Above all, we cannot play ducks and drakes with a native battery of idioms which prescribes such egregious collocations of vocables as the Basic *put up with* for *tolerate* or*put at a loss* for *bewilder*.—*Professor Lancelot Hogben (Interglossa).*
- On the one side we have the free personality: by definition it is not neurotic, for it has neither conflict nor dream. Its desires, such as they are, are transparent, for they are just what institutional approval keeps in the forefront of consciousness; another institutional pattern would alter their number

and intensity; there is little in them that is natural, irreducible, or culturally dangerous. But *on the other side,* the social bond itself is nothing but the mutual reflection of these self-secure integrities. Recall the definition of love. Is not this the very picture of a small academic? Where is there a place in this hall of mirrors for either personality or fraternity? —*Essay on psychology in Politics.*

- All the 'best people' from the gentlemen's clubs, and all the frantic Fascist captains, united in common hatred of Socialism and bestial horror of the rising tide of the mass revolutionary movement, have turned to acts of provocation, to foul incendiarism, to medieval legends of poisoned wells, to legalize their own destruction to proletarian organizations, and rouse the agitated petty-bourgeoisie to chauvinistic fervour on behalf of the fight against the revolutionary way out of the crisis. —*Communist pamphlet.*
- If a new spirit *is* to be infused into this old country, there is one thorny and contentious reform which must be tackled, and that is the humanization and galvanization of the B.B.C. Timidity here will bespeak canker and atrophy of the soul. The heart of Britain may be sound and of strong beat, for instance, but the British lion's roar at present is like that of Bottom in Shakespeare's *Midsummer Night's Dream* — as gentle as any sucking dove. A virile new Britain cannot continue indefinitely to be traduced in the eyes, or rather ears, of the world by the effete languors of Langham Place, brazenly masquerading as 'standard English'. When the Voice of Britain is heard at nine o'clock, better far and infinitely less ludicrous to hear aitches honestly dropped than the present priggish, inflated, inhibited, school ma'amish arch braying of blameless, bashful mewing maidens.

Each of these passages has faults of its own, but, quite apart from avoidable ugliness, two qualities are common to all of them. The first is staleness of imagery: the other is lack of precision. The writer either has a meaning and cannot express it, or he inadvertently says something else, or he is almost indifferent as to whether his words mean anything or not. This mixture of vagueness and sheer incompetence is the most marked characteristic of modern English prose, and especially of any kind of political writing. As soon as certain topics are raised, the concrete melts into the abstract and no one seems able to think of turns of speech that are not hackneyed: prose consists less and less of words chosen for the sake of their meaning, and more of phrases tacked together like the sections of a prefabricated hen-house. I list below, with notes and examples, various of the tricks by means of which the work of prose construction is habitually dodged:

DYING METAPHORS

A newly invented metaphor assists thought by evoking a visual image, while on the other hand a metaphor which is technically 'dead' (e.g. *iron resolution*) has in effect reverted to being an ordinary word and can generally be used without loss of vividness. But in between these two classes there is a huge dump of worn-out metaphors which have lost all evocative power and are merely used because they save people the trouble of inventing phrases for themselves. Examples are: *Ring the changes on, take up the cudgels for, toe the line, ride roughshod over, stand shoulder to shoulder with, play into the hands of, no axe to grind, grist to the mill, fishing in troubled waters, rift within the lute, on the order of the day, Achilles' heel, swan song, hotbed.* Many of these are used without knowledge of their meaning (what is a 'rift', for instance?), and incompatible metaphors are frequently mixed, a sure sign that the writer is not interested in what he is saying. Some metaphors now current have been twisted out of their original meaning without those who use them even being aware of the fact. For example, *toe the line* is sometimes written *tow the line.* Another example is *the hammer and the anvil,* now always used with the implication that the anvil gets the worst of it. In real life it is always the anvil that breaks the hammer, never the other way about: a writer who stopped to think what he was saying would be aware of this, and would avoid perverting the original phrase.

VERBAL FALSE LIMBS

These save the trouble of picking out appropriate verbs and nouns, and at the same time pad each sentence with extra syllables which give it an appearance of symmetry. Characteristic phrases are: *render inoperative, militate against, prove unacceptable, make contact with, be subject to, give rise to, give grounds for, have the effect of, play a leading part (role) in, make itself felt, take effect, exhibit a tendency to, serve the purpose of, etc.etc.* The keynote is the elimination of simple verbs. Instead of being a single word, such as *break, stop, spoil, mend, kill,* a verb becomes a *phrase,* made up of a noun or adjective tacked on to some general-purposes verb such as *prove, serve, form, play, render*. In addition, the passive voice is wherever possible used in preference to the active, and noun constructions are used instead of gerunds.

The range of verbs is further cut down by means of the -*ize* and *de-* formations, and banal statements are given an appearance of profundity by means of the *not un-* formation. Simple conjunctions and prepositions are replaced by such phrases as *with respect to, having regard to, the fact that, by dint of, in view of, in the interests of, on the hypothesis that*; and the ends of sentences are saved from anticlimax by such resounding commonplaces as *greatly to be desired, cannot be left out of account, a development to be expected in the near future, deserving of serious consideration, brought to a satisfactory conclusion,* and so on and so forth.

PRETENTIOUS DICTION

Words like *phenomenon, element, individual* (as noun), *objective, categorical, effective, virtual, basic, primary, promote, constitute, exhibit, exploit, utilise, eliminate, liquidate,* are used to dress up simple statements and give an air of scientific impartiality to biased judgements Adjectives like *epoch-making, epic, historic, unforgettable, triumphant, age-old, inevitable, inexorable, veritable,* are used to dignify the sordid processes of international politics, while writing that aims at glorifying war usually takes on an archaic colour, its characteristic words being: *realm, throne, chariot, mailed fist, trident, sword, shield, buckler, banner, jackboot, clarion.* Foreign words and expressions such as *cul de sac, ancien régime, deus ex machina, mutatis mutandis, status quo, Gleichschaltung, Weltanschauung,* are used to give an air of culture and elegance. Except for the useful abbreviations *i.e., e.g.,* and *etc.,* there is no real need for any of the hundreds of foreign phrases now current in English.

MEANINGLESS WORDS

In certain kinds of writing, particularly in art criticism and literary criticism, it is normal to come across long passages which are almost completely lacking in meaning. Words like *romantic, plastic, values, human, dead, sentimental, natural, vitality,* as used in art criticism, are strictly meaningless, in the sense that they not only do not point to any discoverable object, but are hardly even expected to do so by the reader. When one critic writes, 'The outstanding features of Mr X's work is its living quality', while another writes, 'The immediately striking thing about Mr X's work is its peculiar deadness', the reader accepts this as a simple difference of opinion. If words like *black* and *white* were involved, instead of the jargon words*dead* and *living,* he would see at once that language was being used in an improper way. Many political words are similarly abused. The word *Fascism*has now no meaning except in so far as it signifies 'something not desirable'. The words *democracy, socialism, freedom, patriotic, realistic, justice,* have each of them several different meanings which cannot be reconciled with one another.

In the case of a word like *democracy,* not only is there no agreed definition, but the attempt to make one is resisted from all sides. It is almost universally felt that when we call a country democratic we are praising it: consequently the defenders of every kind of regime claim that it is a democracy, and fear that they might have to stop using the word if it were tied down to any one meaning. Words of this kind are often used in a consciously dishonest way. That is, the person who uses them has his own private definition, but allows his hearer to think he means something quite different. Statements like *Marshal Petain was a true patriot, The Soviet press is the freest in the world, The Catholic Church is opposed to persecution,* are almost always made with intent to deceive. Other words used in variable meanings, in most cases more or less dishonestly, are: *class, totalitarian, science, progressive, reactionary, bourgeois, equality*.

Now that we have made this catalogue of swindles and perversions, let me give another example of the kind of writing that they lead to. This time it must of its nature be an imaginary one. I am going to translate a passage of good English into modern English of the worst sort. Here is a well-known verse from*Ecclesiastes*:

We returned, and saw under the sun, that the race is not to the swift, nor the battle to the strong, neither yet bread to the wise, nor yet riches to men of understanding, nor yet favour to men of skill; but time and chance happeneth to them all. Objective consideration of contemporary phenomena compels the conclusion that success or failure in competitive activities exhibits no tendency to be commensurate with innate capacity, but that a considerable element of the unpredictable must invariably be taken into account.

This is a parody, but not a very gross one. Exhibit 3, above, for instance, contains several patches of the same kind of English. It will be seen that I have not made a full translation. The beginning and ending of the sentence follow the original meaning fairly closely, but in the middle the concrete illustrations — race, battle, bread — dissolve into the vague phrase 'success or failure in competitive activities'. As we have tried to show, modern writing at its worst does not consist in picking out words for the sake of their meaning and inventing images in order to make the meaning clearer. It consists in gumming together long strips of words which have already been set in order by someone else, and making the results presentable by sheer humbug. The attraction of this way of writing is that it is easy. It is easier — even quicker, once you have the habit — to say*In my opinion it is a not unjustifiable assumption that* than to say *I think.* If you use ready-made phrases, you not only don't have to hunt about for words; you also don't have to bother with the rhythms of your sentences, since these phrases are generally so arranged as to be more or less euphonious. When you are composing in a hurry — when you are dictating to a stenographer, for instance, or making a public speech — it is natural to fall into a pretentious, latinized style.

Tags like *a consideration which we should do well to bear in mind* or *a conclusion to which all of us would readily assent* will save many a sentence from coming down with a bump. By using stale metaphors, similes and idioms, you save much mental effort, at the cost of leaving your meaning vague, not only for your reader but for yourself. This is the significance of mixed metaphors. The sole aim of a metaphor is to call up a visual image. When these images clash — as in *The Fascist octopus has sung its swan song, the jackboot is thrown into the melting-pot* — it can be taken as certain that the writer is not seeing a mental image of the objects he is naming; in other words he is not really thinking.

Index

A

Acoustic 1, 19, 23, 38, 39, 40, 54, 55, 56, 60, 69, 70, 74, 83, 91, 98, 99, 105, 111, 128, 131, 132, 135, 137, 139, 145, 151, 152, 158, 181, 182, 183, 198, 199, 204, 213, 218, 224, 225
Apico 25, 27, 34, 45, 98, 140, 142
Articulation 20, 22, 24, 25, 26, 27, 28, 32, 34, 37, 42, 43, 44, 45, 46, 47, 48, 49, 51, 52, 60, 61, 62, 63, 64, 65, 76, 80, 96, 97, 98, 130, 157, 159, 164, 166, 167, 169, 170, 172, 173, 208, 216, 224
Articulatory Phonetics 1
Aspirated 26, 35, 99, 122, 132, 133, 137, 145, 211
Aspiration 21, 23, 26, 35, 101, 136, 160, 162
Assimilation 45, 63, 64, 65, 73, 74, 165, 166, 167, 169, 171, 172, 173
Auditory Phonetics 2

B

Bilabial 27, 28, 33, 64, 76, 78, 80, 91, 99, 101, 110, 140, 142, 166, 167, 169, 170

C

Cardinal 30, 39, 40, 68, 69, 70, 71, 72, 86, 138
Cartilage 17
Constriction 19, 20, 51, 52, 55, 56, 80, 141, 142, 144, 160, 224
Customary 35, 46

D

Diacritics 26, 87
Dialects 14, 23, 25, 31, 32, 40, 41, 53, 64, 69, 72, 97, 114, 115, 141, 156, 161, 262, 277
Diphthongs 5, 12, 13, 29, 31, 32, 37, 40, 41, 44, 53, 73, 106, 115, 147, 148, 149, 150, 152, 153, 154, 210, 211, 224
Dyslexic 8, 9

F

Ferdinand 128
Fricative 19, 20, 21, 22, 23, 24, 25, 27, 28, 32, 33, 34, 35, 43, 44, 51, 52, 64, 65, 76, 77, 78, 79, 80, 82, 91, 97, 98, 99, 100, 110, 111, 112, 113, 130, 135, 136, 137, 140, 141, 142, 144, 145, 206